Step into An IT Career Today: Become A Web Developer

By Caroline Manta
Editors and Publishing Company: Digital Enterprising UK
London 2023

Preface

Welcome to the start of your new career in IT (Information Technology). Starting from today, no matter what knowledge of IT you have alrighty or how little you know about IT. No matter how much previous experience you have in IT or not, what your previous job or work experience was, you can begin a fresh career in IT today. No matter what your age is, your academic attainment and qualification, your background or social status, this book will guide you to start earning in IT today, and may help you secure a job in IT.

Just as stated on the tittle, this is a guide for you to follow, to help you break through into the IT work sector and into a career path of your choice.

The book is one in a series of similar books, each of which describes some of the various pathways to follow in an IT Career and gives more details and practical step-by-step guided tutorials on how to achieve it.

You may desire to know more about a particular field, if so, then please check to see if one of the series offers it. These book series are available on Amazon or SkiBlu, or Digital Enterprising UK.

Content

PART ONE

PART TWO

PART THREE

Introduction to IT and IT technology

Introduction

The IT and Technology work sector offers many various jobs and a lot of opportunities to work in many different companies and aspects of life. These days, in almost every workplace, you are bound to find an IT role of some sort. This work sector does command a relatively high starting salary than many other sectors. In addition, there is also a chance to find flexible working roles, with the increasing rise in remote and hybrid working conditions.

Apart from employment jobs, this sector also offers a huge ground for freelance work opportunities, which creates a chance for you to start your own venture and your own business.

This book offers an overview of the industry and the different career paths that one can take. The book also has practical guides that are simple, logical, and easy to follow. In line with the guides, we will start by creating an IT-style CV, learning a few basics concepts and start applying for jobs proactively. This book also includes a positive step-by-step guide on how to start earning money independent of employment.

The book is divided into three parts. The first part is an overview of the general aspects of the IT sector. If you are already conversant with the IT and Technology industry, then you may choose to skip this part. The second part offers help on how to set up your profile, portfolio, and CV.

The third part is the core subject of the book, showing you a specialise guide of the subject matter by using a follow-on, step by step instructions.

The IT and Technology Industry

IT and Technology does splits into areas of expertise. - Computing, Hardware, Software, Networking, Infrastructure, Data Science. These segments are all connected and tend to overlap, but there are many roles in these various and different aspect of computers.

Computing - is an activity such as algorithmic calculations, study thinking or experimentation processes that requires or are beneficial by the use of a computing machinery. It includes the technical need of creating and developing of both hardware and software for that purpose. Scientific research, engineering, mathematical, technological and some social society solutions all benefit from computing.

Computer Hardware - is the physical computer machine that you can install a software on it, to get it to perform some sort of functions. Computer hardware can be just the parts, such as the case, central processing unit, random access memory chip, monitor, mouse, keyboard, computer data storage, graphics card, sound card, speakers, or motherboard. Other things like the printers, scanners, cables, are also referred to as computer hardware, that is, any physical component that is involved with computing.

Computer Software - is a set of instructions that can be stored and run by a computer hardware. These sets of instructions, called computer programs would be associated with documentations and data, and tells the hardware what to do.

Computer Infrastructure - is the set of facilities, hardware, software, and systems that serves a company's IT system. It encompasses the facilities and services necessary for the firm to function and its IT autonomy.

Computer Network - is a set of computers in one location or in multiple locations that are connected with each other, either using a Cable wire or a Wi-Fi connection or a Cloud CDN. They can see each other by their network nodes, and they can share resources with each other.

Data Science - is a field in computing that uses statistics, scientific computing, scientific methods, processes, algorithms, and systems. It mainly deals with the art of making sense of data, that is, extract structured data from unstructured data, to give insights and predictions.

Pathways in An IT Career

The pathways in an IT career

A Career in IT

There are many kinds of jobs in IT, and many career pathways to follow. However, if you are new to IT, it is advisable to start with jobs, which are classed as entry-level roles.

If you are interested in a particular pathway that is more advance than the entry-level roles, consider it; first, accept what is on offer, then seek to change paths once you are in. People have been known to frequently change from one IT job path to another.

Which path should you go?

It is up to you: You should choose what you are better at, or what you like. If you are not sure, you can try a few pathways before settling on one, especially true if you are young; you should end up choosing one and become a Master of it.

Options for IT career pathways.

Keep it Real – Pls Note   This is just a guide, and not every path is covered here.

JOB TITTLE	OVERVIEW
IT Security Specialist	Also known as cybersecurity or information security analyst. The role involves defending an organization's data and computer systems from outside attacks and also from internal data corruption.
Help Desk Technician	Help desk technicians, also known as IT support specialists, or similar. They provide technical support for their clients, either remotely or on-site. Their job is to diagnose and fix issues with hardware, software, and network, etc.
Mobile Application Developer	Mobile Apps developers build apps for mobile devices such as smartphones and tablets. They may be developing Android apps or iOS apps, or both.

Web Developer	Web developers write codes that build websites and web-based applications. Web developers could specialise in front-end, back-end web or full-stack developing.
Video Game Designer and Game Developer	A Game Designer could also be a Game Developer, or work as a team, which may also include a Game Artist. They create interactive games.
Network Administrator	Network administrators may work as part of a firm's IT department to manage the computer networks and telecommunications systems of the firm. Their main job is to manage the computers and connections for other staff in the company.
User Interface Developer	User interface (UI) developers may be working in a team of software developers, that is working on a big project. Their main role is to create the part of the application that users will see and interact with. They may need to work hand in hand with a UX designer.
UX Designer	User experience (UX) designer's main role is to come up with a design for an application or services that the end users would have a satisfactory experience using it. The design normally come about as a result of research and analysis of the relevant experiences of similar products.
Graphic Designer	Graphic design is all about art, colours and creativity fused down using special computer applications and some coding.
Data Scientist	Data Scientists or Data Analysts deals with data statistics, analysis and making predictions. They may also write programs and scripts to use as their tools.
Health Information Technician	Health information technicians manages patients' electronic medical records and other health data.
Database Administrator	Database administrators (DBA) work mainly with SQL, MySQL, PostgreSQL, Oracle, etc. Their role

	involves inputting and managing the database system.
AutoCAD Drafter	There are special applications that are used for CADD (computer aided drafting and design), like Autodesk's AutoCAD. Drafters learn to use these for designs and drafting.
Software Engineer	Software engineers are software developers who build computer systems and applications that incorporates both computer science and programming skills. It involves – designing, developing, and improving upon programs.
Information Technology Manager	IT manager is a managerial position that involves over-seeing a team of IT specialists and the various tasks, to make sure that the business is running well.
Computer Systems Analyst	Systems analysts may work as part of the firms' IT depart. Their role is to check that the hardware, software, and network devices are working well, or seek to upgrade to newer versions where feasible, in order to secure optimum performance for the company.
IT Project Manager	IT project manager oversees a project that is being carried out by one or more teams in various departments. Usually, the project are external projects of a client.
Computer Programmer	Computer programmers or coders, write codes in specific programming languages, usually as part of a whole software or an application developing team.
Chief Information Officer	CIO is a top managerial position in an IT firm or a firm with a large IT department. The role will involve organisation level decisions making. CIO are now largely being replaced by Director or Information Technology.

Computer Hardware Engineer	Hardware engineers deals with the hardware, be it computer, routers, printers. They may be fixing old hardware or building new ones.
Computer Scientist	Computer scientists, also called information research scientists carry out the researching and analysis of concepts that facilitates the developing of new technologies.
Computer Animator	Computer animators use special graphics and visual effects applications to design, draw and animate characters for cartoons, games, etc.
Computer Network Architect	Network architects would normally manage the whole setup of the IT network. They would have the schema, which is the plan and design of the enterprise computer network.
Robotics Engineers	These engineers research and develop the design and the blueprints for robotic systems, and also build them.
Cloud Engineers	Cloud engineers work on cloud computing solutions. Their role is to plan, develop, and support an organization's cloud-based solutions.
DevOps Engineers	DevOps engineers are usually made up of a team of people, each using their expertise either in programming, testing, integration, systems architecture, and project management, to deliver successful software solutions in one package.
Change Analyst	Involves managing and auditing all changes to the software or systems and oversees the upgrades of the software. It involves stakeholder management and communicating with a wide range of project stakeholders.
Pre-Sales Technical Consultant	Pre-Sales Technical Consultant support and guides customers in a high-level way about products and services on offer. This includes the solution, design, and demonstration of equipment, as well as provide product overviews, updates, and advice to clients on various product range.

Account Manager	It is a marketing department representative, who will source clients, sell, and liaise with the clients for aftersales care and future business relationship.
IT Trainer	Specialises as a training tutor and trains single or groups of individuals on how to use specific parts of the software and systems.
Portfolio Manager	Is in charge of the daily management and colossal overseeing of all old and new software and systems being developed and managed by the company. Usually, it is a position of authority.

Training and Accreditations

Training for an IT Career

As the saying goes, 'learning is lifelong'. The same goes for IT, it is imperative to keep learning and updating your knowledge so that the world does not leave you behind. Learning fuels your ambition in IT and commands advance roles and better pay. In IT, you would find that even if you started out with a degree in computer science or others, you would still need to do some courses along the way in your career journey. More so if you are starting from zero, then certainly start enrolling in some courses as soon as possible.

To Degree or Not to Degree?

Having a degree is always an advantage in today's world. Some IT firms sets a degree as their bottom line to join them. At the same time, a speciality degree does propel you to some specific jobs. Some employment agencies and firms offer a Degree Scheme job intake. Having said that, please don't be put off if you do not have or cannot attain a degree. There are other options, but the choice is yours to make.

Go for what is specific to the job role. Let's say, you are eyeing a job with Google, would it be more convenient to go to university and start a degree in computer science? Or quickly start doing a Google course and obtain a Google certificate, specific to that job role?

What training and certification should you get?

When choosing a course, try to go for what is new and current, not what is obsolete or has already been archived as legacy. IT is fast paced, and always a - 'in with the new and out with the old' environment. For example, what is the point of starting to learn Windows NT now? - Things have long moved on to Cloud Computing and IoT.

Google Career Certificates

Google offers courses and career certificates through a company called Coursera. Coursera calls them; 'job-ready' skills you need to launch your career in Data Analytics, Digital Marketing & E-commerce, IT Support, Project Management or UX Design. Each program is free to try out for seven days with a Coursera trial. After the trial ends, the program will cost $39 a month to keep learning.

https://www.coursera.org
https://support.google.com/cloud-certification
https://cloud.google.com/certification

CompTIA training and certifications

The Computing Technology Industry Association, more commonly known as CompTIA, is an American non-profit trade association that issues professional certifications for the information technology industry. https://www.comptia.org

Microsoft Learn

Microsoft Learn is a free program that anyone, on their own can follow to master core concepts, at their own speed and on their own schedule. At the end, one can take the paid exams and gain the certifications. https://learn.microsoft.com/en-us/certifications

Alternatively, you can book an instructor through one of their Partners.
https://learn.microsoft.com/en-us/certifications/partners

Cisco certifications

Cisco offers free online training and certification programs to address today's dynamic technologies and prepare students, engineers, and software developers for success in the industry's most critical jobs.
https://www.cisco.com/c/en/us/training-events/training-certifications/certifications.html

These places also offer IT courses.

Some are free and some are paid programs.
https://www.udemy.com
https://devpost.com
https://www.codecademy.com/subscriptions
https://www.itcareerfinder.com
http://www.tutorialspoint.com

https://www.w3schools.com
https://codepen.io/pen
https://itcertify.co.uk
http://www.digitalenterprising.co.uk/tutorials
http://www.skiblu.com/tutorials
https://sites.google.com/view/caroline-mant/tutorials

Local Colleges may offer these.

BTEC Tech Award Digital Information Technology
Cambridge International AS & A Level Computer Science
Cambridge IGCSE Information and Communication Technology

Skill Badges vs Certifications

When you have embarked on a course and done the exam and successful passed it, you get sent a proper certificate with your name printed on it, showing that you know your stuff. Badges are just a star, a sticker that a site stamps on your profile to show that you have an idea of your stuff. Usually, you would do a pop quiz on the site and when you get the answers correct, you would get a badge. LinkedIn is one site that does it. Having the badge on your profile is eye-catching when employers are looking at your profile.

Self-Teaching using materials from:

Company's Website – You go to the Docs or Help/Support section of the software company, and you would learn a lot about that software.

Google – Search for 'how to …' - Just searching on google can lead you to someone's blog where they have explained the subject matter in a helpful way.
YouTube – Search for 'how to…' - There are so many people teaching this or that on YouTube.

Communities and Forums

You would learn a lot from other IT guys in a community or a Forum. You can even post your questions to them to guide you. Do look at various ones, here are some examples.

https://www.googlecloudcommunity.com

https://stackshare.io

Coding Bootcamps

Look for online or on site bootcamps and attend them. Bootcamps are short-term, intense educational courses, often conducted online, that focuses on the in-demand technical skills that today's employers want. Their curricula, usually conducted over 3-6 months, can target coding, data analytics, fintech, and other technical disciplines, offering robust learning opportunities and practical experience.

Finding An IT Job

Find a Job in IT

Keep it Real - Advice When looking for a job, don't be put off by the big-named tittle of the job, instead, read the job specifications and skills needed, and look under 'Responsibilities'. You may well have the skills that fits the role. Also, may be the job has been given a different tittle by another company – that's, same job, - different tittle, e.g.
IT Service Desk = Computer Support = IT Support Technician = IT Associate Analyst =
Help Desk Technician = IT Support Specialist = Help Desk Analyst.

Also, look for the meaning of words in the tittle of the job, for different companies may use synonymous, e.g.
Consumer Experience = User Experience = Customer Experience

Look in the section or sections that describes skills and qualification required. If it states them as thus:
Desirable – If you don't have some of these, don't worry; still go ahead and apply for the job.
Required qualifications - If you have some similar qualifications as them, then try applying for the job.
Required Skills and Experience - If you have some similar skills and experience, then try applying for the job.
Must have – If you don't have that requirement; then don't bother apply for that job.

Entry-Level Jobs

At our level, we are going to start at entry-level jobs. IT work is both intellectual, as well as practical with a hands-on approach. Some of the jobs, the skills and knowledge required to carry out the tasks can only be gained through work experience. For that reason, there are opportunities for entry-level roles that mostly come with in-house training and on the job. Below, are some entry-level jobs that we can straightaway start applying for.

Help Desk Analyst.	Database Administrator.
PC or Hardware Support.	Digital Content Writer
Computer Operator.	Website and Content Analyst
Software Developer (Junior).	Change Analyst
Cybersecurity Technician.	Trainee Web Developer
Web Sites Development	Web Manager
UX (User Experience Analyst)	IT Service Desk Team
Front-end Web Developer.	Web Developer
Quality assurance (QA) or Test Analyst	System Administrator

Skills and knowledge Required for Entry-level roles

- The ability to work well with others.
- Basic knowledge of computer operating systems, hardware, and software.
- Analytical thinking skills.
- Basic knowledge of engineering, science, and technology.
- To be thorough and pay attention to details.
- Customer service skills.
- Excellent verbal communication skills.

Where to find IT jobs

Below are a few options of places you can go job-hunting for an IT role. Looking for an IT job requires you to think outside the box and may be, go the extra mile.
Register with an Agency or go the company's website and click on Careers.

https://uk.jora.com/	https://www.cv-library.co.uk/
https://www.jobsite.co.uk/	https://www.createselect.com/
https://cleansheet.org.uk/	https://careers.tiktok.com/
https://careers.byp-network.com/	https://thecareerwallet.com/login
https://www.bame-jobs.co.uk/	https://www.careeraddict.com/
https://uk.jora.com/	https://jobs.womenintech.co.uk/
https://www.jobsite.co.uk/	https://careers.arm.com/
https://cleansheet.org.uk/	https://www.senitor.com/
https://careers.byp-network.com/	https://joblookup.com/uk
https://www.bame-jobs.co.uk/	https://pg-rec.com/
https://www.gumtree.com/computing-it-jobs	https://www.adzuna.co.uk/jobs
https://jobs.theguardian.com/job	https://www.totaljobs.com/
https://www.totaljobs.com	http://www.digitalenterpris-ing.co.uk/jobs
https://uk.generation.org/london/greenjobs	http://www.skiblu.com/jobs
https://www.technojobs.co.uk	https://sites.google.com/view/caroline-mant/jobs
https://www.linkedin.com/jobs	
https://www.risetechnical.co.uk	
https://www.lafosse.com/	

Apprenticeships and Graduates Schemes

https://itcareerswitch.co.uk/
https://careers.dcc.ie

Join IT Social Networking groups

https://www.eventbrite.co.uk/b/united-kingdom--london/business/

Register in User Groups and Communities

Some IT companies actually advertise their jobs amongst these communities, user groups and forums. If you have some time on your hand, you can join a community of voluntary developers, for instance, the people working on an open-source project. You can join them and if a job becomes available, you are already in that team and you may be offered the job. You can also use that for work experience and state it on your CV.

Create a Profile on LinkedIn

LinkedIn helps with your CV, with mini skills courses and skills badges, and proactively assigns upcoming jobs to you. Many agencies and employers also hire from there.

Collaboration

Collaboration is the trendy thing in IT now, and Google is the 'big one' on collaboration with that their Colab. Join Google Colab - Who knows, you might just come up with the solution to one of their research algorithms, and that will surely land you a job.

https://colab.research.google.com

https://opensource.googleblog.com

Hackathon

Hackathon is the latest craze among young people, - running around the country, having themselves a 'hacking fest'? Well, at least it is more profitable than going to Glastonbury or Oktoberfest. If you (both old and young) can attend one of those, or even win the price money, it will surely add a priced value to your CV.

https://www.hackathons.org.uk

Blog Site.

Write an interesting or a helpful blog of any technical topic and post it on your portfolio site. Especially, if it is of a technical content of the job role that you are looking for, it could attract some agencies or employers. Be sure to emphasise your name and contact info and that you are open for work.

The Interview

Interview

Getting an IT job or any job is such a big deal these days, - involving many steps. There may be up to three interview stages, plus an oral and a written assessment of some sort.

1ST INTERVIEW
Telephone interview - Do sound confident (Afterall, you are an IT professional), and bluff your way through (it is widely done in this field).

2ND INTERVIEW
Videocall or in their office - Do appear calm, with a fixed half smile (The person interviewing you was once in your sit, usually a team member and a team leader. The line manager may be there too). Their job is mainly to test your technical knowledge and ability.

3RD INTERVIEW
On-site interview - Don't let your feathers be ruffled (If they need you, they will hire you. Since you've made it this far, it means that they probably need you). Usually, the HR or the hiring personnel may be among the panel.

Before you Attend the Interview

Before you attend an interview, there are certain things you need to do to prepare yourself.

1. Learn some IT terminologies, acronyms and word pronunciations, so that you will 'fit in'. The IT Crowd can be such a snubbish set of people at times. If you don't talk like them, you could be looked down on or even be laughed at. For instance:
- You may hear them say, "JS, JS". Please, don't stop and ask: "What is 'JS?' - It's JavaScript -ok?
- Some words may not be pronounced according to the acronyms or spelling phonics, e.g.-
- SQL – Lots of them would pronounce it as, 'Sequel' (MySQL = MySequel.
- C# = C-sharp
- Amazon AWS, simply as, 'Awis.'
- Xamarin = They would call it out really fast = 'Sham'rin'
- MS Azure = Ayshure.
- Be mindful of UK - American English spelling and pronunciations. For instance, we say, "Colours", they say, "colors".

- We pronounce Route as = "Roo-u-te", they pronounce it, "Raowt".
- Speak with confidence and try to incorporate some latest IT buzz words, but appropriately, and with confidence.

If you speak and pronounce like them, they could be fooled into thinking: "Yeah this guy knows his stuff", but if you go calling, SQL = S-Q-L, then, their jaw will drop, thinking: "What a slow manga".

Research the Company

Please, please, do research the company and don't be like me, who turned up at one interview only to lashed at by one interviewer who couldn't hide his anger at the fact that I had not 'bothered to research the company'. Look on their website, if you can't find much there, then call their receptionist and ask questions, or even the person who is in charge of the department. Find out what they do, their clients, markets, moto, when the company was established, their visions, etc.

Practice Interview Questions

I sometimes thing that interviewers all went to the same school or something, because they all ask the same interview questions, to which they expect the same standard answers, which is a cliché really. Take for instance, 'Why do you want to work for us?'. Anyway, it is not your place to dare to be different, stay safe and give them the expected answer. Look on Google or YouTube or LinkedIn for some interview questions and answers.

Skills Assessments

Before you attend an interview, be prepared for a technical test on the subject matter. Sometimes, you get sent a pre-interview or a job screening assessment to complete online. To prepare yourself, you need to.

- Learn your basic arithmetic.
- Part of the interview assessments will be a timed logic problems solving to see how fast your brain is thinking. Computing is about functions, algorithm, and solutions in everyday life. In those days computer programmers were hired from a stock of people who have gone to university and studied Mathematics, Physics or Computer science. That is because computers work with logical mathematical logic of everyday life.
- Try and improve your typing speed, -using both hands. Have you ever noticed how fast these young IT guys speak, while typing at the same time? Also noticed how well their thinking is; absolutely clear and logical while doing that.

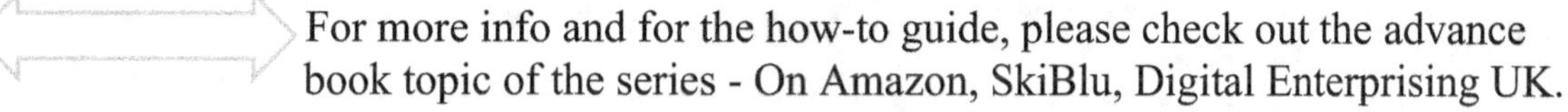

For more info and for the how-to guide, please check out the advance book topic of the series - On Amazon, SkiBlu, Digital Enterprising UK.

Freelance and Self-Employed in IT

Freelance

Information Technology (IT) is not an employment only sector. It has huge doors of freelance work and business start-ups. So, do not restrict yourself to just the job market. In fact, you may be limiting yourself, if you simply resign yourself to just working in an IT firm only. If you can't find a job straight away, start doing something and start earning money in the field. Let me tell you; most of the big IT companies were started by some unemployed guy (guys) in their rooms, or garage, etc.

Microsoft was founded by Bill Gates and Paul Allen on April 4, 1975.
Apple Computers, Inc. was founded on April 1, 1976, by college dropouts, Steve Jobs and Steve Wozniak,
Google was founded in 1998 by Sergey Brin and Larry Page.
Amazon.com was founded in 1994 by Jeff Bezos, a former Wall Street hedge fund executive.
eBay was founded in 1995 by Pierre Omidyar.
YouTube was founded on February 14, 2005, by Steve Chen, Chad Hurley and Jawed Karim.
Facebook was founded on February 4, 2004, by Mark Zuckerberg, along with his Harvard college roommates.

Here are a few steps and guides that you can take to start earning money in IT today, as a free-lancer.

Make money from Adverts on your Blog Site.

Write an interesting or a helpful blog of any topic and post it on your website, then ask Google to start placing ads on your website and get paid for it. (In Part three of this book, we are going to learn how to build a web site, which you can use as a blog site).

According to one blogger: 10 Best Blog Advertising Networks (to Make Money with Blog Ads) in 2022

AdThrive
RevenueHits
Infolinks
SHE Media
Monumetric
Google AdSense
PropellerAds
Ezoic
Media.net
Mediavine

How to Sign up for a monetized Google Ads

https://support.google.com/blogger/answer/1269077?hl=en

Sign into your Google account and go the link above, then follow their guide.

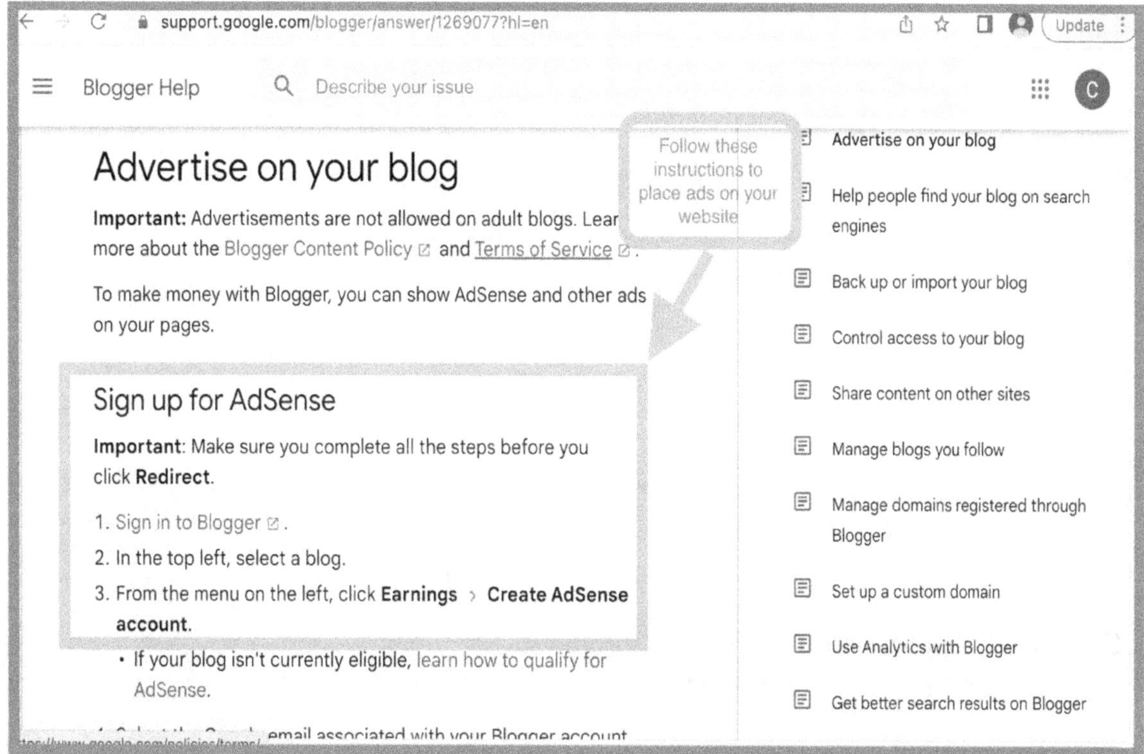

YouTube and Facebook Channels

Produce a video, discussing or teaching some technical topics and upload it onto YouTube and Facebook and get paid for it.

Make money from YouTube

Make a YouTube video, teaching this same topic or other technical topics, then upload it onto your channel. If 1,000 people subscribe to your channel, YouTube will start placing ads on your video and you will get paid per view.

Sign into your Google account and go the content tab, then choose -YouTube.

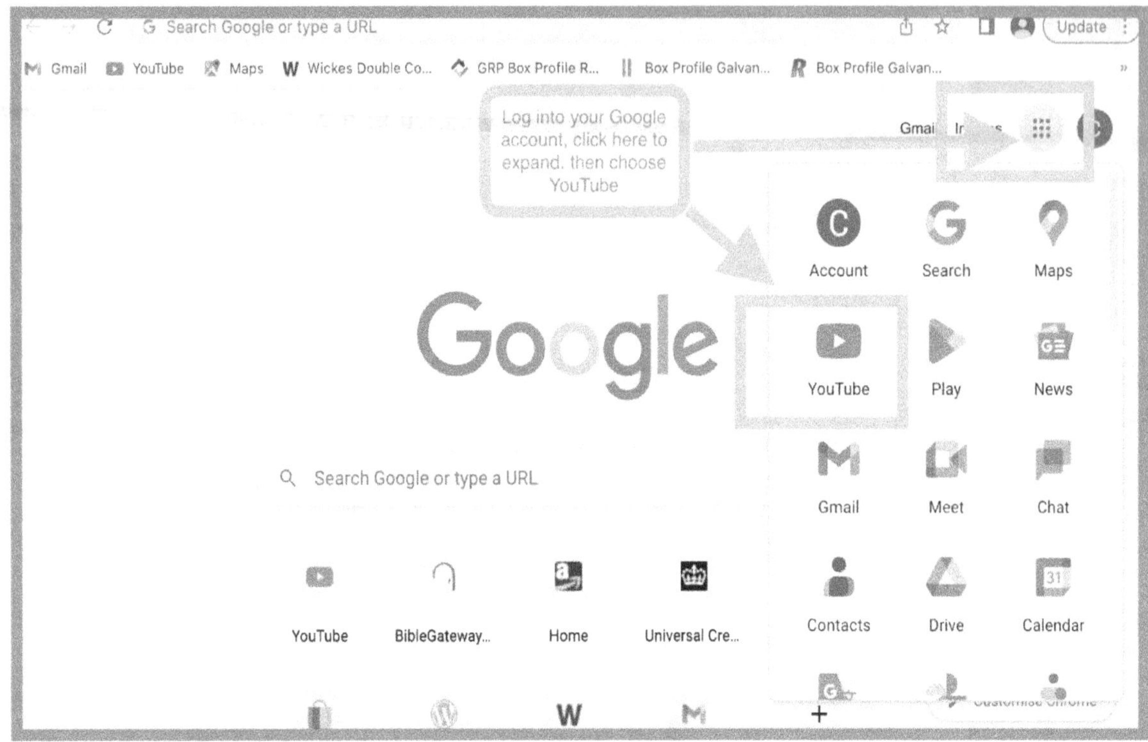

Click on -Upload Video and follow the prompts

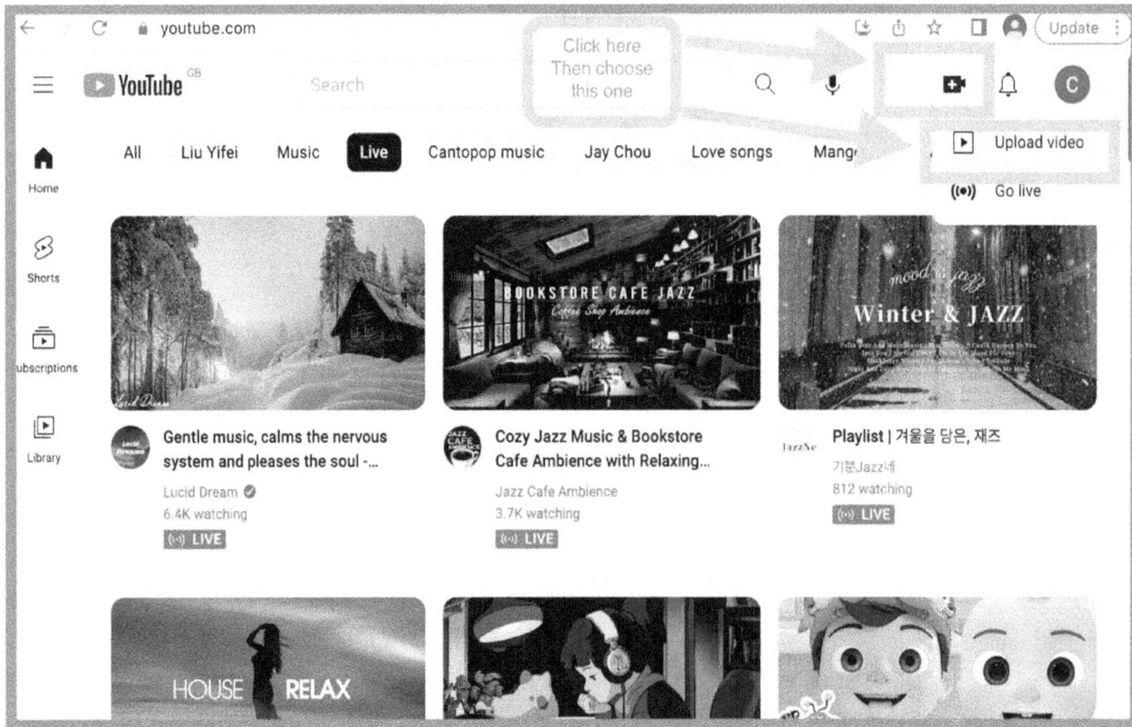

You can insert a logo, banner to brand your channel

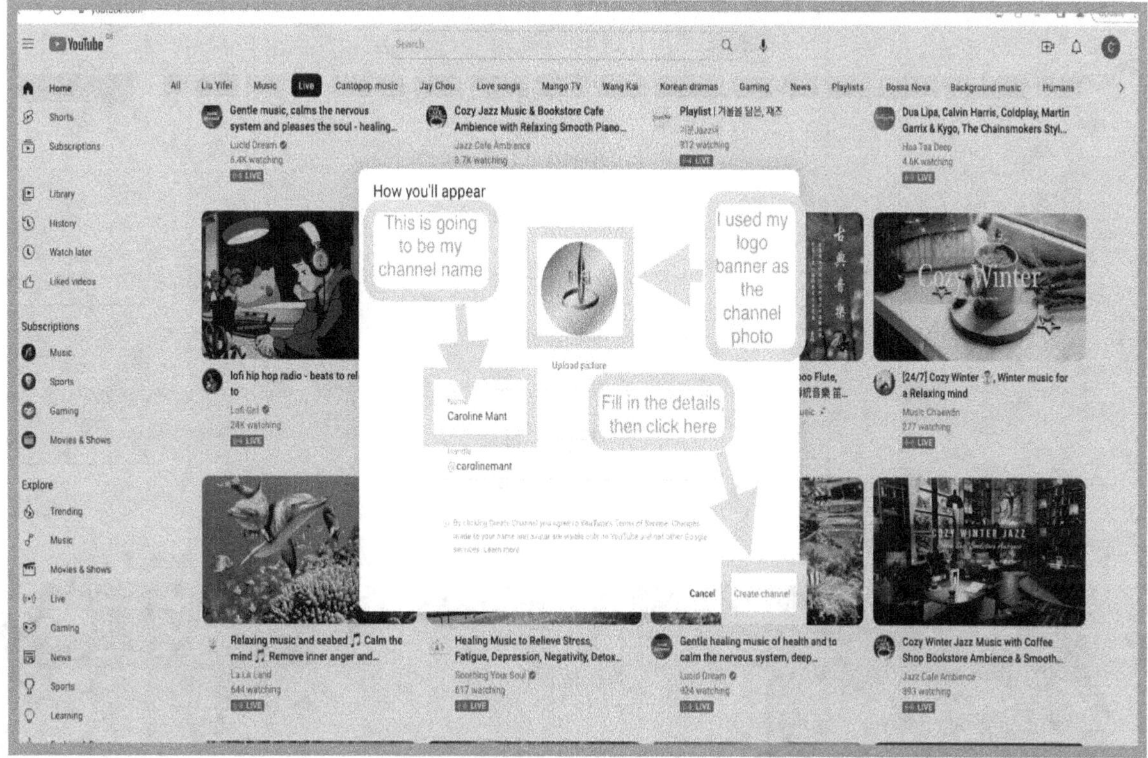

LinkedIn

Styled yourself on LinkedIn that you a freelancer and opened for contracts. Look for businesses on LinkedIn or other social media sites, then send an introductory letter, as below:

Hi,

Hope you're well,
I am writing to you as I have recently come across your business on LinkedIn. I really love how the business looks. I would like to know if a bigger digital presence would help your business get more customers.
I'm an expert on improving brand identity and increasing revenue by giving your website a good feel for user experience.
Would you be open to a short 15-minute conversation to see if this is worth your time?

Thank you and look forward to collaborating with you in the near future.

Caroline

Advertise your services on the freelance platforms

The main platforms for that are below:

Upwork
https://www.upwork.com

Fiverr
https://www.fiverr.com

Gumtree
https://www.gumtree.com/telecoms-computer-services

FIVERR

To advertise on Fiverr, go to their website and click on -Join

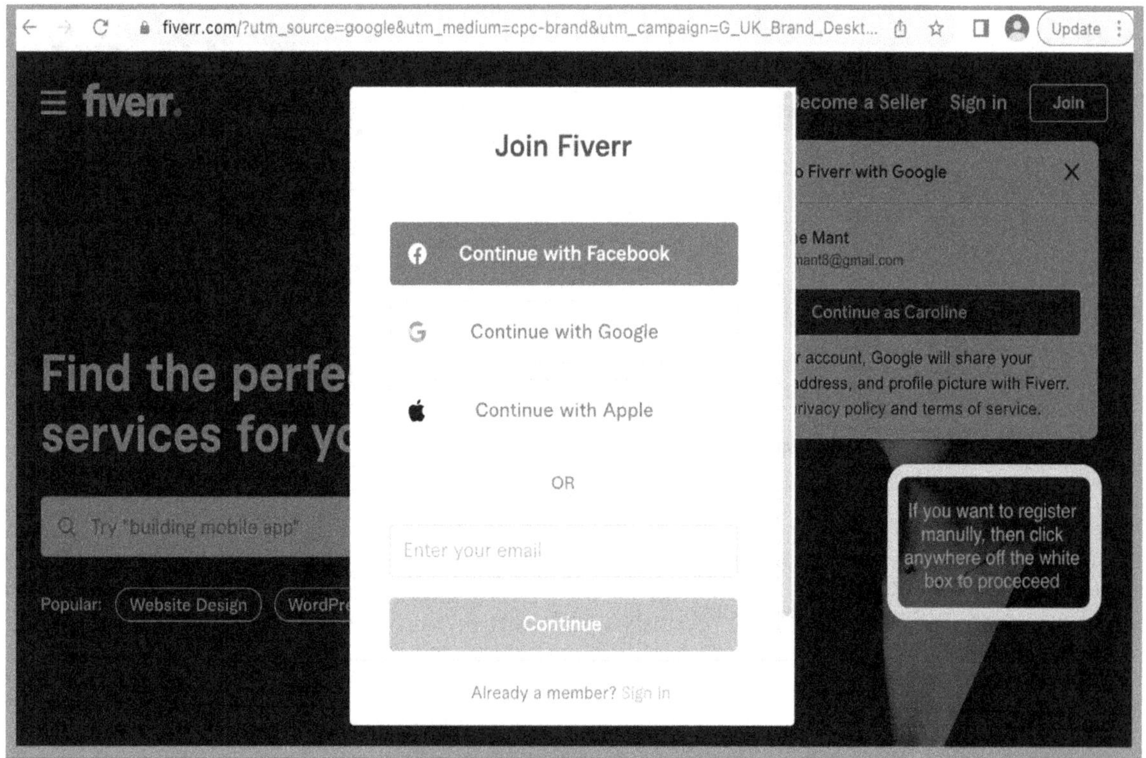

Here are other people's advert (Gig) for hire. Follow their examples.

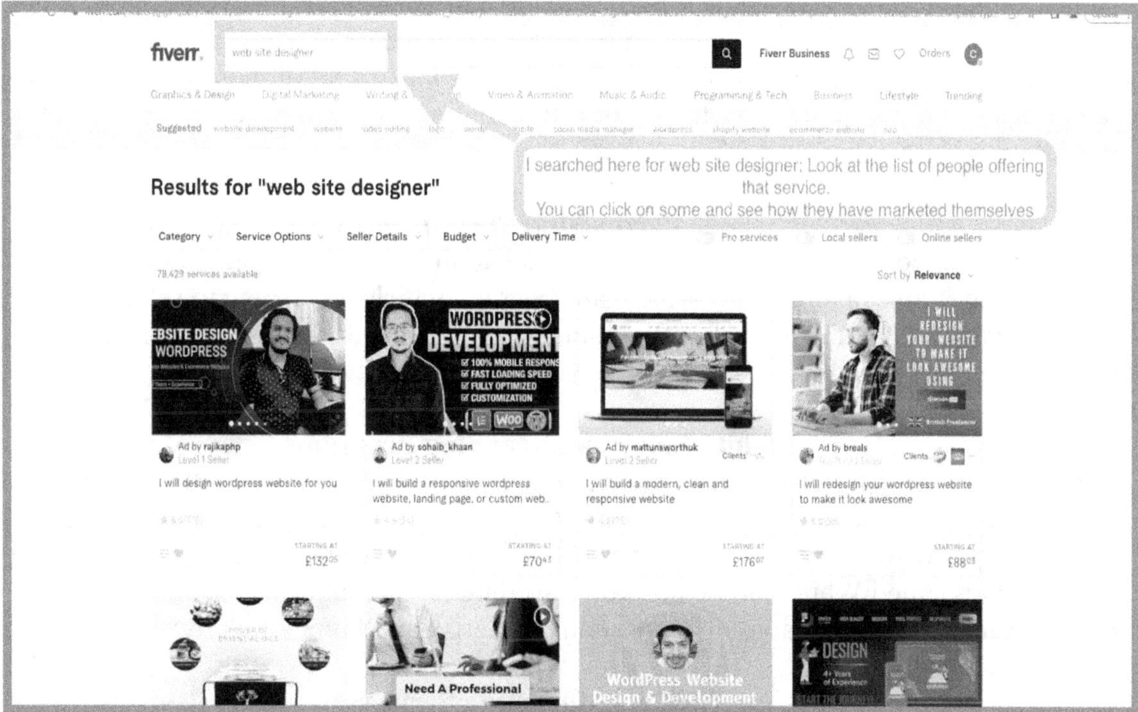

In your Fiverr dashboard, click on your profile and choose -Become a seller. Then follow the prompts.

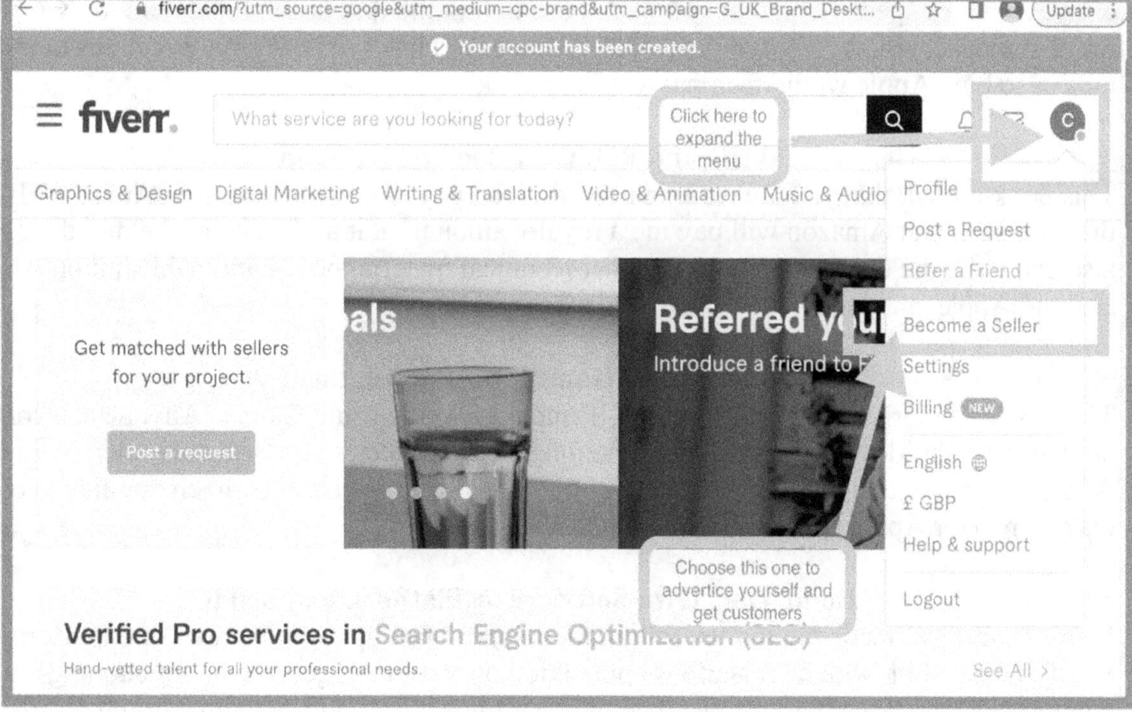

Open an Online Shop

Upload some products and start selling. There are numerous items that you can buy wholesale and sell at a retail price online and make a profit. If you are good at arts and craft, you can sell the things that you make online. I heard of a lady who make a lot of money online just selling 'all things white' for home furnishing. For selling online, you will need a Payment Gateway that allows you to receive payments online.

Partnership Programs

When software companies have built a functional application or program, they need to sell it to the public. You can join their Partnership Program, which allows you to sell their products on commission. I am in Partnership Programs with IBM and 3CX. This means that if I sell any of the products and services, they will pay me a commission.

White Label and Branding Programs

Some software companies may have built a functional application that could be used for a few different uses, and they can customise it for you with your own logo and branding that makes it look unique to your company. This is a sort of buying software, services, concepts, whole-sale, which is called White Label, then you re-selling to your end users using your brand name. Examples are companies that are selling Asterisk and FreePBX software.

Affiliate Marketing Services

You can set up a web site that does a 'description' or 'comparison' discussions of different products and services. For example, if you have a site that compares Google watch and Apple Watch, then you register with Google and Apple for their Affiliate Programs. They would each give you a special link that you would use to link the discussion topic item to their sites. So, if someone, reading your online article, decides to click on the Apple Watch for more details or to buy, Apple would then pay you 'per click'.

Write and Publish a Book on Amazon

This book/e-book that you are reading now, did you pay to download it from Amazon? If yes, then it means that Amazon will pay me a royalty amount on it at the end of the month. You also can write the exact same book or other technical material books and publish it on Amazon and Apple, and Google to earn royalties.

Build Apps, Games and Publish them

There is a big market for Apps, Plug-ins, Templates, Widget and Games. Anyone can come up with a bright idea that could add a functionality to another's core software, then build an App or extension and publish it on the App Store and charge however much you like. You can make Apps for Apple phones, Samsung phones, etc.

Build Your Own Software or Platform and Sell it

Many nerds have made big money selling their small Start-ups Applications and Platforms. So, if you come up with an ingenious application or platforms, get it to be functioning and becoming popular. If the big IT guys, then think that it is a useful thing with a bright future, or they think that it poses a competition threat to them, they would soon ask you to name your price. Like how, eBay has bought Gumtree, or Facebook has bought Instagram.

Graphic Photography

Take powerful photographs and sell them online to stock image platforms. Also, you can use the photos in a creative way to make elegant prints and souvenirs to sell online.

3D models

Some people are gifted in this field. If you are, then make all kinds of 3D models and sell them on the 3D models platforms, such as TurboSquid.

Marketing Yourself and Your Business

You can also increase your freelance revenue by creating and running ads campaigns of yourself or your products and services.

Google Ads. - starts from $15 onwards.

TikTok Ads – free.

Programming Language

Programming Language

How do computers work?

Computers work by reading a line of codes of instructions or program, asking it to do something or to display something on the screen. So, you take a piece of paper and write down, "Computer; do something", then you feed it into the computer and the computer reads it and starts 'doing something'. Say, you write down on the piece of paper, "Computer: 'Say hello world'". The computer reads it, and the computer shows, "Hello world." on the screen.

What is a Programming Language?

'Programming' is writing a set of computer codes to carry out a specific function. A programming language is a coding language. A programming language is the language that the computer understands. Just like human language (French, Japanese, English, Greek), you can tell the computer to do the same thing in any programming language, although some programming languages are better suited for certain instructions than others.

The computer sits like a UN convention moderator. So, one person gets up and introduces himself: "Hello, I am French, and I am going to give you the solution for the global warming problem, in French." So, the computer orders: "All change our runtime environments to 'French.'" The same solution could also be given in Latin and other languages, and as long as the computer knows which programming language it is dealing with, it can interpret and output the solution to the global warming issue.

Programming languages are man-made – that is, invented. There are many programming languages out there, and more are still being invented. Don't be surprised; you go to sleep tonight, and by the time you wake tomorrow morning, some guy - brain still buzzing, couldn't sleep, and rather than counting sheep to try to sleep? No, he gets out of bed and start making up his own programming language??? The good news is that, once you've learned one programming language, the learning curve for another programming language becomes less steep, simply because you are now in the game of programming languages.

As new programming languages are coming up, some are becoming obsolete. So, before you start learning a programming language, check first, to see if it is relevant to the job you are applying for, or if it is still in active development, that is, if it is still getting regular updates. You don't want to be the only person left behind when everyone has packed up and left the 'ghost town'.

Programming languages operates on a design method of programming, such as object-oriented, imperative, procedural, and functional programming, but object-oriented takes top grade amongst them. Object-oriented programming uses a model that organises software design around objects, which makes it quicker and easier to reuse codes.

Here is an overview of some programming language. This is put here in no particular order.

Programming Language Brief Description

Programming Language	Brief Description
Python	Python is a free open-source programming language with extensive support modules and community. It is a general-purpose scripting language with syntax that is very simple and close to human language, making it easier to learn than some other languages. Python is also known for its broad range of libraries that allows you to extend the language to do more. Python is used for data analysis, machine learning, server-side web development. Also has been used to develop 2D imaging and 3D animation packages like Blender, Inkscape, and Autodesk and video games. Python developers can work in job roles such as a data scientist, a software engineer, and an artificial intelligence (AI) researcher.
Java	Java, owned by Oracle Corporation, is a general-purpose programming language with its object-oriented structure. It is a solid programming language that is used across platforms, that is on Mac, Windows, Android, iOS, because of its Write Once, Run Anywhere (WORA) capabilities. The Java Virtual Machine lets Java run on virtually any hardware and operating system. It is commonly used on the back ends of software applications and mobile apps. Some large-scale enterprise websites that used Java, include Google, Amazon, Twitter, and YouTube. The Android OS is based on Java Java frameworks include Spring, Struts, and Hibernate. These have a good online communities.

| **HTML** | I heard that HTML, technically, is not actually a programming language. However, you do need it for the internet. If you write a text on a notepad and feed it into a computer to display it on the internet web. In order for your browser to interpret it and show it, you will first have to select every word on the page and change the text to 'Hyper-Text'. Sort of like 'activate it' for the computer to recognise it as marked up. That is what it is – a flat bit of text turned into a hyper-text - Hyper-Text Markup Language (HTML). In development, you can introduce the whole document as HTML at the very top and save it with the .HTM file extension.

While HTML is just a flat piece of content and structure on a web page, CSS is the tool that makes that web page to look 'pretty'. That is, colours, styling, etc. Those two, work hand in hand with another programming language called 'JavaScript', which tells the web page to 'do something'.

So, you open a web page - you see the written content = HTML, on a colourful background, with nice buttons = CSS. You click on the button, and something happened = JavaScript.

HTML (Hyper-Text Markup Language) is the standard language for creating web pages and web applications. You can use HTML to add images, links, and other types of content to your web page.

HTML5 provides better multimedia and interactive features like video and audio elements, local storage, and 2D/3D graphics, but it is not very secure to use just on its own.

W3C HTML is the current HTML standard
https://www.w3.org/html |
| **CSS** | CSS (Cascading Style Sheets) is a set of rules for styling and decorating web pages for the browser to recognise. It controls the look and style of HTML or XML file in a |

	set of ways. CSS dictates the colour of the text, background, the size of the columns, buttons, indents, etc. You can put a style definition on each section of the HTML document individually, or you can write one style sheet and link each section to use it, or you can link the sections to a third-party style sheet somewhere across the net. Popular framework for CSS is Bootstrap, which has responsive designs.
JavaScript	JavaScript was created in 1995 and was initially known as Live Script. It's the most popular programming language, as it is one of the core technologies of the World Wide Web, but it is complex to learn, especially for advance programming. JavaScript is a client-side programming language, primarily used on the front end of websites and applications to make them dynamic and interactive. It can also be use on the server-side with frameworks like Node.js. JavaScript is also an excellent language for developing intuitive designs, therefore used for web apps, UI/UX designs, full stack developing, and software engineering all work with it. Frameworks include, Angular, React, Vue.
C	C is one of those foundation languages that is considered, a lower-level language because it has syntax that is closer to machine code (a very low-level, entirely numerical language that runs computer processes). It involves problem-solving and has more complex syntax than some other programming languages. It is probably the oldest programming language, it is popular and is the root of some programming languages such as C++, C#, Java, and JavaScript. C is most commonly used for desktop applications, operating systems, and databases.

C++	C++ is also a popular programming language that was built on top of C, resulting in an added enhanced sophistication. The name comes from the "++" operator in C, which adds a value of one to an integer. It is fast and powerful, uses Classes and Objects that allows you to represent real-life objects in the code. It supports OOP (Object Orientation Programming), generic, and imperative programming. C++ is used to build sophisticated things where performance is a critical issue, like systems, or application software, drivers, client-server applications, web browsers, embedded firmware, and video games.
C#	C# was developed by Anders Hejlsberg of Microsoft in 2000 to run on its .NET platform for Windows applications and other GUI-based desktop applications, but now it is compatible with Linux. C# is an object-oriented programming language that branched off from C, but has a simple syntax and well-defined class hierarchy, giving it a fast performance and improved stability. C# is used on the back end of several popular websites like Bing, Dell, Visual Studio, Unity game engine, 2D and 3D games, mobile phones, and enterprise software.
Ruby	Ruby is a server-side scripting language, developed in the 1990s. It uses object-oriented architecture that also supports procedural and functional programming notations too. It has a more English-like syntax; therefore, it is considered, a relatively simple programming language to learn. Its open-source framework, Ruby on Rails ("RoR") is one of the most stable options for website development applications because of its security and low maintenance. Square, Shopify, Airbnb, and Hulu are built on it.

PHP	PHP is an open-source programming language created in 1990. It is a server-side scripting language, used in web development to build dynamic web pages. PHP is the core language for WordPress and other content management systems like Joomla. Programmers can also use this language to write command-line scripts, as well as server-side scripts and to develop desktop applications. PHP is known for its many frameworks on the market. Fat-Free Slim PHPixie CodeIgniter Laravel Laminas CakePHP Yii Phalcon FuelPHP Symfony
SQL	SQL (Structured Query Language) is the standard programming language for managing relational databases. A relational database is one in which data in two or more tables are related to each other. SQL is used to access and manipulate this data in the database. It allows you to add data to tables, extract data from tables, and change data. When dealing with data in a database, you can either use SQL admin or write SQL scripts that run automatic jobs that involves storing, fetching, and analysing data. SQL is widely used in many applications and environments, such as web applications, data warehouses, and e-commerce applications, making it very useful for data analysts, product experts, business analysts and data scientists. MariaDB, PostgreSQL, and MySQL are other database applications, very similar to SQL.

NoSQL	While SQL is relational database language, NoSQL databases is the opposite- that is, it is a non-relational database. NoSQL databases are often used in big data applications where data is distributed across many nodes and may need to scale down or up quickly. This design provides high performance and scalability. There are four key concepts that a NoSQL databases employs. Key-Value Stores Columnar Stores Document Stores Graph databases.
Swift	In 2014, Apple developed Swift for Linux and Mac applications, a programming language to develop iOS and macOS applications. Swift is an open-source programming language that has relatively straightforward human-readable syntax and it is a flexible language when it comes to mistakes. It is also a very scalable language, which makes it easy to translate your projects from small experiments into full-blown apps. Swift supports almost everything, including Objective-C and it can be used with IBM Swift Sandbox and IBM Bluemix. Swift is used in popular iOS apps like Mozilla Firefox, SoundCloud, and many more.
Go	Go (also known as Golang) is a general-purpose programming language created by Google in 2007 to support software development projects, namely, APIs and web applications. It is similar to C, but with easier syntax and some added functionality to support more efficient building and more scalable projects. Some people see Go as combining the more user-friendly aspects of several programming languages into one.

	Go is now being used for cloud-based applications, AI and machine learning, web servers, data tools, and command-line tools. Some of the best job roles for Go developers include software engineers, data scientists, back-end web developers, and AI researchers. Companies using Go as their programming language include Google, Uber, Twitch, Dropbox.
Kotlin	Kotlin is a general-purpose programming language originally developed and unveiled as Project Kotlin by JetBrains in 2011. The first version was officially released in 2016. It is interoperable with Java and supports functional programming languages. Kotlin is used extensively for Android apps, web applications, desktop applications, and server-side application development. Most of the Google applications are based on Kotlin. Some companies using Kotlin as their programming language include Coursera, Pinterest, PostMates.
R	R is an open-source programming languages with an active online community. R is essentially a version of the S language and bears great similarities. Applications built with the R language are used for processing statistics, calculations, testing, visualisation, and analysis. Applications coded using R can interface with a number of databases and process both structured and unstructured data.
Matlab	Matlab is a proprietary programming language owned by MathWorks and originally released in the mid-1980s. It is built specifically for use by scientists and engineers, who uses it to analyse data, create algorithms, process images, and verify research. Programmers use Matlab to build machine learning and deep learning applications.

TypeScript	TypeScript was developed in 2012 by Microsoft. It is a typed version of JavaScript that is well suited for large code bases. TypeScript is used to create JavaScript-based projects with typing in both client-side and server-side development, and it is useful for catching errors and preventing systemic issues.
Scala	Scala is a general-purpose, type-safe Java virtual machine language that combines the best OOP and functional programming languages into one special high language. Scala is ideal for reducing and removing bugs in large complex applications. It supports both object-oriented and functional programming. Programmers can use Scala for any task that they normally would use Java for. Scala is a complex language, but that complexity gives it a lot of flexibility. Companies that use Scala include Netflix, Twitter, and the New York Times.
Perl	Perl was originally developed by Larry Wall in 1987 as a general-purpose Unix scripting language to make report processing easier. It is a versatile and powerful, high-level programming language. It is used for various tasks, including web development, network programming, system administration, and more.
Dart	Dart was developed by Google in 2011. It is an object-oriented programming language, designed for client-side development, such as for the web and mobile apps, but the Dart virtual machine can be used on the server-side. Python and Dart have similarities, and Dart is similar in syntax to C# and Java. Dart is used in Flutter template for developing the frontend hybrid mobile apps, but if creating native apps for android only, then using Java is better. Its framework is Flutter.

Which Programming Languages are the best or are still active?

Here are two lists that I got from two blog sites.

Top 13 Programming Languages to Learn in 2023

Python.
Java.
Kotlin.
Swift.
C#
C and C++
Go.
PHP
Matlab
R Programming
Scala
Ruby
TypeScript

20 Most Popular Programming Languages to Learn in 2023

JavaScript
2. Python
3. Go
4. Java
5. Kotlin
6. PHP
7. C#
8. Swift
9. R
10. Ruby
11. C and C++
12. Matlab
13. TypeScript
14. Scala
15. SQL
16. HTML
17. CSS
18. NoSQL
19. Rust
20. Perl

I cannot confirm if the programming languages in the tables above were put in a particular order of importance / in-demand or not. All I can say is; if these two experts say that these are
the ones to focus on in 2023, then so be it. I, myself, have not analysed the data in their research to verify it.

Choosing which programming language to learn as a newcomer depends on the job in sight
and the career pathway of interest. In summary, if you are going to be using it for.
Client-side programming - JavaScript
Server-side programming - Python, PHP, Go, and Ruby
Web application development - C#, JavaScript, Java, Go, and Ruby
Database management – SQL
Game development - C++, JavaScript, and Java
Mobile App development - C++ and Java. (Swift for developing iOS Apps).
GUI applications (desktop apps) - Python, C#, PHP, Java, and Go
Data processing - Python, SQL, and Ruby

Fintech

Fintech (Financial Technology) refers to firms using IT technology to manage and to deliver
financial services. In Fintech, software and technologies are made specific to the need of the
banks and the finance industry. These software for fintech are used for Bank transactions, Encrypted Authentication, Artificial intelligence, Blockchain, Cloud Computing, Big Data, and
Machine learning for predictions. Python is commonly used, as the Python libraries are good
for tasks like fraud detection, customer rating, etc. SQL is also used for the data manipulation
and statistics.

Scripting Language

A Script is a small piece of instructions that you give to the computer or other software to
carry out a small function at a crucial time within a particular runtime environment. Examples
are; performing some configurations, extracting data from data sets or to automate a task exe-
cution, such as initiates a backup, autosave, and others.

A script is coded using a Scripting Language. Some scripting languages are also programming
languages. However, the script is specific to that platform and have not been compiled as part
of the original application, rather they are like little injections into the runtime executions,
such as, Bash for the GNU operating system or VBA for Microsoft Office.

Top 13 Scripting Languages You Should Pay Attention to in 2023
JavaScript/ECMAScript
PHP
Python
Ruby
Groovy

Perl
Lua
Bash
PowerShell
R
VBA
Emacs Lisp
GML

Template

A Template is a flat coded design model for a software or an application or part of a program that has been made and set aside to be copied and build upon. Software templates saves a lot of time when building similar applications. The developer using a template would simply just build on it, then make small changes, like colours, if wanted. Templates are usually open source, with a free to modify licence of some sorts. Some plates are licenced and are for sell, mostly marketed by freelance developers, but the licence should also allow modifications and onward sale of finished products. Application templates, like the ones you find in Ms Word and Ms PowerPoint are also free to use and modify and to sell the end products afterwards.

Framework

A framework is more like a car plant, which has a ready-made schema and pre-fabricated templated moulds that has already been prepared halfway, for you to build on. It comes with added items necessary for building a particular program of that model. Frameworks offer built-in features that are automatically loaded up for you when you create a project for a similar program. A framework is usually based on a particular programming language and may be platform-specific of cross-platforms.

Most frameworks are open-source software that are maintained by a community group. Every day, there are new frameworks based on the various languages coming up. Each framework does come with a learning curve to be able to use it and to master that specific framework, and they can sometimes create a programming restriction.

All templates, frameworks and extensions are there just to make life easier for you. Some good fellas have done all that hard work, so you don't have to. So, do appreciate it, - and use it. And don't forget to say, 'Thank you'.

Platform

A platform is like a movie set, with a stage for performing. It will have templates, tools, programming frameworks for software building. A platform offers built-in features to improve software development lifecycle. These features increase development speed and improve performance within a team by lowering the workload of the developers. Some platforms are programming language specific, while others are broad languages. Some platforms providers may include access to storage and databases as well. You can download a platform for use on a server, but most are now online, on the cloud systems, and that makes for an easier work collaboration.

Bugs, Debug, Debugging Tools

Software bugs are tiny errors that you found in a software that makes it difficult to use that application properly or makes the application to keep crashing. It may not affect the functionality too badly, but it makes for an irrigating user experience and rough future upgrades of the software. The bug can be caused by a syntax error, typing error, a wrong formular and algorithm, misinterpretation of a business logic or a malicious injection by a third party. It is a source of a big headache and frustration for coders and a fair good amount of programmers' time can be wasted on trying to find the bug, and to fix the problem.

Thankfully, many platforms and IDE (Integrated Development Environment) now come with Debugging Tools for errors - correcting. There are also specialist third party debugging tools that the DevOps and testing teams can use to debug applications.

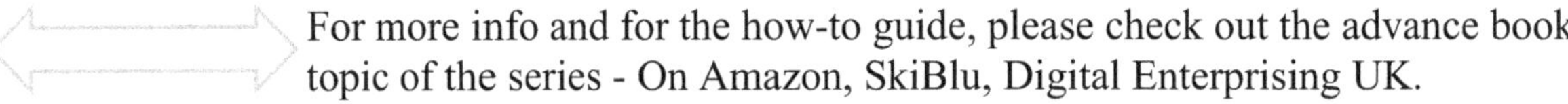

For more info and for the how-to guide, please check out the advance book topic of the series - On Amazon, SkiBlu, Digital Enterprising UK.

Graphic Design

Graphic Design

Graphic design is about visual communication of ideas or concepts in IT; where fine art, colours, creativity, innovations, and lateral thinking is transmitted digitally. It is used for Typography, logos, branding, etc.

There are professional and academic disciplines such as BA Hons Graphic Design degree that you can undergo for a career in Graphic Design, however, this career field is more like a 'gifted' vocation, and it involves a lot of practice. There are downloadable Graphic Design software that you can start using right away, but with Graphic Design software, you need a high spec machine, containing a lot of hard disk space and RAM. Instead, there are also online tools and platforms that you can do your work online.

Online Graphic Design Tools

Figma

Figma is a tool that has all the elements you need to create amazing logos, social media graphics, presentations and more. Their Starter Plan free, but paid plans will offer more advance features.

https://www.figma.com

NX CAD

NX CAD is a Powerful 3D modelling software with advanced freeform modelling, assemblies, and sheet metal design.
The NX cloud-connected Core Designer supports Synchronous modelling, combines parametric and direct modelling to provide designers with greater versatility and product design flexibility. Provides an end-to-end mechanical product design solution with a rich set of supporting tools, including rapid prototyping, design review, and validation.
You can sign up for the NX Core Designer free trial.

https://trials.sw.siemens.com

Adobe Creative Cloud Apps

Adobe Creative Cloud - All Apps

Adobe Creative Cloud includes industry-leading graphic design apps for £51.98/month.
It includes many apps like,
Premiere Pro
Illustrator
After Effects
Adobe Express
Animate
Adobe Photoshop

Adobe Illustrator is a vector graphics editor and design program developed and marketed by Adobe Inc. Originally designed for the Apple Macintosh, development of Adobe Illustrator began in 1985.
https://www.adobe.com

Adobe Fuse (Beta) creates 3D human models and characters that can easily import into Photoshop projects to pose and animate the new characters.
https://www.adobe.com/wam/fuse.html

Downloadable software – You can also download each of the applications singly for a licence fee.
If you are new to Adobe, Adobe would let you try Adobe Creative Cloud Apps for free for 30days, then after that, you have to subscribe to carry on using.

For students and teachers, you can try applying for the discounted subscription of £16.24/month.
https://www.adobe-students.com

GIMP

GIMP is a free and open-source raster graphics editor used for image manipulation and image editing, free-form drawing, transcoding between different image file formats, and more specialized tasks. It is not designed to be used for drawing, though some artists and creators have used it for such.
https://www.gimp.org

OpenShot Video Editor

A free and open-source video editor project started in August 2008 by Jonathan Thomas.

Krita

Krita is a free and open-source raster graphics editor designed primarily for digital art and 2D animation. It has been around since 1998. The software runs on Windows, macOS, Linux, Android, and ChromeOS, and features an OpenGL-accelerated canvas, colour management support, an advanced brush engine, non-destructive layers and masks, group-based layer management, vector artwork support, and switchable customisation profiles.

https://krita.org

CorelDRAW

CorelDRAW is a vector graphics editor developed and marketed by Corel Corporation. It is also the name of the Corel graphics suite, which includes the bitmap-image editor Corel Photo-Paint, as well as other graphics-related programs.

https://www.coreldraw.com

Blender

Blender is a public project hosted on blender.org, licensed as GNU GPL and owned by its contributors. For that reason, Blender is Free and Open-Source software.

https://www.blender.org

Autodesk 3ds Max

Autodesk 3ds Max, formerly 3D Studio and 3D Studio Max, is a professional 3D computer graphics program for making 3D animations, models, games, and images. It is developed and produced by Autodesk Media and Entertainment.

https://www.autodesk.co.uk

Ms PowerPoint, Ms Microsoft Paint, Ms Fresh Paint and Apple Paintbrush

Don't overlook these powerful graphics editors. I have done a lot of artworks using these. Ms PowerPoint even has suggestions on designs.

Unreal Engine and Epic Games and Metahuman

Unreal Engine is a 3D computer graphics game engine developed by Epic Games, first showcased in the 1998 first-person shooter game Unreal.
https://store.epicgames.com

Epic Games, Inc. is an American video game and software developer and publisher based in Cary, North Carolina. The company was founded by Tim Sweeney as Potomac Computer Systems in 1991
https://www.unrealengine.com

Metahuman is a framework for creating a character with human superpowers, by doctoring its features. This is used for Unreal Engine characters in games creation.

Unity

Unity is a cross-platform game engine developed by Unity Technologies, first announced, and released in June 2005 at Apple Worldwide Developers Conference as a Mac OS X game engine. The engine has since been gradually extended to support a variety of desktop, mobile, console and virtual reality platforms.
https://unity.com

VLC media player

VLC media player is a free and open-source, portable, cross-platform media player software and streaming media server developed by the VideoLAN project. VLC is available for desktop operating systems and mobile platforms, such as Android, iOS and iPadOS.
https://www.videolan.org

TurboSquid

TurboSquid is a digital media company that sells stock 3D models used in 3D graphics to a variety of industries, including computer games, architecture, and interactive training.
https://www.turbosquid.com

Font Awesome

Font Awesome is the Internet's icon library and toolkit, used by millions of designers, developers, and content creators.

https://fontawesome.com/start

Mixamo

Mixamo is a 3D computer graphics technology that empowers creativity with animated 3D characters company. Based in San Francisco, a child the company Adobe was found in 2008, com. It develops and sells web-based services for 3D character animation. Maximo's technologies uses machine learning methods to automate the steps of the character animation process, including 3D modelling, rigging, and 3D animation.

https://www.mixamo.com

Plug-Ins and Extensions

Plug-Ins and Extensions

Plug-in

A plug-in is a third-party software or component that adds new functions to the core main open-source software, without altering the core main open-source software. Basically, a plug-in provides extra functionality, but it does not modify the core functionality of the original software. It allows the ability to extend new capabilities beyond the original open-source software.

For example, WordPress is an open-source software, but calendar is not included. If I want to incorporate a calendar on my blog, I will buy a Calendar Plugin (some are free) and install it on my WordPress blog, then my blog would show a calendar.

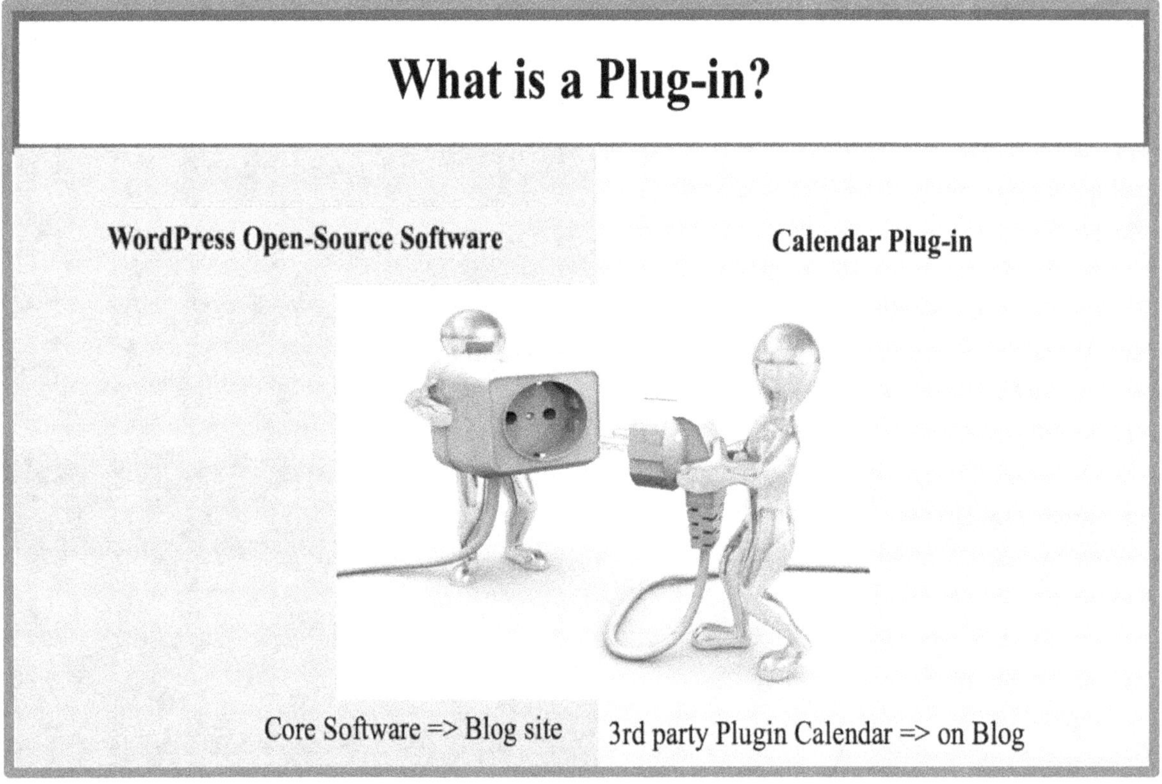

Plugins are made by individuals or companies, not necessarily related to the company that made the core main open-source software. They either sell them or allow free downloads. Plugins can be made to serve more than one core main open-source software. For example, I can build a Calendar Plugin that can do the same thing on WordPress or Jooma!, with a little tweak.

Extensions

An extension is made for modifying the functionality of the core main open-source software. An extension may be provided due to a change in versions, or for a quick bug fix or an improvement of the core main software. To use an extension, the holder of the core main software (open-source or propriety) must be in agreement. Extensions are specific to the particular application, and it will extend functionality of that particular application or software only.

WHERE TO BUY PLUGINS AND EXTENSIONS

https://wordpress.org/plugins/acf-extended
https://extensions.joomla.org
https://plugin.company
https://chrome.google.com/webstore

APP and API

APP

The APP craze seems to be slowing down now – Everyone was heating up on creating / owning an APP. Even kids have their own APPs these days.

An APP (Application) is a computer program or software application designed for a particular function. It is basically, a mini version of the Applications that you have on your desktop computer. The popularity of APPs took hold with the invention of Internet Mobile phones. The phones are small, so APPs were needed to fit into that small space and screen. Many APPs are just a gateway, denoted with the logo /icon of the actual Application that are normally located in some big servers on the internet. So, you click on an APP, it takes you straight to its parent server for further ado. You would have to download and install the App on your device to use it. APPs are able to contact their parent servers using APIs.

There are three types of APPs
Desktop APP – Installed on a computer or laptop. Windows 10 practically runs many Applications via Apps, using App installers.
WebApp – Runs off a browser like Chrome.
Mobile App - Designed to run on a mobile device such as a phone, tablet, or watch.

Native or Hybrid App
Developers in apps development would usually use one of these routes when developing an app - Native or Hybrid

Native App
A native application is a software program developers build for use on a particular platform or device. Native Apps uses the programming language and database provided by the platform owner and run directly on their operating system. Because developers build a native app for use on a particular device and its OS, it has the ability to use device-specific hardware and software smoothly.

Microsoft Native Apps are mainly desk top Apps, developed using Microsoft Platform and Programming language. Examples are Microsoft Edge, Windows Apps, etc.
Google Android Apps are mainly mobile Apps, developed to run on Android phones.
Apple iOS Apps are developed in Apple ecosystem for iPhone and iMac.

When it comes to developing Native Apps, developers find Apple Native Apps to be easier, because Apple has set its iOS and framework in a way that streamline all apps to have a consistent look and feel, by using the provided templates, icons, and graphics. Google, on the other hand, presented a platform for just getting the basics of Android OS, and developers were left to struggle with the UI themselves. Things are changing now though, with Google now trying to standardize the UI, so the Apps can look and feel similar and nicer.

Hybrid App Development

Hybrid App Development develops an App that would be installed on both Apple iOS and Android. This is usually achieved with a neutral programming language like React.JS, and on a neutral platform. After the App has been developed, it would then be streamlined into an Android version and an iOS version by making small alterations, here and there.

FIREBASE – Google's platform for building Hybrid Apps. Allows you free hosting for the app and gives a database as well. There are paid plans that offer more.
https://firebase.google.com

.NET MAUI (formally, Xamarin) – Microsoft's platform for building Hybrid Apps. You can host on a hosting plan on a free trial period, then may need to start paying on a pay-as-you-go plan.
https://dotnet.microsoft.com/en-us/apps/maui

XCode Cloud - Apple's platform for App building, though it is not so big on hybrid systems.
https://developer.apple.com/xcode-cloud

Publishing and Selling Apps

If you have created a useful App, you can publish it on the App stores to sell or share it out free. You can equally download other people's Apps from the App stores.

Google Play charges developers only a one-time registration fee of $25 to publish an App, while Apple has a $99 yearly developer fee, to be paid every year if you want your app to continue being on the Apple AppStore.

Google Play Store
https://play.google.com

Apple AppStore
https://www.apple.com/uk/app-store

Microsoft App Store
https://apps.microsoft.com/store/apps

API

Now people have left APPs and moved on, crazy, crazy, on to API.

An API (Application Programming Interface) is a way for two or more computer software to communicate with each other. It is a type of software interface, offering a service to other pieces of software or applications.

An API works as a set of secret codes that an application on a computer in one company will use in order for another computer application in another company open the gate / door and talk to it and form a link or bridge of communication between the two of them. So, you are at home sleeping at night, and your computers and website are busy having a life out there, heh?

Here is how it works:
Supposing the Council insists on setting up a direct debit for the council tax and scheduled it for the first day of each month. So, I give them my bank details, which they passed on to their bank manager, who then sets up a Direct Debit. At midnight of the last day of last month / the first day of this month, the banking software on the computer at the council's bank will contact the banking software on the computer at my bank, to try to yank out the amount it's been told - It will be lucky if it gets any money there?!? – Cheeky computer application!

This fintech application on the computer at the council's bank was only able to enter my bank account because my bank had already shared its secret code word for accessing their bank and my account. These secret code words (mini encrypted computer programs) are called API KEYS.

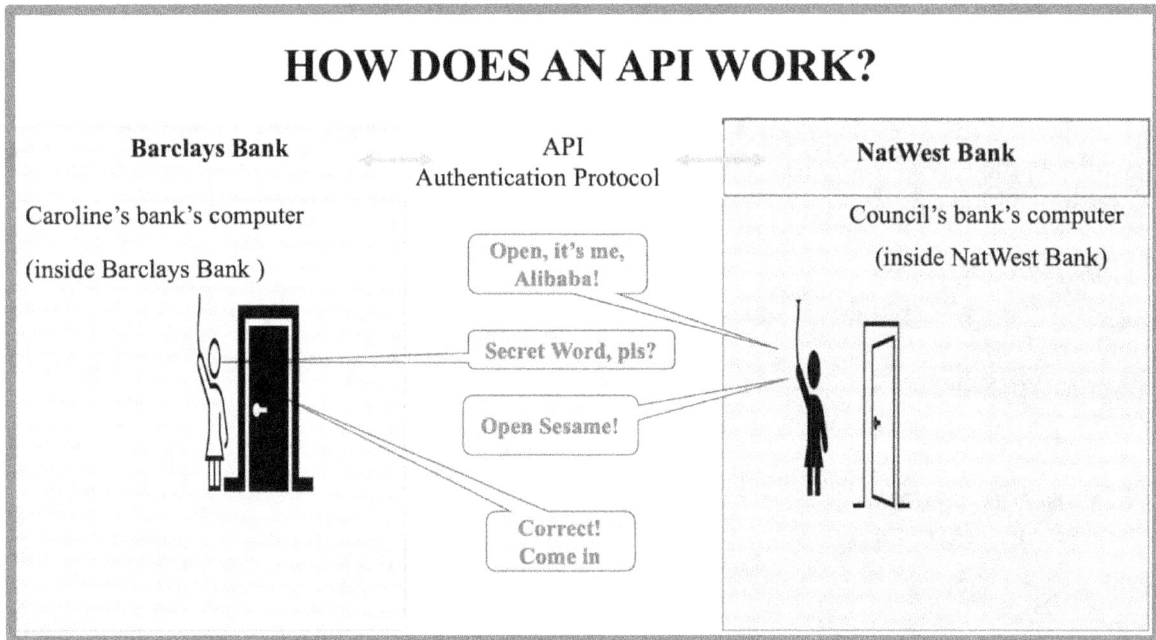

Payment Gateways, E-Commerce

E-commerce

E-commerce or Ecommerce or eCommerce or E-Commerce or e-commerce or ecommerce or Ecommerce = Electronic Commerce.

E-commerce is commercial transactions conducted electronically on the internet. That is, the buying and selling of goods and services, or the transmitting of funds or data electronically over the Internet. A business can have products to sell, create a branded and a store experience, run adverting campaigns to attract customers and do all kind of things as it is done in the physical, except that the business models are carried out digitally and money takes the form of electronic transactions only.

An ecommerce web site is the digital storefront of the business on the internet. The business can have its own ecommerce site on a dedicated domain, with a payment gateway system that facilitates the selling of the goods to completion. Or the business may simply have a storefront on a multi-channel selling platform like Shopify, WooCommerce, which takes care of the payments, and only charges a transaction fee.

The Most Common Types of Ecommerce Business Models

B2C (Business-to-consumer) – A business selling directly to their end-users. E.g. Tesco sells milk and bread to customers.

B2B (Business-to-business) – A software company rebranded its white labels software with the logo of another smaller provider of it services to end users.

B2B2C (Business-to-business-to-consumer) – A big supplier selling to customers through a middle retailer's storefront. Dropshipping through platforms like AliExpress or Printful.

B2G (Business-to-government) – Big firms that bids for government contracts, e.g. Microsoft selling cloud services to the MOD.

C2B (Consumer-to-business) – Individual consumer selling services to a firm. E.g. Affiliate marketing services.

C2C (Consumer-to-consumer) – People buying and selling to each on a marketplace platform like eBay, Gumtree, Amazon, Facebook Marketplace

Some Marketplace Platforms

https://www.bigcommerce.com
https://sell.amazon.com
https://www.shopify.com
https://woocommerce.com
https://www.ebay.com

Payment gateway

Payment Gateway and Checkout

If you are going to accept payments online, you would need an online Checkout and a Payment Gateway. Online checkouts are just like the checkouts in the supermarkets. You pick up an item, then go to the checkout, where it is scanned, and the total is calculated for you to pay. You pay for it and gets given a receipt. On the web, it is exactly the same. Usually, the software that is used to build your web site, would have a build-in checkout (Ecommerce Software).

For the person selling online, in order to be able to receive the payment, you need to contact some payment gateway providers (operates just like Marchant banks). They will give you details on how to set up your online checkout and payment system, so customers can send money to you, via them.

Payment Gateway Providers

There are many payment gateway providers, but here are the well-established ones over time.
STRIPE
https://stripe.com

PAYPAL
https://www.paypal.com/us/business/accept-payments

AUTHORIZE
https://www.authorize.net

Newer ones

WORLDPAY
https://worldpay.fisglobal.com

APPLE PAY
https://www.apple.com

GOOGLE PAY
https://pay.google.com

ALIPAY
https://global.alipay.com

Sandbox Account

Sandbox Account is the test account that the Payment Gateway Provider gives you to test things first, before going live. If you are a developer setting up a payment system, do try to use the Sandbox Account for security reasons.

Wallet

Wallet is an app on your Phone and Watch that functions just like an ordinary purse, except it is not physical. You connect your bank cards and your bank account to this app and organise what cards you prefer to pay what with. You use your phone ID to sign into the Wallet, effectively turning your smartphone or watch into a digital wallet that is secure, easy and convenient to pay everyday things with. The wallet, not only organises your credit and debit cards, it can also store boarding passes, tickets, loyalty cards and help to keep track of your money, track allowances and cash withdrawals, all in one place.

Samsung Pay Wallet
https://www.samsung.com/uk/samsung-pay

Google Wallet.
https://wallet.google

My Wallet
https://mywallet-app.com

Apple Wallet
https://www.apple.com/uk/wallet

Cash App (Used locally to send money between friends and family)
https://cash.app

QR Codes

If you go the supermarket and pick up an item on the self, it will have a barcode on it. Then when you scan it on the barcode scanner, it will decode it to show such information like the name of the item, the shop stock number code for the item, the price, etc. See, that is a lot of information that has been reduced to just that small graphics matrix. The standard barcodes that shops use is one-dimensional, can only be read in one direction - top to bottom and stores only a small amount of information.

The QR (Quick Response) code is a type of barcode that is two-dimensional (2D barcodes). The information is encoded on a 2D graphics matrix. QR reads information in two directions, that is, from top to bottom and right to left. This allows it to house much more data than the one-dimensional barcode. They can include between 3000 - 4000 Characters on a very small space.

The Japanese company, Denso Wave, a Toyota subsidiary invented the QR code in 1994. They developed the QR code, a type of barcode that could encode kanji, kana, and alphanumeric characters within the 'iconic' Square box. That was for them to use to track all vehicles and parts conveniently and accurately during the manufacturing process.

Denso Wave made their QR code publicly available and declared that they would not exercise their patent rights. This meant anyone could make and use QR codes freely. The original version of the QR code created by Denso Wave in the 1990s is called QR code, but since then, there have risen different variations (Aztec code, Maxi code, PDF417 code, Semacode).

QR Code Generator

To create a QR code, you use a QR Code generator. Simply enter the information that is going to be stored on the QR code (your text, URL, SMS, telephone, or vCard contact information). The QR code will be generated automatically, then you either download it or transfer it as a data to mobile devices and it can be saved in vector graphic formats - EPS and SVG, as well as high-resolution PNG, GIF or JPEG raster graphics formats. QR generator normally create QR codes image with the information being encoded according to ISO/IEC 18004:2006 standard, that is, in Black and White Dot pixel matrix. However, some generators can help you to create your customized QR Code with your styles, logo, frame, colours, etc. QR codes are static, but now, there are platforms that offer dynamic QR codes, using their QR-Server management system.

QR Code Generator Sites.

https://www.qrcode-monkey.com
https://www.beaconstac.com/qr-code-generator
https://www.adobe.com/express/feature/image/qr-code-generator
https://goqr.me
https://www.qrstuff.com
https://www.canva.com/qr-code-generator
https://www.qr-code-generator.com

Parts of a standard QR code

How does a QR reader decodes the QR?

A QR reader decodes a QR code in a sequence of events:

A QR reader firstly, has to identify if the shape is a standard QR code or not, by scanning the outer borders of the shape – the **Quiet Zone**.

Next, it looks for three black squares in the top and bottom left, and top right corners. These squares – the **Finder Pattern** tells the QR reader the starting boundaries of the QR code.

Next, it scans the smaller square contained, a bit up from the bottom right hand corner. This is the **Alignment Pattern** that ensures that the QR code can be read, even if it is skewed or at an angle. Then it uses the **Timing Pattern**, an L-shaped line that runs between the three squares in the finder pattern as a guide to scanning the matrix. The timing pattern helps the reader to identify individual squares within the whole code and makes it possible for a damaged QR code to be read. Then it reads everything within the **Data Cells**, which is the rest of the matrix pattern that contains the actual information.

The patterns within a QR codes represent binary codes that can be interpreted to reveal the code's data. The QR reader then analyses the QR code by breaking the whole thing down to a grid. It looks at the individual grid squares and assigns each one a value based on whether it is black or white. It then groups the grid squares to create larger patterns.

How do I scan QR codes?

Most smartphones have built-in QR scanners, which are sometimes built in the camera. A QR scanner is simply a way to scan QR codes. Some tablets, such as the Apple iPad, have QR readers built into their cameras. Some older devices may require a particular app to read QR codes – these apps are readily available on the Apple App Store and Google Play.

Scanning a QR code is just like taking a photo of the QR code using your device. Open the QR reader application or the camera on your smartphone. Point it at the QR code – you should be able to point your camera from any angle and still receive the necessary information. The data will be instantly shown on screen – for instance, if the QR code contains contact details, your phone should be able to instantly download these.

Barcode and QR Reader / Scanner APPs

Barcode Scanner, Kaspersky QR Scanner - Android-based devices).
QR Code Reader - On iOS-Devices like iPhones
ScanLife
CodeBot

Free Online Barcode Reader

http://www.the-qrcode-generator.com
https://online-barcode-reader.inliteresearch.com
https://cmbdn.cognex.com/free-barcode-scanner
https://products.aspose.app/barcode/recognize

QR Codes Are Used

- In advertising campaigns, because it provides a faster and more intuitive way to direct people to websites, than by entering URLs manually.
- To link directly to product pages online.
- By businesses that need to keep a close eye on products and supplies, such as the construction, engineering, and retail industries.
- In Tracing Apps, such as in a pandemic.
- In the classroom and in the library to find books
- By postal services around the world to tract parcels.
- As barcodes on the packaging of some product types.
- For websites URL links that consumers can scan to open landing pages, websites, and online stores instantly.
- To generate marketing leads with Email QR Codes that takes the person direct to your customer sales or support team.
- In SMS QR Code to send predefined texts to a group.
- For storing a local business telephone, so that all your customers need to do, is scan the QR Code and it makes a call for them.

- To increase social engagements, like Facebook QR Codes and YouTube QR Code
- On posters or included on the product tags.
- To give out Digital coupons connected to promotions.

Do QR codes collect my personal information and data?

QR code-generating software does not collect personally identifiable information.
The data it does collect – and which is visible to the code's creators – includes location, the number of times the code has been scanned and at what times, plus the operating system of the device which scanned the code (i.e., iPhone or Android).

Are QR codes safe?

QR codes on their own are secure, however, attackers can embed malicious scripts that intercepts the QR code and inject malware that either re-direct the customers to their URLs and tricks them into sharing confidential information. Or the malware will install an unsuspecting program on the mobile device when scanned, which could then extract data from a mobile device or corrupt it. Some scammers can also use your brand and logo to send fake QR codes to your customers.

Cryptocurrencies

A cryptocurrency, sometimes called crypto-currency or crypto is a digital virtual world currency that is secured by cryptography, which makes it nearly impossible to counterfeit or double-spend.

Cryptocurrencies were introduced with the intent to boycott centralised intermediary financial infrastructure, i.e., banks and monetary institutions by presenting a new, decentralised paradigm of a monetary system. In this system of cryptocurrencies, financial watchdogs are not necessary to enforce trust and police transactions between two parties. Cryptocurrencies promised to make it easier to transfer funds directly between two parties, without the need for a trusted third party like a bank or a credit card company. It is a relatively new technology, where the decentralized transfers are secured using Public Keys and Private Keys encryption, and other proofs of ID, along with proof of the source of the money.

The cryptocurrency system functions on networks based on blockchain technology, which runs on networks of computers that is parallel to the normal internet. It was thought that this system eliminates the possibility of a single point of failure, such as a large bank failure setting off a cascade of crises around the world.

In Cryptocurrencies world, you can take a loan, which are processed without a backing collateral, you can invest and trade on the crypto markets, which can generate profits, although the market has seen a rise and fall in recent years, and there are fears of market manipulations. Any investor can purchase cryptocurrency from popular crypto exchanges such as Coinbase, apps such as Cash App, or through brokers. Within the United States, Bitcoin are available on the Chicago Mercantile Exchange.

Bitcoin is by far the most popular and valuable cryptocurrency, followed by Ethereum, Binance Coin, Solana, and Cardano. Bitcoin was invented by an anonymous person, called Satoshi Nakamoto, who introduced it to the world via a white paper in 2008.

Although cryptocurrencies are considered a form of money, you cannot go to the shop to buy anything with it (well, except in El Salvador and the Central African Republic).

Currently, cryptocurrencies such as Bitcoin is being tested as an intermediate currency for streamline money transfers across borders. Thus, a flat currency conversion and with a flat fee across all borders.

Due to the lack of coherent regulations, there are few protections against deceptive or unethical management practices and since it is not backed by any public or private entities, many investors have lost large sums to management teams that failed to deliver a product. Now many governments are seeking to regulate and vet cryptocurrencies for securities and currency values.

In the past, the Securities and Exchange Commission (SEC) in the USA took the stance that Bitcoin and Ethereum were not securities; however, in September 2022, SEC Chairman, Gary Gensler stated that he believes cryptocurrencies are securities. This stance implies that cryptocurrency's legal status may become subject to regulation.

Cryptocurrencies are legal in the European Union and in June 2021, the European Commission released the Markets in Crypto-Assets (MiCA) regulation that sets safeguards for regulations. China has banned cryptocurrency exchanges and mining, while Japan's Payment Services Act defines Bitcoin as legal property that requires checks.

On May 20, 2021, the U.S. Department of the Treasury announced a proposal that would require taxpayers to report any cryptocurrency transaction of $10,000 and above to the IRS for income tax purposes. The IRS (Internal Revenue Service) treats cryptocurrencies as a financial asset, same as a property, and if you reap capital gains in selling or trading cryptocurrencies, the government wants a piece of the profits.

Cryptocurrencies are generated by mining, and it is said that anyone can mine them using a computer with an internet connection. However, mining popular cryptocurrencies requires considerable energy costing too much, that only the large firms whose revenues run into the billions of dollars can afford to mine.

Though cryptocurrency blockchains are highly secure, other crypto repositories, such as exchanges and wallets can be hacked. On top of that, many investors and merchants rely on exchanges or other custodians to store their cryptocurrency, of which theft or loss of data of one of these third parties could result in the loss of one's entire investment. Also, some assets are becoming inaccessible due to lost passwords or incorrect sending email addresses. Cryptocurrencies have become a popular tool for money laundering and illicit purchases, that now, the Federal Bureau of Investigation randomly checks users.

Blockchain

A blockchain is digital information collected in groups and stored in a database or ledger that is shared among the nodes of computers in a virtual private network that runs parallel to the internet. The information in the database is stored in a set of blocks. Each block would contain a maximum set of information that has been verified by each member of the network, then time-stamped and stored. The information in each block is set (like set on stone) and cannot be changed. Any new information after that is then collected and stored in the next block, which sits after the first block, like a chain of blocks.

This is an innovation that guarantees the fidelity and security of a record and makes it almost impossible to forge transaction histories of the data and thus generates trust without the need for a trusted third party.

Cryptocurrencies such as Bitcoin functions on this concept of blockchains and the technology may well serve other industries, like supply chains, and processes such as online voting and crowdfunding and some financial institutions.

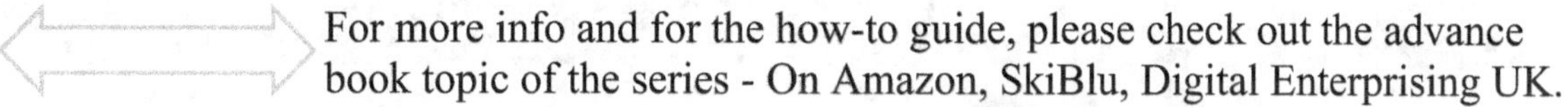 For more info and for the how-to guide, please check out the advance book topic of the series - On Amazon, SkiBlu, Digital Enterprising UK.

Images, Logo, Colours

Images, Logo, Colours

All images are copy-righted, though some sites allow you to use some for free. Before you copy or download any image or photo from the internet to use in your work, make sure it says, 'Free image + Royalty-free'. On the other hand, you could take your own pictures using your mobile and upload them onto your computer and use on your site.

These sites allow you to use their images free but do check up on Royalty first.
https://unsplash.com
https://www.pexels.com
https://www.freeimages.com
https://www.freepik.com/popular-photos
https://depositphotos.com
https://favpng.com
https://www.pexels.com/ - (free image option only)
https://www.pexels.com/videos
https://www.freeimages.com

How to copy an image
To copy an image, either use the download button or right-click on the image and choose 'Save Image As'.

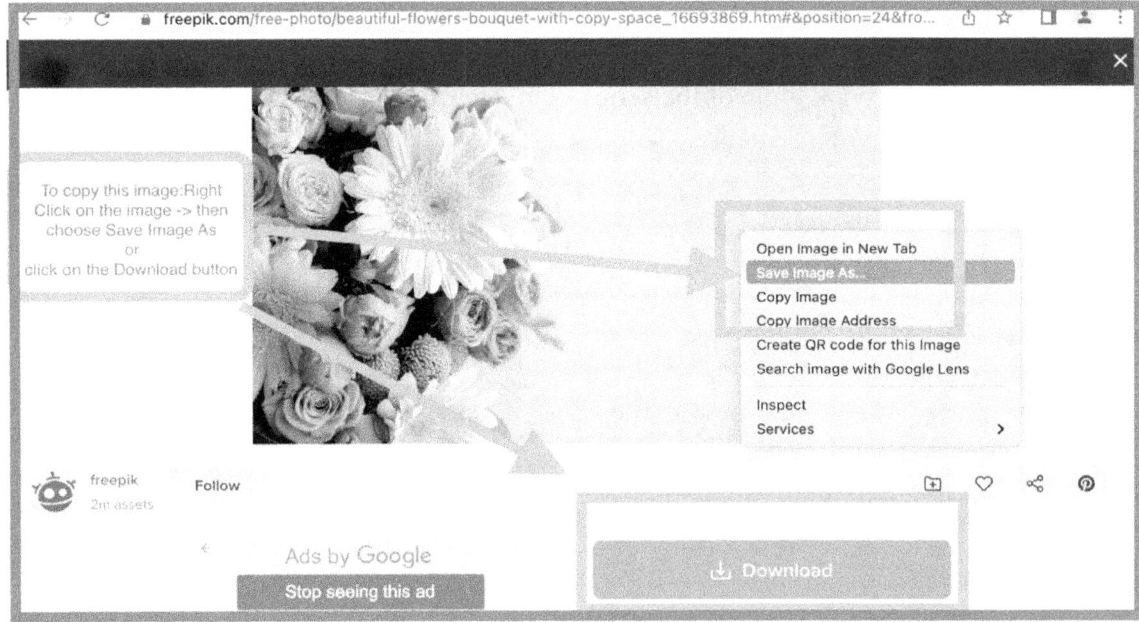

There are two types of Images Formats.

Raster – Raster images are taken in pixels and can only be resized to enlarge them just a little, before they become pixelated (blur). Their file extensions are - JPEG, GIF, and PNG.

Vector - Vector Image formats are constructed using proportionate formulas and are more flexible to resize. Therefore, they are used for logo and banner making. Their file extensions are -SVG. Unlike raster images, vector images retain quality when resized.

High Resolution and Low Resolution

Image resolution is measured in DPI (dots per inch) or PPI (pixel per inch). Image quality may be resolution 72dpi (low resolution), going up to 300dpi (high resolution). For use on web sites, the low-resolution images are good enough. However, to get a quality photo print, it is best to start with a high-resolution image.

File Extension for saving Images and Photos

Image File Extension	Brief Description
JPEG and JPEG 2000	JPEG stands for Joint Photographic Experts Group, an international organization that standardised the format during the late 1980s. JPEG is a commonly used method of lossy compression for digital images, particularly for those images produced by digital photograph and complex still images. When you compress an image using lossy compression, you determine the file size and image quality trade-off (e.g., smaller files = worse image quality). The more editing and saving of a single image you do, the worse the quality of the image will be. A less common version of the JPEG format, the JPEG 2000 format improves quality and compression ratios at the expense of processing power. These files are commonly used in the entertainment industry for movie editing and distribution. Use Cases: Use JPEG 2000 to edit cinema quality video.
PNG Portable Network Graphics	Lossless compression saves your images in an entirely different format (usually PNG). Here the image quality is never sacrificed because no information is eliminated and

	so the final file size of the image will always be bigger than with lossy compression. PNGs are low resolution, but you can edit them and not lose quality. You can save your image with more colours on a transparent background, making for a much sharper, image that will be amazing for interactive documents such as web pages. The PNG file format supports transparency. This means that objects within an image can be rendered transparent.
GIF **Graphics Interchange Format**	GIFs are most common in their animated form, in pop up pages and in banner ads. In their more basic form, GIFs are formed from up to 256 colours in the RGB colour sphere. Due to the limited number of colours, the file size is drastically reduced. This is a common file type for web projects where an image needs to load up very quickly. It also support transparency rendering. Use Cases: Used for creating simple images, logos, and simple animations.
TIFF **Tagged Image File**	A TIF is a large raster file that doesn't lose quality. This file type is known for using "lossless compression," meaning the original image data is maintained regardless of how many times you copy, re-save, or compress the original file, making them good for frequently edited images. When used with a program like Photoshop, they can store tags, layers, and transparency. TIFF files are quite large and can take forever to load up on websites, TIFF files are also commonly used when saving photographs for prints, used in publishing and desktop publishing software.
BMP **bitmap image files**	BMPs are a raster image format popular on Microsoft Windows systems, especially the older Windows systems. Though they can be easily opened in most image editing applications and browsers, they are not used frequently on the web due to their size.

SVG **Common Vector Image File**	SVGs are the most common vector image files. They retain image quality no matter how large or small the image is made, because it uses polygons to retain image quality. Use Cases: SVGs are ideal for responsive web design, as well as for when creating company logos.
PDF **Portable Document Format**	PDFs are Adobe's proprietary document format. They are designed to store more than just images and are usually used for documents containing both rich text and multimedia. Use Cases: PDFs are useful to print documents forms, as form tends to fit onto a single page. Adobe provides a free Acrobat Reader to open PDFs. Most browsers can open them, and they can be converted into Ms Word documents.

Common Image File Conversions

Images can be converted from one file format to another. For example - JPG to PNG, JPG to SVG. There are tools on the internet that are used to convert images. Some of them allows you to convert the images for free.

https://image.online-convert.com/convert-to-jpg
https://convertio.co/image-converter
https://www.freeconvert.com/image-converter
https://www.simpleimageresizer.com/online-image-converter

Image Resize

There are tools on the internet to use for image resize. Some are free.

https://www.adobe.com/express/feature/image/resize
https://www.resizepixel.com
https://promo.com/tools/image-resizer
https://picresize.com

Tools to convert a raster image to a vector

Adobe Illustrator - paid tool
Adobe Photoshop – paid tool
GIMP – free tool
BMP (.bmp, .dib)
PDF (.pdf)

Logo

You can make a logo easily with a little bit of imagination and creativity. Logos are linked to the brand, so that anyone; just seeing your logo, would know that it's your web site or business. Logos are saved with .PNG file extension.

Tools for making a Logo

Ms PowerPoint
Adobe Suite
GIMP
Logo Wizard on your webhosting dashboard

Or use these free online tools

https://looka.com/logo-maker
https://www.adobe.com/express/create/logo
https://www.freelogodesign.org
https://www.canva.com/create/logos

Banner

You can take your logo (or any of your product branding image) and resize it to enlarge into a long rectangular banner, according to the size required. Banners are like the flag for your shop.

Favicon

Favicon is a smaller version of your logo that sits in the browser, right at the beginning, before the characters in the URL of your site. It loads up before the page comes into view. If someone minimises your site to the bottom, it will be the small image icon that represents the site. When constructing a web site using a wizard, the wizard may automatically re-size and convert a copy of your logo into a favicon and put it there for you. Favicon is saved with the .ICO file extension.

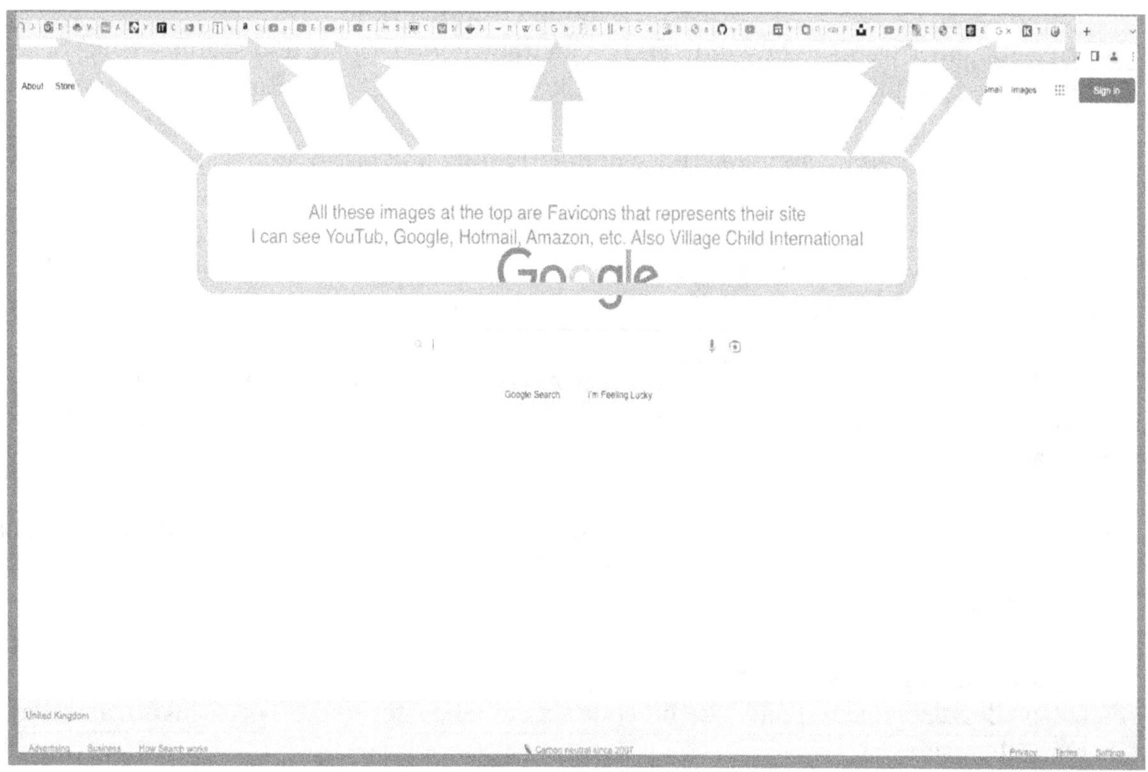

TAG and TAGLINE

Tag

When you put something on the internet that you want people to find when they are searching for that type of item, you tagged it to a keyword. Example: I have a shop online, selling milk and bread, and my shop's name is Tesco. So, I would tag 'milk' with a few keywords (Tesco, Milk, Fresh Milk, Full Cream, Fat-free, Organic Milk). These are all the possible scenario of words that a customer might type in Google search. That way, my milk will also come up along with the others. Similarly for Bread, I would tag to keywords (Tesco, Bread, Fresh Bread, White bread, wholemeal bread).

Tagline

A Tagline is catchy phrase; a slogan or a Motto slang, that is linked to your product brand for the sake of advertisements. You would put it across or next to your Brand name or Logo. When people hear it anywhere, anytime (even in their sleep), immediately your shop / product brand will come to their mind. For example.

Nike – "Just do it'!

Tesco – "every little help"

MacDonald – "I'm Lovin' it"

Homebase – "Make a house a home"

Search Engine Optimization

When a customer wants to buy milk and bread, they go to Google and search 'Milk' or 'Bread', if I want the customer to see my milk and bread first (Top Ranking), before the others (which translates to a high probability of buying from me, instead of from the other shops that are also selling milk and bread). I will tag my milk and bread with as many keywords as possible, to try and get to first position in the list of milk and bread that comes up.

Ok - In the real world; just tagging will not secure me 1st position in a searched list. This is because Google has already sold all the top-ranking positions for top Dollar.

Search engine optimization (SEO) is the process of improving the quality and quantity of website traffic to a web site or a web page from search engines. SEO targets unpaid traffic rather than direct traffic or paid traffic.

Big shops have a whole team of people called Search Engine Optimization Analysts /Managers/ Consultants, or something, whose job it is to sit there and do all kinds of jiggery-puckery to get to that Top Ranking, and stay there!

There are some IT Consultation / Marketing companies that offer these services for a fee. You can also advertise yourself and take on contracts to take sites to the Top Ranking and thereby, increase their sales.

Colours

Colour Picker

Colour Pickers are tools that you can use to pick colours for your site or applications, that would work in harmony with each. When doing colour combinations, you want colours that would complement each other, while still each having its own mood. Colour Pickers can also help pick colours that will give contrast, so as to make readability better.

Operating systems such as Microsoft Windows or macOS have a system colour picker, which can be used by third-party programs. Mixing colours and colours gradient, masking or fading of colours can also be done there.

With online tools, you can upload an image or provide a website URL and get the RGB Colour or HEX Colour codes.
https://imagecolorpicker.com/color-code
https://htmlcolorcodes.com/color-picker
https://www.w3schools.com/colors/colors_picker.asp

When working with colours in computing, natural colours that we have in everyday life have to be translated into computer codes. There are three main models of colours in computing.

RGB

The RGB (Red, Green, and Blue) colour model is this – if you add the three colours - Red, Green, and Blue in the right proportion, you will get a colour of the mathematical proportions of how much of each that you put in. For example, if you add an equal amount of Red, Green, and Blue, you get pure Black (Elementary school Arts class). So, the coordinates for getting pure Black are Red, Green, and Blue = 0, 0, 0. That is the three colours cancels the power of each other exactly.
Colour Black = RGB (0, 0, 0)

CMYK

The CMYK colour model works by using printing ink colours - Cyan, Magenta, Yellow, and Key (Black). This model works by subtracting colours proportions from the 4 starting colours. If you take the printer and remove the colour ink cartridges, then you will be left with only pure Black printing. That is, [(cyan, magenta, yellow, and black)} – [(cyan, magenta, yellow)] = black. The degree of any of the four colours that you take off, you will be left with a colour that is proportional to it. Colour Black = CMYK (0, 0, 0, 100).

HEX

Hex model uses hex triplet numbers or degrees using the 360o colour spectrum. A hex triplet is a six-digit, three-byte hexadecimal number used in HTML, CSS, SVG, and other computing applications to represent colours. The bytes represent the Red, Green and Blue components of the colour spectrum. One byte represents a number in the range 00 to FF (in hexadecimal notation), or 0 to 255 in decimal notation. The Hex code for the colour Black is = #000000. The hex value of a colour is in computer language, so, you just have to find the collect codes for the colour that you want. There are many online tools to help convert colours to hex.
https://htmlcolors.com/cmyk-to-hex
https://colordesigner.io/convert/cmyktohex

COLOUR	RGB	CMYK	HEX Key
Black	0, 0, 0	0, 0, 0, 100	#000000
White	255, 255, 255, 1	0, 0, 0, 1	#Ffffff
Red	234, 18, 2, 1	0, 92, 99, 8	#Ea1202

Domain, Domain Name, Website Address

Domain, Domain Name, Website Address

Domain

A domain simply means having my own structure area or sphere within a bigger sphere (the world), be it in the real world or in the virtual world (World Wide Web).

Say, I found myself a nice little shop (domain) in the shopping centre, I get to decide how to organise it and what to do with it, like erect shelves on the walls and sell milk and bread in the shop. Since I don't want my customers to keep referring to it as, 'The shop that sells milk and bread', so I give it a name (domain name) say, - Tesco. In case I fear someone else might steal my shop's name, so I register it (registered domain) with the authorities – Tesco.co.uk. Now, I want customers to know where my shop is, so I assign the shop name to the building address and show it as my business address (website address).
So, where my real shop address would be – Tesco, 1 High Street, London, UK, my virtual address will be – www.tesco.co.uk and the internet surfing address will be – http://www.tesco.co.uk.

ICANN

ICANN (Internet Corporation for Assigned Names and Numbers) is the authority that domains are registered with.

ICANN (Internet Corporation for Assigned Names and Numbers) is a private, non-government, non-profit corporation with responsibility for Internet Protocol (IP) address space allocation, protocol parameter assignment, domain name system (DNS), management and root server system management functions.
https://www.icann.org.

WHOIS Lookup

Before I can register my domain – tesco.co.uk, I should check to see that no one else has already registered that domain name as theirs, by doing a WHOIS Lookup.

WHOIS is a query and response protocol that is widely used for querying databases that store the registered users or assignees of an Internet resource, such as a domain name, an IP address block or an autonomous system, but it is also used for a wider range of other information. WHOIS is a public database that houses the information collected when someone registers a domain name or updates their DNS settings. ICANN, the International Corporation for Assigned Names and Numbers, regulates the WHOIS database. They've done so since 1982.
https://www.whois.com/whois

Register A Domain Name

Keep it Real - Beware   Do not register a name that another business has already registered a trademark on or is known with. For example, take Tesco – everybody knows that it is a well-established supermarket in the UK. If I then decide that since my shop is in India, I go and registered my domain as – www.tesco.in or www.tesco.net.

Or a popular word linked with someone, like 'Posh Spice', which was linked to one of the singers in a popular UK girl band. If I go and pay and register my domain as – www.posh-spice.com. If that singer or Tesco should complain, the domain would be transferred to them, and I would have lost my money, plus any work I had already done on the site.

If you fail to renew your domain registration on time, anybody can then register it after a warning period. Also, some Hosting Providers may quickly renew it on time and then try to sell it to you later at a higher price.

Can you buy a domain that was already registered?

Yes, there are people selling and buying domain names all the time. If there is domain name that matches your business, you can look up the owner on Whois, then contact them to buy it, or go through your Web Hosting Provider. Although now people are paying a few extra dollars to hide their details from the public lookup. This site sells and auctions Domain Names. https://www.namecheap.com/market

Domain Issues Help

If someone steals your domain or your Web Hosting Provider are maltreating you, you can contact ICANN
ICANN Global Support Center
globalsupport@icann.org

Web Hosting Provider

If you want to register a domain, you don't go direct to ICANN, you will normally look for a Web Hosting Provider. They would have a Domain Name Generator on their site to help you in picking a domain name that best matches you.

Web Hosting Providers provide web hosting for sites. To host your web site means that all the files concerning your website are installed and stored on a special server called a Web Server, and it is linked to the internet, so that people can find your site. You can buy a web server and place it under your desk at home and placed all your website files on it and link it to internet. The only trouble with that, is that the traffic coming through your broadband might not be allowed by your broadband provider. Also, no matter what, it would be slower than the service provided by the Web Hosting Providers. Another thing is that you will also need a database server, where the information about the items and the others are stored. Web Hosting Providers usually offer both servers as part of a package.

Web Hosting Providers of January 2023

Hostinger
Bluehost.
BigRock.
Hostgator.
GoDaddy.
A2 Hosting.
Interserver
IPage
MochaHost
InMotion
A2 Hosting
GreenGeeks
Namecheap
Digital Ocean
CloudWays
DreamHost

Keep it Real - Beware   The list above is in no particular order and there is affiliation with these companies. You need to go to each and check out what they are offering, and their prices.

Types of Web Hosting Services

There are different types of web hosting services a provider can offer -: Shared Hosting (Free or Paid Plan) Virtual Hosting, Dedicated Server Hosting, Cloud Hosting.

Shared Hosting (Free or Paid Plan) – You share the Web server with other companies, but your data and workspace will be in your own separate, secured compartment. This is the cheapest, and the best one to start out on, because most of the set-up have already been done, and they provider would be able to guide you a lot.

Dedicated Server Hosting – Like above, except that you have a whole server to yourself. This is only needed for big sites.

Virtual Hosting – This is for highly technical web developers, who have a lot of time on their hands to set up things and manage every little thing themselves. Digital Ocean is one provider that sells such a hosting entity. Here, you are left to set up your web server, database server, etc. Amazon also provide this service with their AWS Tier1

Cloud Hosting – This is for the big guys who need to spread their wings out in the cloud. Amazon also offers this service.

For people who are new to this field, it is best to go for shared hosting, because it will come with a wizard that does the setting up job for you. And usually, they would have support teams that will guide you if you are stuck.

Here is a quick guide when choosing a web host provider

Support – is there a live person on the chats. Is there a 24hr telephone helpline?

How much - is the plan and what is thrown in with the plan?

Domain – do they give a free domain name?

DNS – is it free? And can you get access to it?

SSL certificate – is it free, or how much?

Security wise - will your data be secured?

Web hosting server – how much space and bandwidth?

Softaculous installer – what software is included?

Domain Transfer – is it easy and straight forward to transfer out?

Migration – will they help you with migration?

The World Wide Web

The World Wide Web - also known as the web, WWW or W3, refers to all the public websites or pages that users can access on their local computers and other devices through the internet. These pages and documents are interconnected by means of hyperlinks that users click on for information.

HTTP (Hypertext Transfer Protocol)

The Hypertext Transfer Protocol is an application layer protocol in the Internet Protocol suite model for distributed, collaborative, hypermedia information systems.

HTTPS (Secured Hypertext Transfer Protocol)

Hypertext Transfer Protocol Secure is an extension of the Hypertext Transfer Protocol. It uses cryptography for secure communication over a computer network and is widely used on the Internet. In HTTPS, the communication protocol is encrypted using Transport Layer Security (formerly; Secure Sockets Layer).

A domain validated certificate

A domain validated certificate is what validates your web site and put the padlock to show people that your site is secure. This certificate is part of the SSL (Secure Sockets Layer) certificate that you register and buy from a Certification Authority (CA). Certification Authority is an entity that stores, signs, and issues out these digital certificates. The certificate also provides secure emails from your site. Your Web Hosting Provider will either sell you one or give you one free for some time.

The 's' in the website address shows that the site has registered with the Certificate Authority.

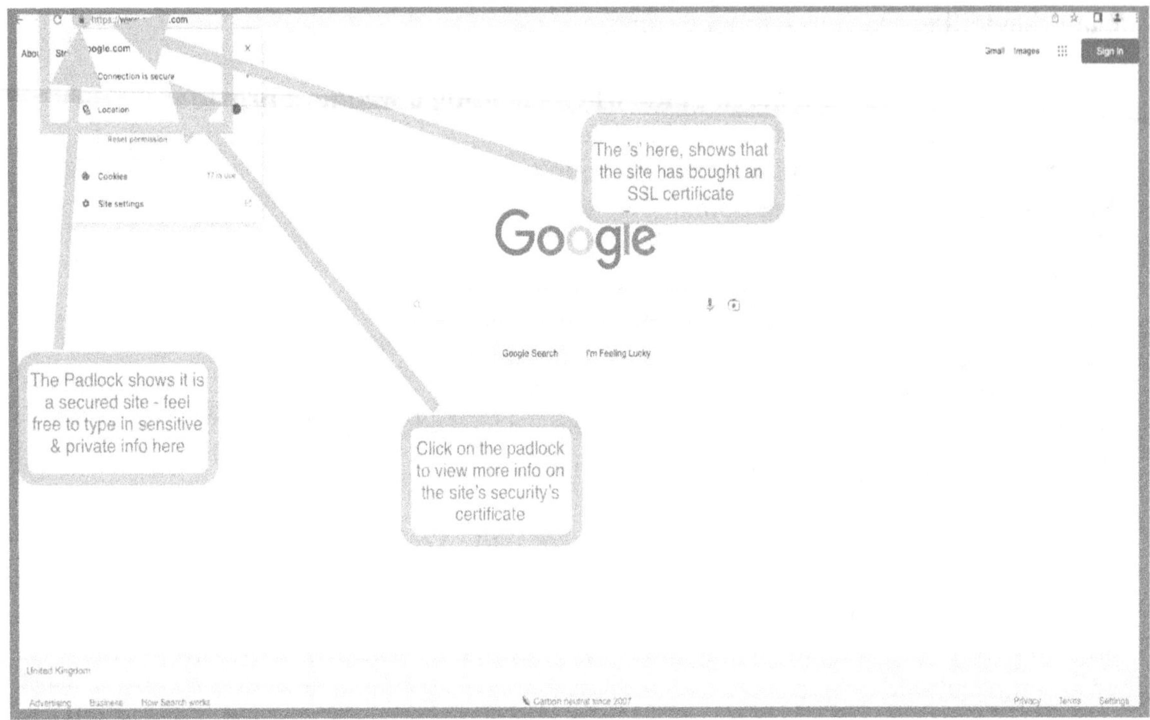

There is no 's' here, so it means that the site cannot proof its SSL certificate.

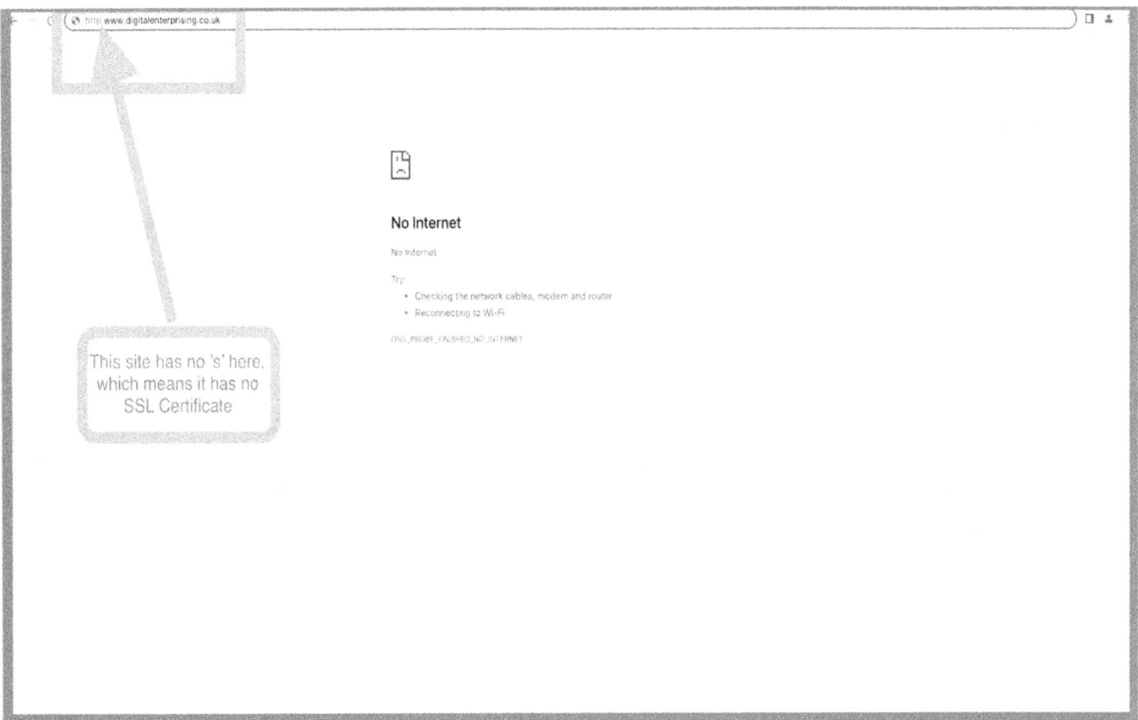

If you click on further info, it will tell you that the site is not secured.

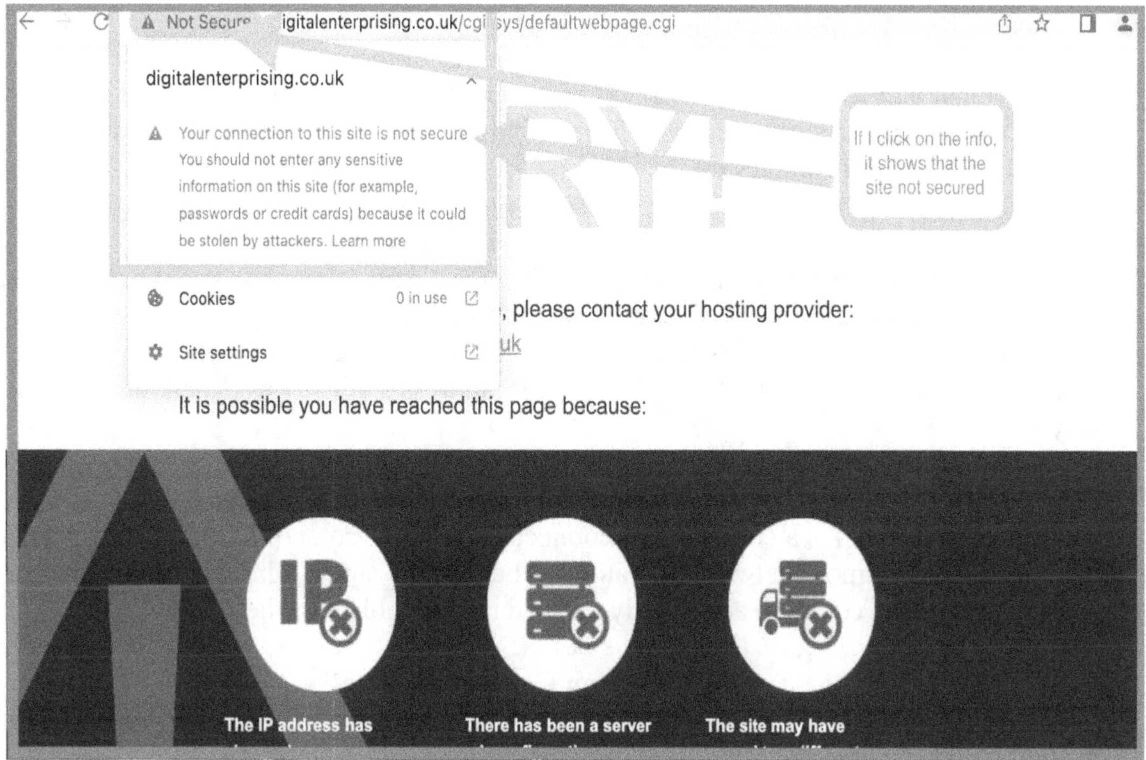

Website Address

Website Addresses are not domain names. A Website Address is a domain name address that has been mapped to a DNS server and has been resolved to an exact Web server, plus then had the internet protocol http or https added to it. Say, if my domain name is tesco.co.uk. Then if I don't host it on a web server, you would not be able to find my shop, because there is no web site address attached to it. If then I host it on a web server and map it on a DNS, the web site address will then become http://www.tesco.co.uk or https://www.tesco.co.uk, if I have paid for a security certificate.

URL

URL (Uniform Resource Locator). A URL is the exact address of a given unique resource on the web. Say, supposing my web site address is www.tesco.co.uk. Then I am selling milk, which is on Aisle1, on the Top shelf, the item is -fresh whole milk-1pint. To get directly to that milk, the URL will be = www.tesco.co.uk/aisle1/topshelf/item-freshwholemilk-1pint.

Resource

A resource (Res) is anything that is valuable for an event or for an activity to function effectively or can be used as an asset to add good value to things, activities, etc. A bottle of milk is a resource for making tea and a great resource for children's growth. A book is a resource for note taking. Even a person is classed as a resource in the workplace.

DNS

DNS (Domain Name System) is one of the foundations of the internet, a web infrastructure in the background that serves as the internet's phone book. It is a server service that matches domain names to their associate various information in order to give the names of web sites. It also resolves singular resources on the net.

Dynamic Host Configuration Protocol

The Dynamic Host Configuration Protocol (DHCP) is a network management protocol used on Internet and Intranet Protocol Networks for automatically assigning IP addresses and other communication parameters to devices connected to the network, using a client–server architecture. The opposite of a DHCP, is to have the IP address statically assigned, however, this costly.

Autonomous system

An autonomous system is a collection of connected Internet Protocol routing prefixes under the control of one or more network operators on behalf of a single administrative entity or domain, that presents a common and clearly defined routing policy to the Internet.

Transmission Control Protocol

The Transmission Control Protocol (TCP) is one of the main protocols of the Internet Protocol suite. It originated in the initial network implementation in which it complemented the Internet Protocol. Therefore, the entire suite is commonly referred to as TCP/IP.

Ethernet

Ethernet is a family of wired computer networking technologies commonly used in local area networks, metropolitan area networks and wide area networks. It was commercially introduced in 1980 and first standardized in 1983 as IEEE 802.3.

Cookies

Cookies are small bits of our information that websites collect and keep. When you visit their site, spywares capture your details, so that they can use it to determine what things you are interested in, and then they can start bombarding you with the products' adverts.

You can view or block cookies.

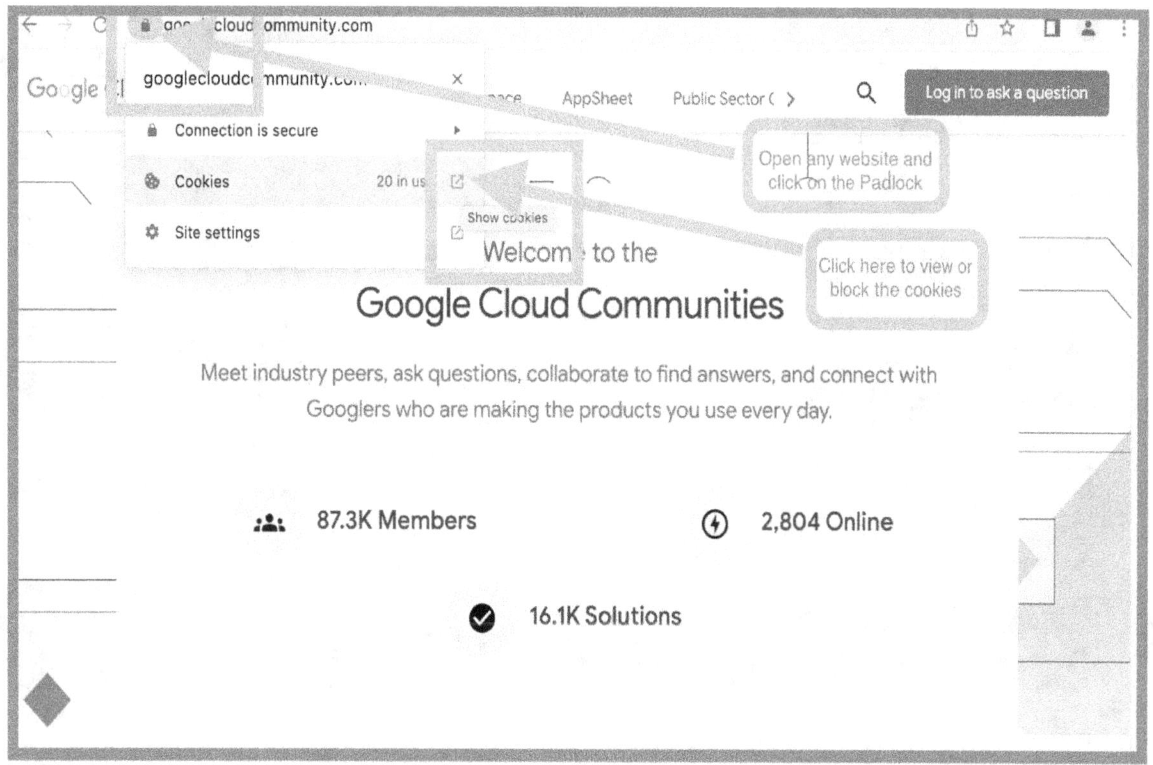

If a site is going to be viewed in the EU or the UK, the site must put up a Cookie Warning, with the option for the person to accept or not. Some sites do not allow you to view their sites if you reject a cookie policy.

Cookie Policy is governed by GDPR (General Data Protection Regulation. The General Data Protection Regulation is a Regulation in EU law on data protection and privacy in the EU and the European Economic Area. The GDPR is an important component of EU privacy law and of human rights law, in particular Article 8 of the Charter of Fundamental Rights of the European Union.
https://gdpr-info.eu
https://www.gov.uk/data-protection

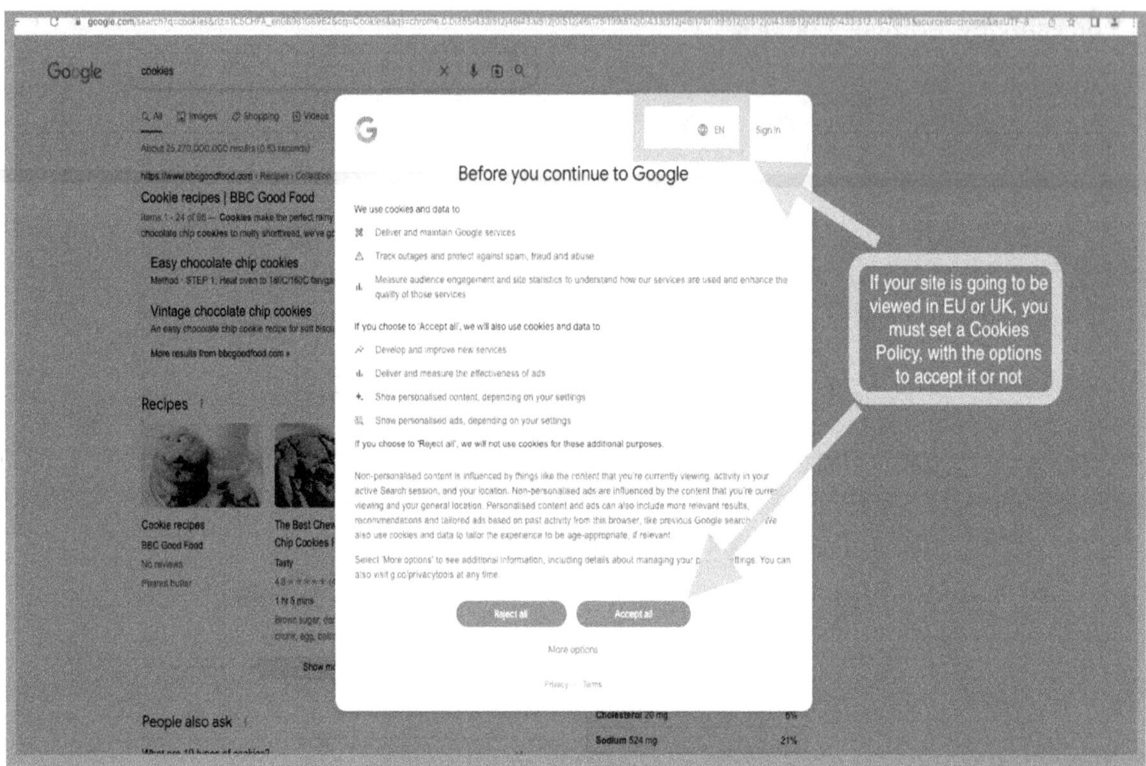
Google
cookies
Before you continue to Google
If your site is going to be viewed in EU or UK, you must set a Cookies Policy, with the options to accept it or not
Reject all
Accept all
More options

IP and IP Address

IP and IP Address

What is An IP Address?

Let's say that there is a shop in UK that sells milk and bread, and I, who lives in Canada want to buy milk and bread. So, I physically set out to go to the shop to my milk and bread. To get there, I would use the Travel Protocol (travel way of going about it).

Travel Protocol

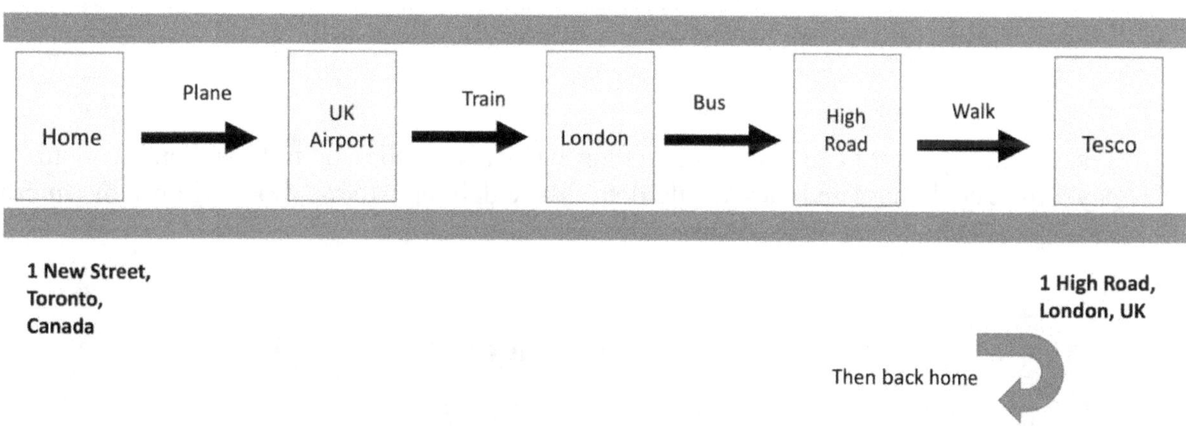

Supposing I found out that I can post a cheque to Tesco, and they will post the milk and bread to me? So, I will use the Postal Protocol (postal way of going about it).

Postal Protocol

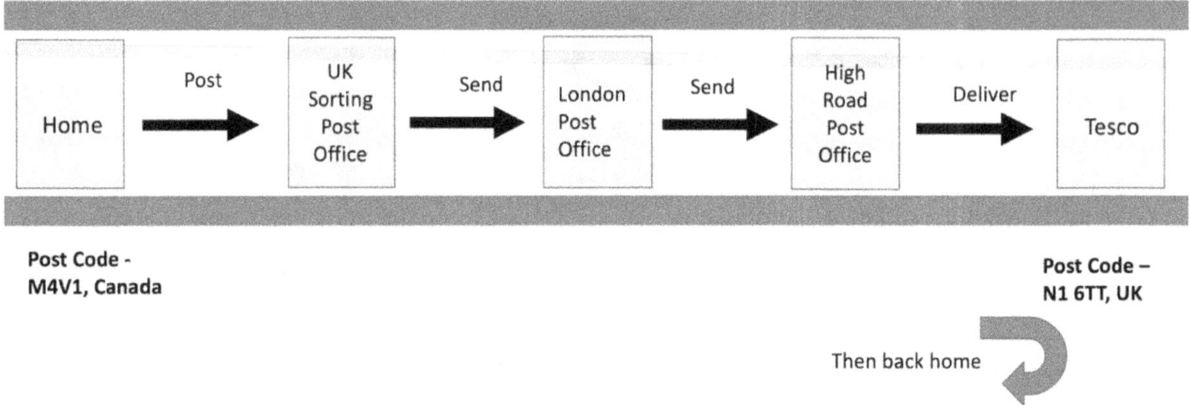

Tesco then says that I can simply go to their website and click on milk and on bread, to buy, pay with a credit card and they would do a 'home delivery' to me. So, I will use the Internet Protocol (Internet way of going about it).

Internet Protocol (IP)

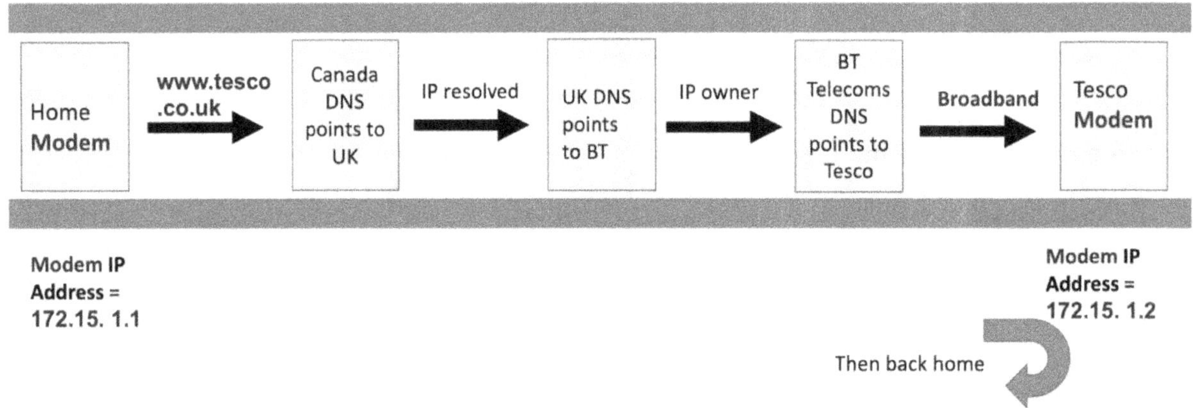

Tracing IP

Supposing you got bored at home and started being mischievous, hacking into a government site, or start trying to crash down Tesco's website, because you are angry that they have sent you expired milk and refused to refund your money. Can you be caught? Yes, the IP address that the attacks came from will be traced out to the telecoms company, BT that owns that

External IP address. BT will then match it to your broadband because they assigned that IP to your home when you purchased their broadband.

Supposing the IP traces back to your home; 1 New Street, Toronto, Canada, however, there are three people living there, using their personal computer or laptops, can they trace it to you? Yes, the IP that comes via the broadband, when it reaches the modem, it branches out into the internal IP Network IP addresses. Then each one goes to a laptop. How would they know which went to yours? Every computer device has a network card that has been stamped with a MAC address, which is unique to that device. The IP will report that the originator of that illegal activity was your MAC address - there = caught!

What is my IP Address?

To check the external IP of your machine that is showing your machine on the internet, click on any one of these website addresses from your machine. Shamelessly, they will show up your IP address and if possible – your location as well.

https://ip-lookup.net/
https://www.iplocation.net/
https://whatismyipaddress.com/
https://nordvpn.com/ip-lookup/

Internet Service Provider (ISP)

An Internet Service Provider is an organization that provides services for accessing, using, or participating on the internet. They are telecom companies that provide you broadband connection and gives you the modem to use. ISPs can be organised in various forms, such as commercial, community-owned, non-profit, or otherwise privately owned. Examples are BT, Sky, Virgin. When you buy the broadband from them, they assigned you an IP address to the house.

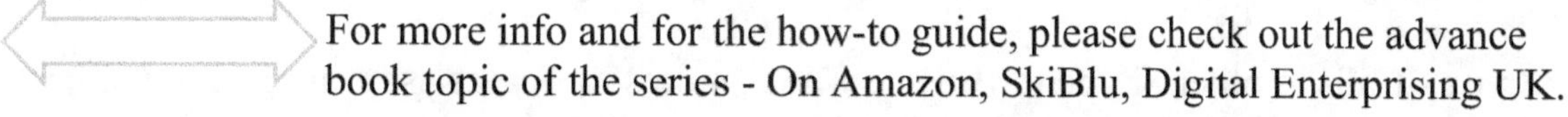 For more info and for the how-to guide, please check out the advance book topic of the series - On Amazon, SkiBlu, Digital Enterprising UK.

VOIP

VoIP

VoIP – Voice over Internet Protocol

If you have a smart phone (internet phone), and you have paid for mobile internet data from your ISP or the phone can connect to the home broadband, then you would be able to send pictures, images, video clips from your phone via the internet.

If your mobile phone is not a smart phone (that is, analogue phone), you won't be able to send pictures and videos. You can only make voice calls and SMS (short messaging service). When we speak into an analogue phone, the voice data is converted into electronic pulses (radio signals) that travels along on copper wires called, Analogue Lines. The analogue line service is referred to as POTs (Plain Old Telephone Service) and it supports home phones, basic mobile phones, faxes, and modems.

Mobile phones are grouped in terms of their age and functionality; with the old, basic ones being -1G (1st Generation), through to the more smarter ones (with Wi-Fi, Bluetooth, videocalls, etc), being 5G.

VoIP (Voice over Internet Protocol)

VoIP (Voice over Internet Protocol), sometimes referred to as VoN (Voice over Network) or VoB (Voice over Broadband) or Internet Telephony or Voice over IP.

With VoIP, the voice, or media data travels along the IP (Internet Protocol) on the internet. So, if I start a call from my smart phone, to go to my friend's smart, who is also online, my phone's IP address would channel through my broadband / phone data, then through the internet, until it connects with my friend's phone IP, then deliver the voice data.

Popular examples of voice calling and video calling platforms that uses VoIP are.
WhatsApp – Free calls and videocalls to other WhatsApp users.

Skype - Calls to other Skype for Business and Microsoft Teams users are free, but other non-Skype users, need to check out the Microsoft Calling Plans.

Video Conferencing

Using this ability to video-call over the internet, groups and companies can have video conference calls with participants from all over the world. Popular examples of video conferencing platforms that uses VoIP are.
Zoom – You can have a Zoom Meeting with up to 100 concurrent participants for free the first 40mins.
https://zoom.us/pricing

Microsoft Teams - No free minutes.
https://www.microsoft.com/en-us/microsoft-teams/microsoft-teams-phone

Google Meet – Free video conference with friends.
https://apps.google.com/meet

But paid plans for workplace teams.
https://workspace.google.com

Cisco Webex - You get 40min free with up to 100 members.
https://www.webex.com

Apple FaceTime – Free video conference with friends with up to 32 members.
https://apps.apple.com/us/app/facetime

Wi-Fi

Wi-Fi is the radio signals sent from a wireless router to a nearby device, such as a laptop, mobile phone that translates the signal into data for you to see and use. Wi-Fi is essentially a very advanced digital radio over short distances, using frequencies between 2 gigahertz and 5 gigahertz in the electromagnetic spectrum, which is around the same range as microwave ovens. Wi-Fi technology is a family of wireless network protocols based on the IEEE (Institute of Electrical and Electronics Engineers)802.11 family of standards, which are commonly used for wireless networking. Wi-Fi is not an acronym; it is a brand name created by a marketing firm that's meant to serve as an interoperability seal for marketing efforts.

Wi-Fi or Wireless routers are the hardware devices that the Internet Service Providers sends to you when you subscribe to their internet service.

Bluetooth

Bluetooth is a short-range wireless technology standard that is used for exchanging data between devices, usually, a mobile device and an earpiece headset.

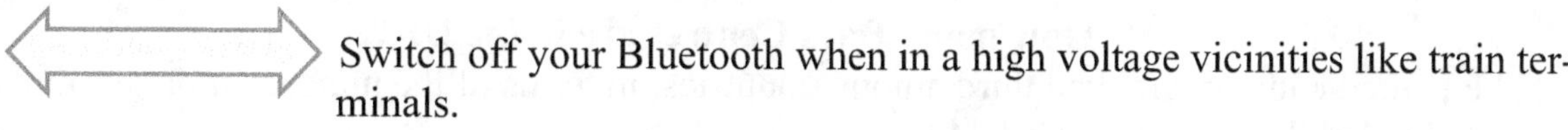 Switch off your Bluetooth when in a high voltage vicinities like train terminals.

Data, Data Centre

Data Centre

Question: Have you ever wondered how Google performs searches in such quick time, even across the globe?

Answer: Because Google has installed Data Centres all over the world and their Cache Data is stored as copies, spread in those data centres.

What is a Data Centre?

Data Centres are the large data facilities that large computer companies, such as Google, uses to store date and to provide their services from. It is usually a large warehouse / building that housed the huge computer servers (mainframes) with data on them. These huge server systems would usually comprise of large storage drives, computer nodes - organised in racks, in aisles, with cabling that connects internal and external networking. The main functions of a Data Centre are to store data securely and to route data coming in from different destinations and going out to different destinations.

Two keywords in a Data Centre are.

One is **High security:**

It needs to be able to safeguard the data, both physically and cyber-wise. Imagine, the UK Ministry of Defence has given their data to Microsoft to house in one of their UK Data Centres. So also, some NHS Trusts. All those patients' private sensitive information and MOD top secrets must be guarded well.

The second Keyword is **Uptime:**

The stored data must be available for access at any time of the day (some people don't sleep at night for the sake of work?). Alright, not just that, it is because there are different times zones. And also, the internet doesn't sleep at night. Internet traffic must be able to find its connecting routes from one data centre to another.

How many Data Centres are in the UK?

The United Kingdom ranked third among countries, in terms of the number of data centres with 456, while China recorded 443.

Number of data centres worldwide in 2022, by country.

Country	Number of data centres
USA	2701
Germany	487
UK	456

China	443
Canada	328
Australia	287
Russia	172
According to the company – Statista	https://www.statista.com

Who owns a Data Centre?

All the big players (plus a few middle-weight companies)-
Google, Microsoft, Amazon, BT, Cisco, IBM, Salesforce, etc

These companies have their own physical locations scattered all over the place. They either own the building / premises or use a service called colocation, where they rent out some space from each other to place their mainframe servers there. And if that is not possible, they would also take out a paid plan from each other as necessary. All this is done to keep them evenly distributed and well-connected.

BT London Data Centre

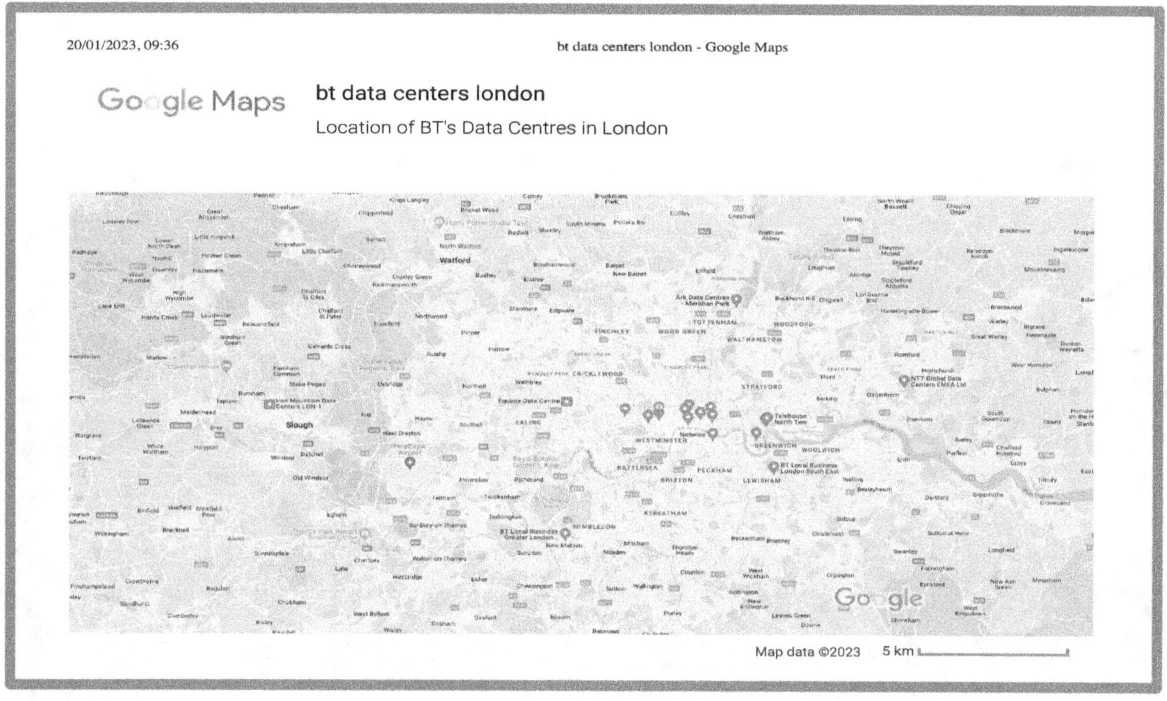

Google London Data Centre

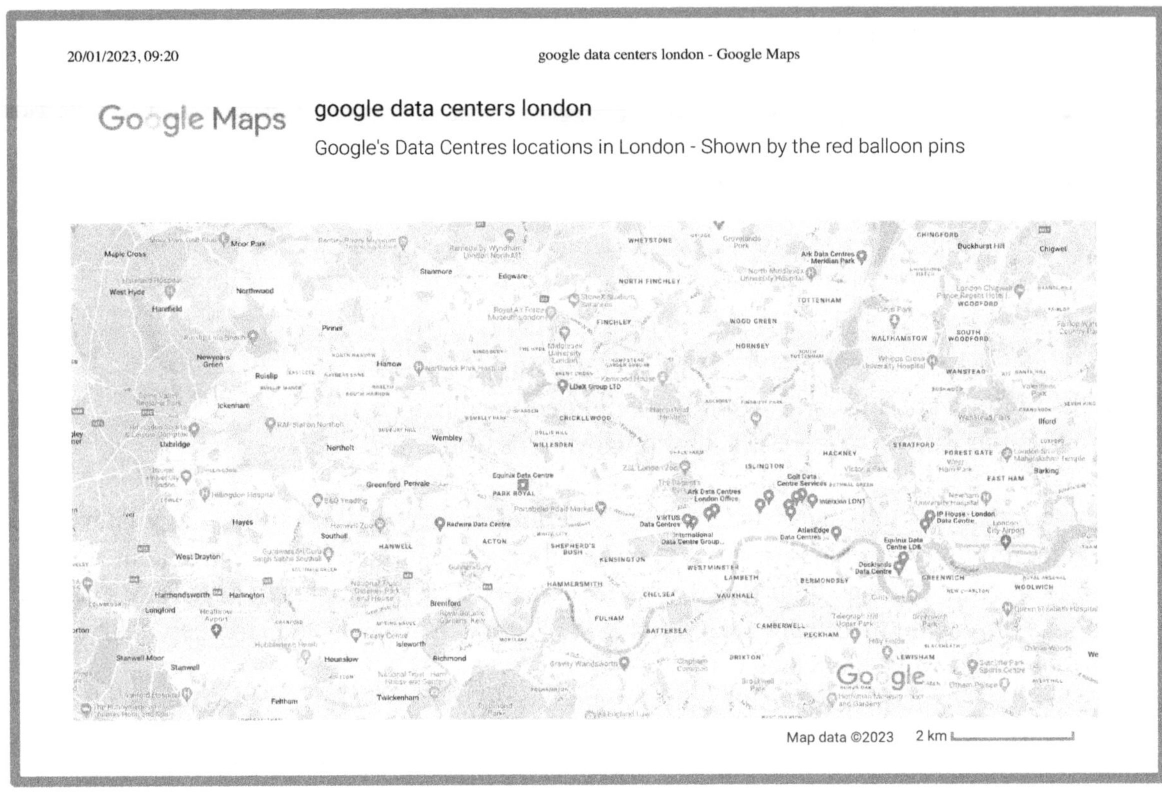

Google UK Data Centre

Microsoft London Data Centre

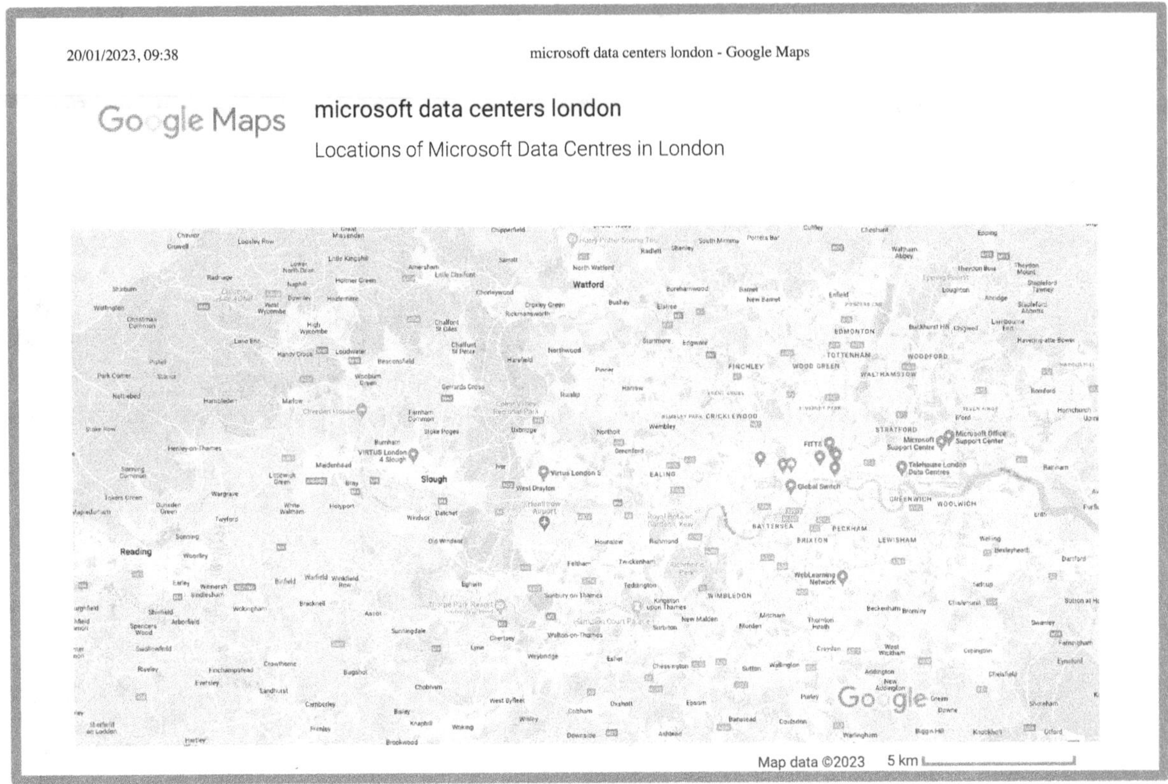

Microsoft London Data Centre

Amazon London Data Centre

IBM London Data Centre

Data Centres and Co-locations around the World Interconnects to form a GCDN (Global Content Delivery Network)

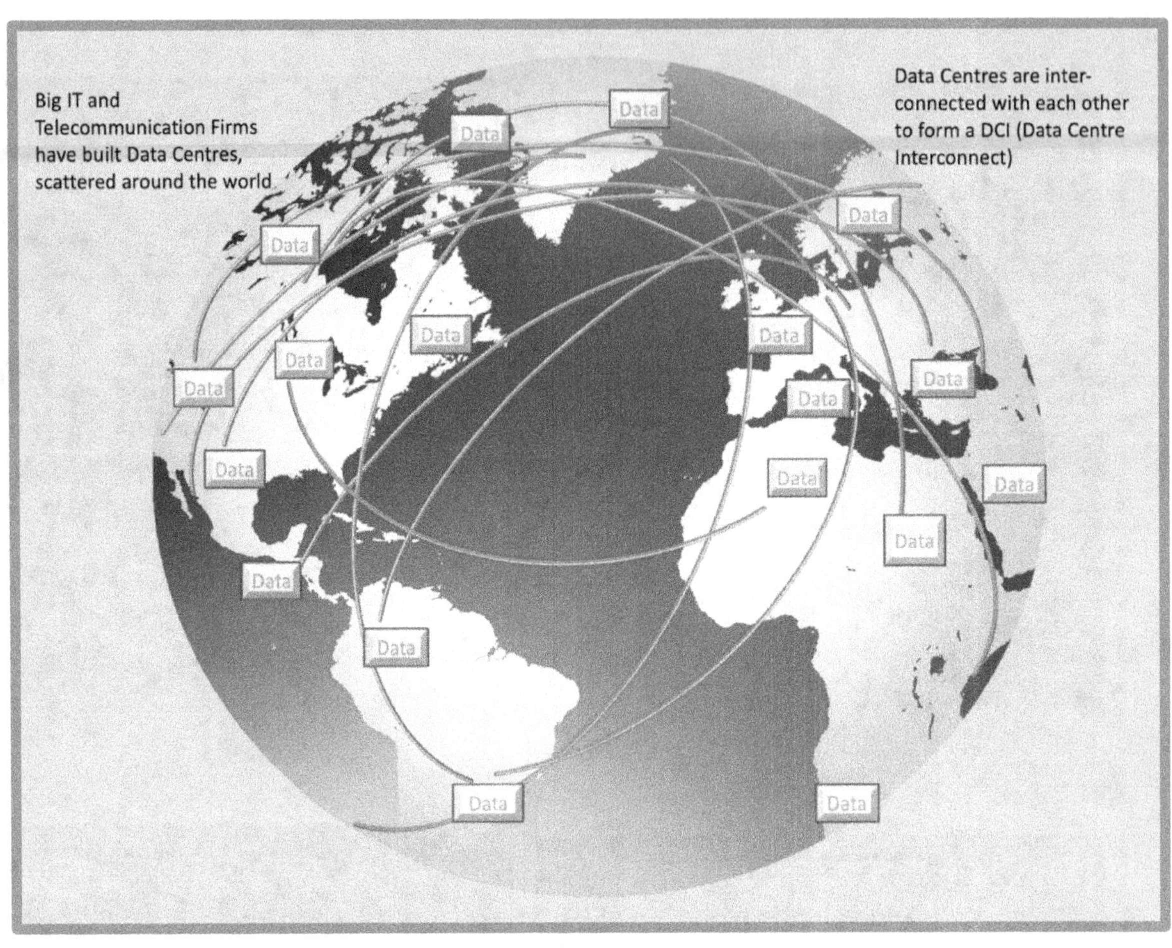
Big IT and
Telecommunication Firms
have built Data Centres,
scattered around the world
Data Centres are inter-
connected with each other
to form a DCI (Data Centre
Interconnect)
Data
Data
Data
Data
Data
Data
Data
Data
Data
Data
Data
Data
Data
Data
Data
Data
Data
Data
Data

Cloud Computing

Cloud Computing

I once watched a documentary of Sir Richard Branson swigging in a hammock in the paradise garden of his Caribbean home, with a thin laptop on his lap. The reporter asked him if he was on holiday. He said that he was working then, and that was his office. How does he run his business empire from there? - Cloud Computing!

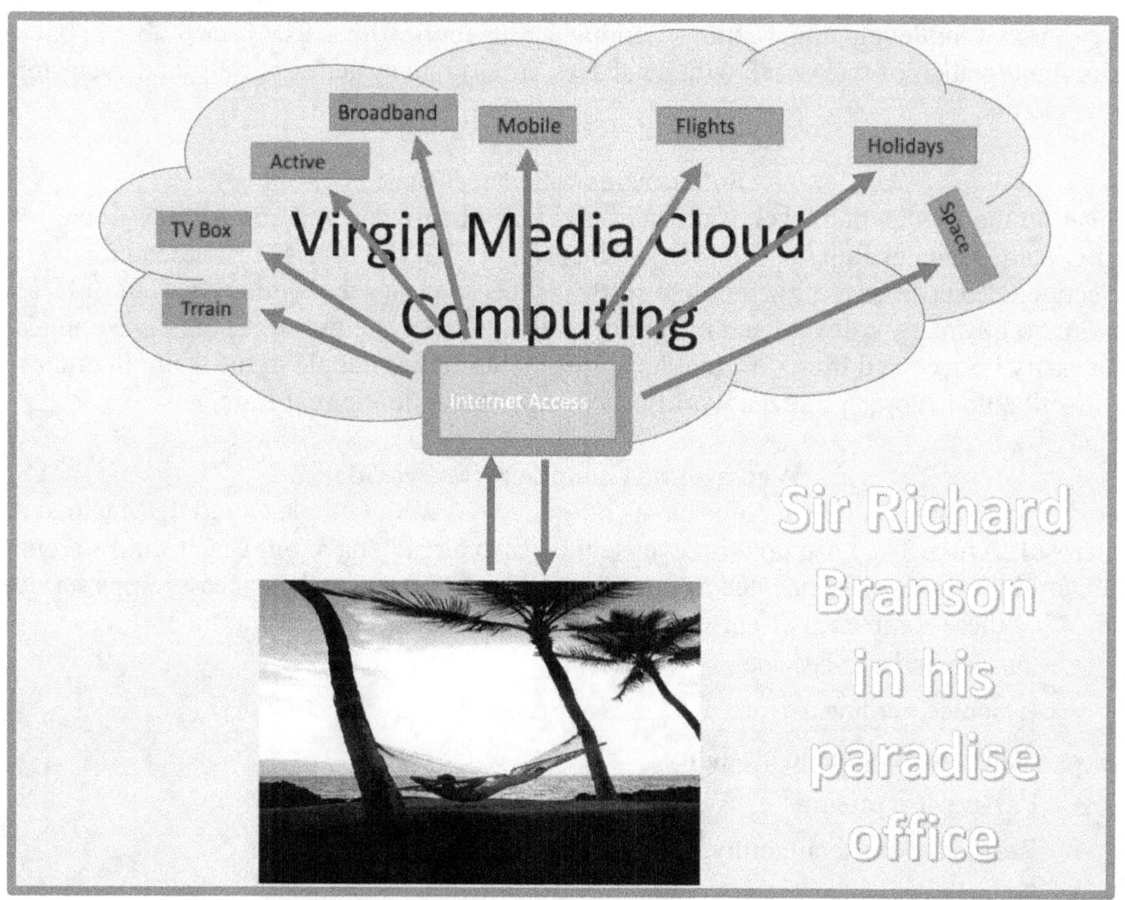

Cloud Computing

Cloud computing is the on-demand availability and delivery of computing system resources, and computer services. Computer system resources includes storage, databases, software, etc. Computer services include networking, analytics, and intelligence over the internet, in the cloud. Cloud Computing is divided into three segments:

Infrastructure as a Service (IaaS).

Platform as a Service (PaaS).

Software as a Service (SaaS).

Infrastructure as a Service (IaaS)

This is at the infrastructure level. It provides a virtual powerful computer machine, other virtual hardware, network, and storage resources as a package to consumers, on-demand, over the internet and on a pay-as-you-go basis. Using cloud infrastructure on a pay-per-use scheme enables companies to save on the costs of acquiring, managing, and maintaining their own IT infrastructure. Plus, the cloud is easily accessible. Most major cloud service providers - including Amazon Web Services (AWS), Google Cloud, IBM Cloud and Microsoft Azure, offer IaaS with their cloud computing services.

Platform as a Service (PaaS)

This is at the Service-level. It provides the user, a complete access and functionality to a cloud environment for developing, running, and managing applications. The user is able to have a virtual integration of their work with databases, messaging systems, portals, and even storage components.

Software-as-a-Service (SaaS).

This is at the Application level. It includes all kinds of software and applications, including CRM (Customer Relationship Management) and ERP (Enterprise resource planning) applications. Companies use SaaS online software access via a subscription. Instead of IT teams having to buy many software and installing on individual systems, rather the same application can easily be accessed from different locations by numerous people in the team, in order to aid work automation, optimized workflows and collaboration in real-time.

Who are the Cloud Service Providers?

Most IT big wigs - including Amazon Web Services (AWS), Google Cloud, IBM Cloud and Microsoft Azure. They can do this because they each already have big Data Centres around the world that are well-connected to provide speedy data storage, data access, Apps services, etc. What these companies promise to offer as part of their cloud computing are:

- On-demand self-service.
- Resource pooling.
- Scalability and rapid elasticity.
- Pay-per-use pricing.
- Resiliency and availability.
- Security.
- Broad network access.

In fact, 'Scalability' is the main word that Microsoft is using to justify its cloud computing. Its meaning is this: – "Calling, calling, all you, computer nerds around the world. Ditch your computers and servers at home/office and scale down to just a thin laptop with not much on it, then come, let's all work in the cloud…". It sounds like the 'home of the happy people', right? Until you see the monthly bill of the 'Pay-per-use' total sent to you.

Cloud Service Providers sell their services in grade plans as below.

Private clouds: A company has a whole cloud to themselves, they either build one of their own – e.g., Amazon Cloud, mainly for selling its goods or rents it.

Public clouds: Small companies buy cloud spaces from Cloud Service Providers, and they would be sharing a cloud with others.

Hybrid clouds: A company combines it's on-premises private network and infrastructure set up with a third-party public cloud services to form a single, flexible infrastructure for running critical applications and workloads. It is a way of expanding, without necessarily buying new hardware.

Multi-clouds: A company is using more than one third-party public cloud services to provide a resilient and cost effective network for its business. They may have their data on two different Data Centres that are being run by the same or two different companies.

Why go for the cloud?

DevOps – It offers a good size environment for development, testing, and production. Imagine trying to spin a bowl of soup in a huge source pan – more room to manoeuvre.

Big data analytics – The cloud is vast and well-connected, so businesses on the cloud are exposed to more customers' information derived from consumers' buying patterns. They can then study the statistics for the sake of channelling adverts of products to the end users.

Cloud data storage elasticity - I once started a Social Networking site that reached 2 million users within a very short time (true story). I woke up one day and found that the site was down. I contacted my host provider, and they said that they couldn't cope with the bandwidth and the storage. What?! Anyway, the moral of the story is, if it was a cloud storage, the bandwidth and storage would have just automatically expanded to accommodate the demand. The only thing is that I would be charged more at the end of the month.

Disaster recovery and data backup. We all know that even bullet-proof plans can go wrong. With the cloud, there is a continuous data replication across two or more data centres. So that if one data centre fails, all eyes will immediately divert to the other data centre and … ahh - life is back to normal again withing minutes. There are also usually automatic backups and a team of people that ensure backup validity and data restorations if needed. Small businesses and individuals often pay little regards to backups, until one day things go wrong. They cloud system guards against that.

Artificial Intelligence (AI). AI is simply 'VIKI' (Virtual Interactive Kinaesthetic Interface) in Will Smith' 2004 movie, I, Robot. VIKI grew into the person she became by teaching herself through data that was inputted and by observations, called Machine Learning. IA is used in the science and engineering of making intelligent machines and intelligent computer programs.

Machine learning – Simply put, is machine teaching itself. It combines Computer Science and Artificial Intelligence's use of data and algorithms to understand human intelligence and to imitate the way that humans learn, gradually improving its accuracy and performance. Businesses use this to gain deeper insights into product buying and consumer behaviour.

Cloud API

In Cloud Computing, in order for your machine to talk to your cloud, or another cloud to talk to another cloud, or components in each cloud to talk to each other, they need APIs. A Cloud API (A cloud application programming interface) is a software interface that allows developers to link cloud computing services together, that enables applications to communicate and transfer information to one another in the cloud.

There are different APIs for each of the four major areas of cloud computing - PaaS APIs, SaaS APIs, IaaS APIs, Cloud provider and cross-platform APIs.

Ecosystem

What is an Ecosystem?

Ecosystem

IT World Ecosystem

Here goes- Ecosystem in IT is this: Let's take the Apple ecosystem for our example.

Once Upon an Apple Ecosystem...

This morning, someone called me on my **i-Phone**, but I couldn't find it between the couch, – so, I quickly borrowed my **i-Watch** to answer the call on behalf of my **i-Phone**. Should in case this happens again, or I lose my **i-Phone** one day, -so I got my **i-Phone** to upload my contacts to my **i-Cloud**. I also remembered and set up my **i-Locator** on my **i-Phone** and linked it to my **i-Watch**.

After that, I went jogging; I used my **i-Pods** to listen to music from my **i-Tunes**. I wore my **i-Watch** to monitor my jogging data. Since the **i-Watch** is small, the data was being transferred to my **i-Phone**. When I got home, I uploaded the data to my **i-Cloud** for storage. On the way back, I took a picture using my **i-Phone**, but there was not enough space on my **i-Phone** to store it, - so, the **i-Phone** borrowed the space on my **i-Cloud**.

Later on, I set out to drive to work, but couldn't find my satnav, -so, I went to my **i-Shop** via my **i-Phone** App. I used my **i-Pay**, which was in my **i-Wallet** to pay for an **i-Map** App, using my **i-Finger-print ID** to authenticate the purchase. I got the App downloaded onto my **i-Phone** and used it.

At work, a colleague sent me an **i-FaceTime** invite on my **i-Phone**, but the screen was too small to see properly, - so, I transferred the facetime call to my **i-Pad**.

I wanted to edit the picture I took earlier to send to the colleague, so I got my **i-Mac** to contact my **i-Cloud** for it. After editing it, I wanted to send it to him via my **i-Messages**, - so, the **i-Messages** on my **i-Mac** linked up to the **i-Messages** on my **i-Phone** for that.

I was setting up an **i-FaceTime** video conferencing and wanted to invite team members, so I told my **i-MacBook** to get the contacts from my **i-PhoneBook**. When I tried to log into my **i-MacBook** in the office, my **i-Apple ID** sent a Two-factor authentication request to my **i-Phone**.

At lunch time, I went out and bought the new **i-Phone** upgrade and when I had placed it next to my old one, the new **i-Phone** then asked my old **i-Phone** to send a copy of all it's got, huh? This helping of each other, by borrowing and sharing between my **i-Devices** went on and on, and they even started doing their own thing - sharing data automatically, calling it – **i-Synch** (synchronising data).

During coffee break, a friend sent me a text message link of trending videos on YouTube, so I passed it over to my **i-Pad** to watch on a wider screen. By the end the day I got home, tired; I slumped onto the couch, and shouted out: "Oi, Oi! - Will one of you **i-Thingy,** switch on that **i-AppleTV** box for me?!" –What an obedient set of **i-Things**.

In a nutshell – here:

Happy Apple Ecosystem

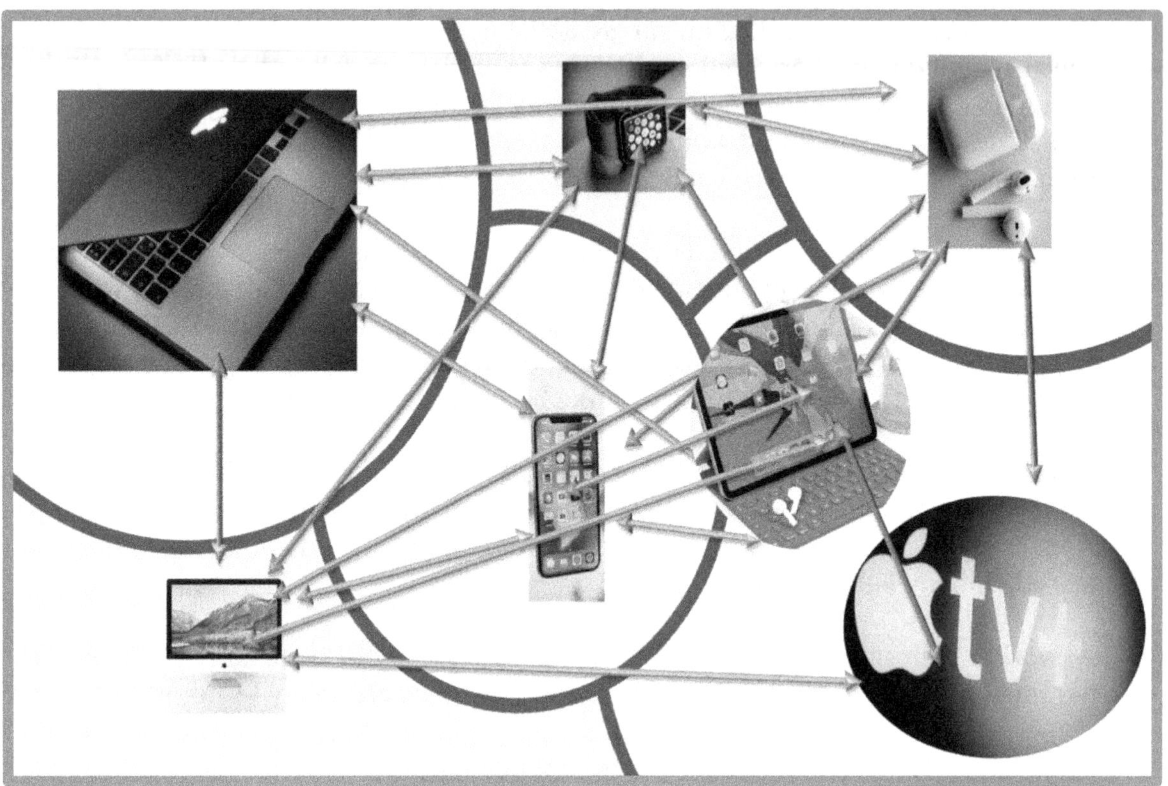

Apple says that it is an ecosystem of their devices sharing in harmony with each, and that it makes for a simpler and better user experience. In truth, newbies to this system would relish the enjoyment of this awesome experience for while (…until the whole thing starts to irritate them, I guess).

The above device ecosystem that the user sees, and feel is powered behind the scenes by, yet another ecosystem called the **Component Ecosystem**. Where the Apple iOS on these devices is sharing components such as the UI, Templates, drivers, APIs, libraries, etc, which are called re-usable codes.

Google Ecosystem

Google's tagline on the ecosystem is - "Better Together". Their focus is on the Android OS, the OS that powers over half of the world's smartphones, but they are also integrated with other facet of the Google lines such as the AndroidTV, Wear OS (smart watch) and the Chrome OS.

Microsoft Ecosystem

Microsoft's Ecosystem comprises of 5 distinct pillars within the Microsoft stack. It is a cloud-based business applications platform that combines components of Customer Relationship

Management (CRM), and Enterprise Resource Planning (ERP), along with Productivity Applications and Artificial Intelligence (AI).

Internet of Things (IoT)

An IoT is an internet ecosystem concept of devices and other things living in their own little world, where they share data with each other, analyse data, carry out tasks without a human interaction (or with very little initial set up interaction). The devices or things must have internet access, special sensors that communicate with other related devices in their ecosystem across the internet. They must have special processors to act on the information they get from one another and the ability to analyse the data. The devices would have had pre-programmed instructions on how to access the data, what gateway to use and how to send data to the cloud storage or others. Apart from physical devices that have built-in communication hardware, an animal can be implanted with a biochip sensor and set to join an IoT ecosystem.

Some organisations use IoT to study customers buying patterns and also to improve decision making on how to operate the business efficiently, in order to enhance customer experience.

Save, Save-As, Backup

Save, Save-As, Backup

Save

I can't seem to emphasise this enough, because of hard lessons learned from my many personal experiences of not saving as I go along. Every few minutes – save your work! Some Applications like Ms Word have the functionality of Auto-Save, but even then, do check that that feature has been enabled in your application, and in between the Auto-Save, save your work.

To enable Auto-Save, to automatically save your file changes; put a tick on Auto Save in the main File menu.

Save-As

Before you make a major change to your work, do consider saving a copy under a different name by doing 'save-as'. You should also consider saving your work to different locations.

USB (Universal Serial Bus). Use a USB stick, but then make sure that it is kept clean and secured.

SSDs (solid state drive). This is an extension of the computer / laptop's hard disk, that did not come with the original computer. It may be internal or external, but mostly, they are external mini devices bigger than a USB that you can send data to, then unplug it and keep safe.

Cloud Storage. These days, the quickest and easiest way to save a copy of your work is to upload it to a cloud storage provider. There are many storage providers out there who offer storage systems in one of their data centres or data centre clusters. These are usually paid plans, but some of them do give a starting limited amount of space free.

Microsoft OneDrive
https://onedrive.live.com

Google One
https://one.google.com

Apple iCloud
https://www.icloud.com

Kinsta
https://kinsta.com

DropBox
https://www.dropbox.com

These offer expanding cloud storage and are intended for the consumer market for personal, to small businesses. The storage would include access to Global Content Delivery Network.

Backup

All large organisations do include daily backups in the list of tasks that their IT Administrator does every day. The backup makes a copy of all data, then burn onto CDs or recorded to tapes, which are properly labelled and stored, either on-site or off-site.

Hard Drive Cloning

While you can save your input data by means of a backup and others, when it comes to the whole state of the computer, you could do a hard drive cloning, using a hard drive cloning App. A hard disk cloning app can be used to create a local backup of hard drives. you can use the software to create a bootable USB or CD/DVD drive.

List of some hard disk cloning software
AOMEI Backupper Standard
O&O Disk Image
MiniTool Partition Wizard
Macrium Reflect
EaseUS ToDo Backup
Acronis True Image 2020
Clonezilla
Paragon Software Hard Disk Manager

You can also clone only your Apps, instead of a full backup.

List of come App cloning software
DO Multiple Accounts
Island
Dual Apps
Multiple Accounts
Water Clone
Super Clone
Multi Parallel
Clone App

Zip and Unzip

Another way to store files in a small space, is to Zip them, and then, unzip or extract the files when needed later. Zipping the file, or group of files inside a folder is compressing them to shrink into a small purse (space). It is easier to email files attachments by zipping them. You can email zipped files to yourself, that being a second copy of your work in your email inbox.

Archive

You can archive old files and documents that are not being used currently but may be needed in the future. When the computer archives a document for you, it compresses it and stores it in compartment, so it stays dormant and not consuming much space and processor's power.

Security in IT

IT Security

When working in IT, you would need to be security conscious, especially if you are dealing with third-party data that may be sensitive or private. You would have to learn how to keep your own designs, patents, codes under wraps until you are ready to unveil them to the world.

Antivirus and Firewalls

The first step in security is to use antivirus, and or firewalls.

If you are using windows10, Microsoft has this to say on security:
"Windows 10 and 11 include Windows Security, which provides the latest antivirus protection. Your device will be actively protected from the moment you start Windows. Windows Security continually scans for malware (malicious software), viruses, and security threats."

And Apple has this to say about their macOS:
"The technically sophisticated runtime protections in macOS work at the very core of your Mac to keep your system safe from malware. This starts with industry-…"

Free Antivirus Products
Apart from those above, you can install an an-virus software.
AVG
https://www.avg.com

TOTALAV
https://www.totalav.com/mac-free-antivirus

Other Top Licenced Products.
Bitdefender Antivirus Plus.
Webroot SecureAnywhere AntiVirus.
McAfee AntiVirus Plus.
ESET NOD32 Antivirus.
G Data Antivirus.
Malwarebytes Premium.
Norton AntiVirus Plus.
Sophos Home Premium.

Firewall and Proxies

Do consider using a firewall on the computers and network. A firewall is an additional security wall that blocks all things that are not on its list. This prevents unauthorised upgrades or silent installation of applications.

A proxy is when the network traffic is made to go through a proxy server for extra security precautions.

Cloud Data Security and Encryption

If your data is on a Cloud Storage, you need not worry about security, because the cloud storage provider deals with the security issues.

Two-Factor Authentication

Two-factor authentications are the new in-thing now, they provide extra verification steps required for access. Two-factor authentication IDs may even include end-to-end encryption. It helps protect you from fraudulent attempts to gain access to your site or account. When you build websites or software for a client, be sure to recommend a requirement for a Two-factor authentication to them.

Device Security

As much as possible, do make sure that your devices are password-protected and that users do keep their passwords or smartcards safe and are used by themselves alone. Try not to travel with a business laptop that contains sensitive data, but if you must, then make sure that you hug it tight to your chest and not forget it on the train.

Premises Security

Do provide a 24-hour security of some sort for the premises or office where your computers, hardware, network cables and backup tapes are kept. Report all intruders to the police immediately.

Privacy, Data Confidentiality and Security Policy

If you work for a company, you most certainly be asked to sign a client data confidentiality clause. And you would be expected to adhere to the company's security policy. Every IT business has to have a Security Policy. An IT security policy lays out the rules regarding how the company's IT resources can be used. It would define acceptable and unacceptable behaviours regarding the hardware, software, networks. It will lay out rules on access controls and resource sharing between teams and cross departments. And it will outline potential consequences for breaking the rules.

Security in IT is governed by organisations such as ISO/IEC 27001. ISO/IEC 27001 is a standard for information security management systems (ISMS) and their requirements. Best practice in data protection and cyber resilience are also covered by more than a dozen standards in the ISO/IEC 27000 family.

https://www.iso.org

Third Party Software

Be very wary of third parties' software. Do not download applications randomly from just about any site. Do try to use the developer's site or trusted outlets.
Be careful not to accept or scan QR codes from just any source; only accept from a trusted or personal sender.

Before you download software and apps, read the third party's Data Safety Info label on that app. The label will show a symbol and explanations concerning data collections, types, and data sharing in regard to that application. Similarly, before you can publish your app to the app stores, you be sure to include this fact sheet on the app too.

DATA SAFETY INFORMATION SYMBOLS

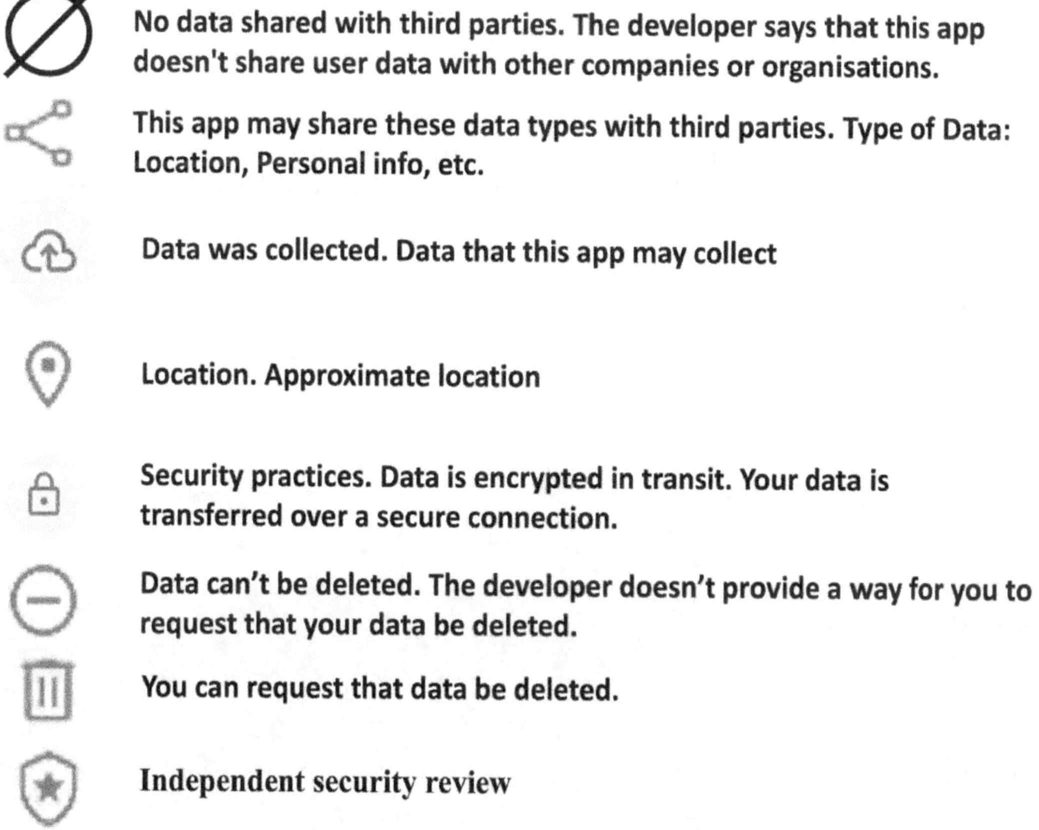

No data shared with third parties. The developer says that this app doesn't share user data with other companies or organisations.

This app may share these data types with third parties. Type of Data: Location, Personal info, etc.

Data was collected. Data that this app may collect

Location. Approximate location

Security practices. Data is encrypted in transit. Your data is transferred over a secure connection.

Data can't be deleted. The developer doesn't provide a way for you to request that your data be deleted.

You can request that data be deleted.

Independent security review

Security Breach

Sites may have a security breach through means such as Hacking, Spyware, Botnets, DDoS.

Hacking – To crack codes of a computer program or to break into a site belonging to other people. Usually, a government site, to steal private information – very naughty!

Spyware - Is any software that installs itself on your computer and starts to monitor your online activity without your knowledge or permission.

Botnet Attacks - A robot like program (a small script) that sends a large, expensive SQL queries, in an attempt to bring down the database server, or keep it too busy from others.

DDoS (Distributed Denial of Service) Attacks - A robot like person keeps sending continues requests to the site via it's IP, in an attempt to crash the site down.

Device Lost - Physical theft of the device or loss of the device that contains the data information.

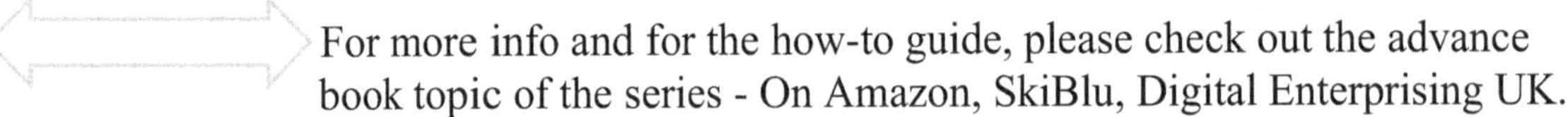

For more info and for the how-to guide, please check out the advance book topic of the series - On Amazon, SkiBlu, Digital Enterprising UK.

Software License

Software Licence

Licence

IT and Software license is covered by the Intellectual Property law. Intellectual Property law covers patents, copyrights, trademarks, trade secrets, etc. This law is International, which means that, while I am in America, I can sue someone in China for software theft or copyright infringement.

Software licence falls under these categories:

Licenced Proprietary Software - 100% belongs to the company. You need to purchase their licence to use it.

Beta ware - Software that is in the beta phase of testing, which the company allows you to use freely for that period of testing, with the hope that you would give them feedback on how to improve it.

Freeware - The company allows you to use it free anytime.

Community version - The company provides a water-down version of their propriety software on their website for free use. All you need to do to use it, is to join their community and abide by their rules to use it. It could also be in the form of Open-Source versions.

The rule on using someone else' software is this:

Activity	ILLEGAL	LEGAL
If I take Microsoft Word - rename it to Caroline Word - That is copyright theft.	X	
If I bought or download Windows 10, burn it onto CDs and start selling them in the market - That is selling stolen goods - Software Piracy.	X	
If my friend allows me to install their copy of Windows 10 on my computer - That is using an Unlicenced Software	X	
If I crack the codes of Microsoft Word, then re-package it and call it Caroline Text Editor - That is Copyright Infringement. I won't be able to get far with it, even if Microsoft does not chase after me for that; I will not be able to publish it in the App Store, Google Play Store or sell it to big companies.	X	

<table>
<tr><td>However, I can do what Apple did - That is tear down Microsoft Word, see how it was put together, then build the exact similar thing from the ground up, that does the exact same thing, or may be with a bit extra or different things and called it Apple Pages.
The same with The Document Foundation that build a free and open-source office similar to Ms Office, called LibreOffice -That is Cloning a software.</td><td></td><td>√</td></tr>
</table>

Software Cloning

Is cloning a software allowed?
<u>No</u>, and <u>Yes</u>.

You can't just clone someone's software and save it as yours – That is theft. On the other hand, you are allowed to clone someone's software or entire website, check how it was built, what ingredients went into it and then build your own exactly similar. Note: I said, 'Similar', not copy it word for word. You should show some improvements on some features at least. Like how Apple cloned Ms Word, but then again, Microsoft built Ms Word by cloning some Legacy software and so on and on.

Web Site Cloning

You can clone a web site using a tool called a Website Ripper. A website ripper enables you to download an entire website and save it to your hard drive for browsing without any internet connection. Some website rippers in the market are:
Octoparse
HTTrack
WebCopy
Getleft

Codes Snippets, Copy-Pasting

If someone say to me, "Could you type out the codes for 'Hello World'?". Would I? Absolutely not – how ridiculous! I will simply Google; 'codes for Hello World', sieve through for the free ones, then copy and paste it – Done!

Is it okay to copy and paste codes?

In answer to that, here is a quote I came across from someone on one Forum:
"Among friends, it's colloquially referred to as "stealing code from stackoverflow".
On resumes you call it "implementation of externally-optimized solutions for 'known problems.'". "Not only is it okay, it's a "best practice" and many languages have built-in systems for distributing these solutions (my favorite implementation is Ruby's "gems")".

Where do I find Code Snippets?

Stack Overflow. - https://stackoverflow.com

Search on Google – You find a geek who has shared the codes on his blog site.

Code Pen (Public only) - https://codepen.io

CodeProject - https://www.codeproject.com

Stack Overflow has been the best place to get codes snippets from. It has a lot of pieces of different types of codes, in different languages and frameworks. If you start building a software or start writing a program and then you get stuck, so you go to Stack Overflow and post your problem there. In no time at all, some nice, clever dude (computer geek) will post you the solution or the codes free! – So helpful? – Yeah!

Keep it Real - Beware   Okay, do go easy on this copy-pasting business. Be discriminate; especially if you are working for a company or on a client project.

Open-Source Software

Open-Source software is the original source codes of a program that is made freely available for anyone to use, modify, and may be redistribute.

Big software companies sometimes have a free version of their software. It would normally be placed in a public hub, like GitHub or on their web site. This would come with a GU or a MIT licence, or other types, meaning that you can download it, modify it, and use to build something beautiful and useful.

In fact, it is recommended that if you are building something (e.g., mobile phone software) that you Do Not start from scratch! - What an idiotic time wasting! Rather, you should you look for the open-source type of the software and build on it. You can find open-source software on GitHub, or their company's website.

Here is an open-source software for download.

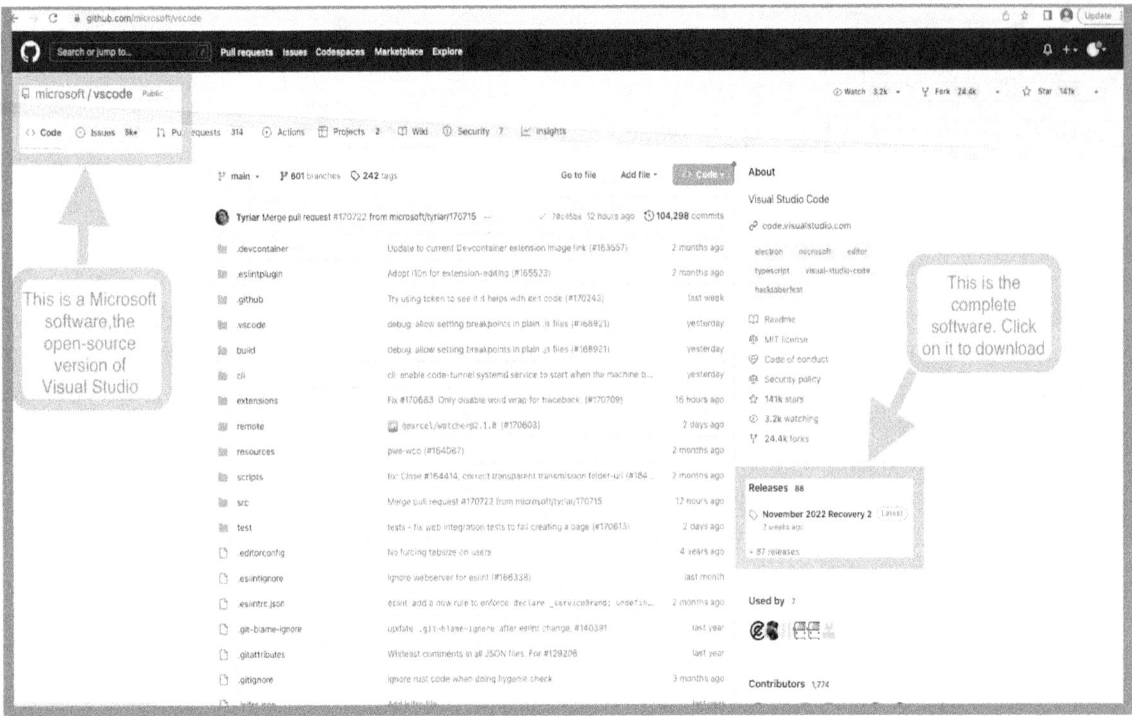

Before you download a software, check their licence agreement first.

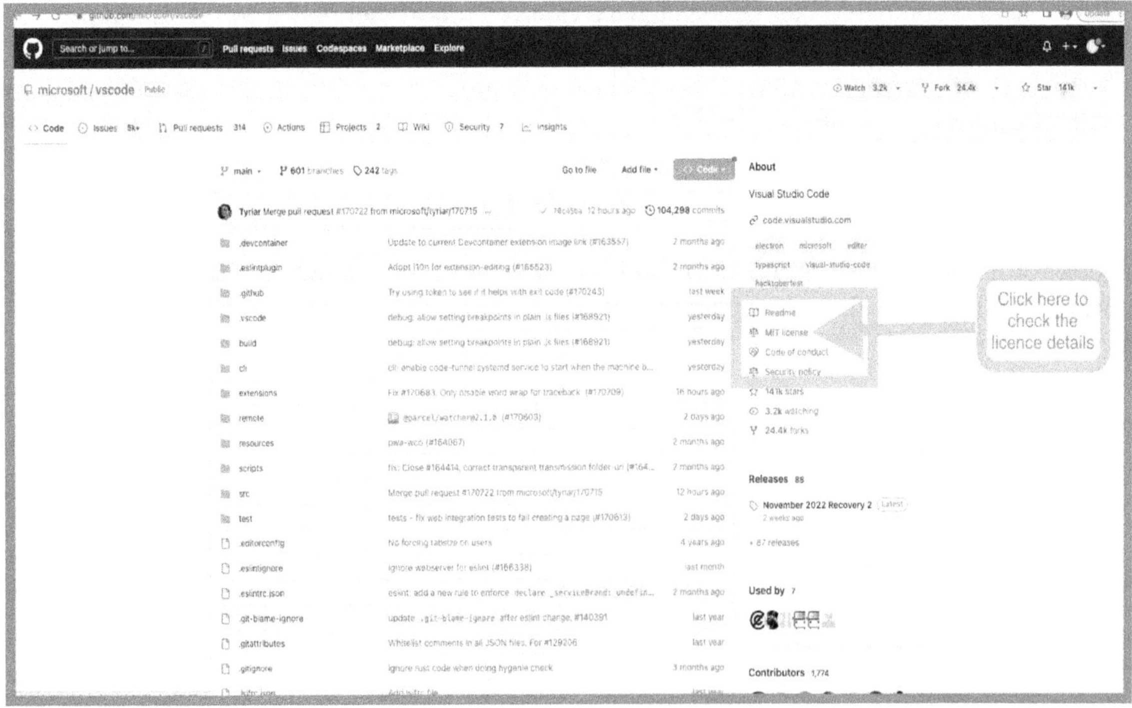

Here is the use definition

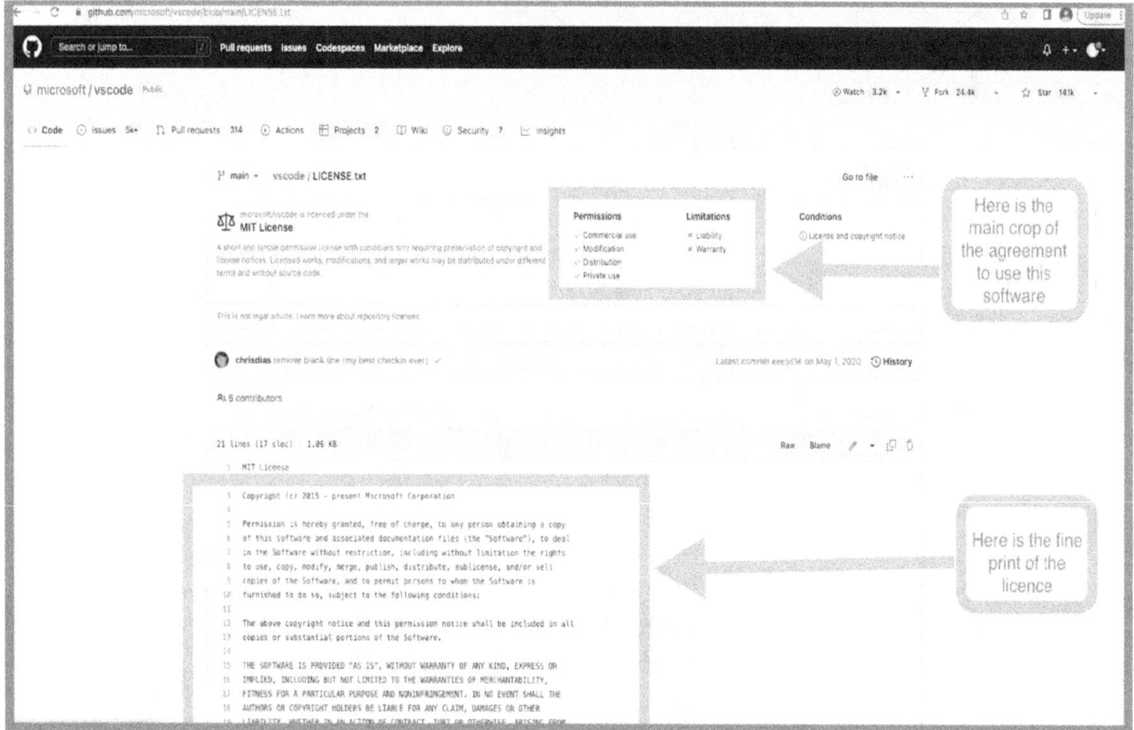

Can you sell Open-Source Software?

You cannot sell open-source software; it is not yours, and the licence holder is still the original person who coded that software or whom a legal authority has been given to. If you want to sell/make money from an Open-Source Software, there are three highly followed ways to generate revenue from Open-Source software:

1 Build something on top of it, licence it and sell.

2. Provide support as a service for users of the Open-Source software and charge for the service.

3. Create extensions/add-ons/plugins and charge for it.

Why do companies give their software for free?

Promotion! They give the software, either initially for free or a reduced version of it for free. This; they hope, would get more people using and talking about it until it becomes a 'household name'. What better way of advertising than that? So, do feel free to use any software that is given out free.

Types of Software Licence

LICENCE NAME	OVERVIEW
GNU General Public License	The GNU General Public License is a series of widely used free software licenses that guarantee end users the four freedoms to run, study, share, and modify the software. https://www.gnu.org/licenses/gpl-3.0.en.html
GNU Lesser General Public	The GNU Lesser General Public License (LGPL) is a free-software license published by the Free Software Foundation (FSF).
MIT License	The MIT License is a permissive free software license originating at the Massachusetts Institute of Technology in the late 1980s. As a permissive license, it puts only very limited restriction on reuse and has therefore, high license compatibility.
Apache License	The Apache License is a permissive free software license written by the Apache Software Foundation. It allows users to use the software for any purpose, to distribute it, to modify it, and to distribute modified versions of the software under the terms of the license, without concern for royalties
Unlicensed	The Unlicensed is a public domain equivalent license for software which provides a public domain waiver with a fall-back public-domain-like license, similar to the CC Zero for cultural works. It includes language used in earlier software projects and has a focus on an anti-copyright message. By default, creating a new project on Github that is public and without any explicit license terms falls under the "All rights reserved" category, and not to be taken as it were 'unlicensed'.

Common Development and Distribution License	The Common Development and Distribution License is a free and open-source software license, produced by Sun Microsystems, based on the Mozilla Public License. Files licensed under the CDDL can be combined with files licensed under other licenses, whether open source or proprietary.
BSD licenses	BSD licenses are a family of permissive free software licenses, imposing minimal restrictions on the use and distribution of covered software. This is in contrast to copyleft licenses, which have share-alike requirements.
Copyleft Granting	Copyleft is the legal technique of granting certain freedoms over copies of copyrighted works with the requirement that the same rights be preserved in derivative works. Copyleft is a general method for making a program (or other work) free (in the sense of freedom, not "zero price"), and requiring all modified and extended versions of the program to be free as well. The simplest way to make a program free software is to put it in the public domain, uncopyrighted.

Copyright Holder

All software is copyright-protected, and the copyright is enforceable for 95 years, no matter what. By default, creating a new project or software without any explicit license terms falls under the "All rights reserved" copyright. It means that others should contact the copyright owner to clarify/get written permission before using it. If you are the copyright holder, and someone failed to contact you, but has used your software, then you may have to go through a lengthy court case to proof that the software was yours originally and they have violated your copyright. As soon possible, do register a copyright to your software codes, pattern, design, project, etc.

Registering A Copyright In UK

https://www.gov.uk/register-a-design/

Go to this website and follow the prompts to register a copyright.

IPO Information Centre

Contact the IPO Information Centre if you have a question about international copyright.
IPO Information Centre
information@ipo.gov.uk
Telephone: 0300 300 2000
Monday to Friday, 9am to 5pm

Registering A Copyright In USA

https://www.copyright.gov
Go to this website and follow the prompts to register a copyright. You can also get details of the current copyright holder of software from there.

Non-Disclosure Agreements

Before you give someone outside your company your new unpublished or unlicenced work to look at, first, you should get them to sign a Non-Disclosure Agreement (NDA). With this document, you can take legal action against them if they steal your work or share it with a third party without your authorisation.

Download the form from the UK Gov website here:
https://www.gov.uk/government/publications/non-disclosure-agreements

All Rights Reserved

By default, creating a new project on Github that is public and without any explicit license terms falls under the "All rights reserved" category.

Software Copyright Infringement

Although the law upholds justice for copyright infringement violations, the courts are too careful not to encourage it. This is for the same reason that software cloning and codes sharing are encouraged. They are encouraged:

- In order to stop monopoly in the market by software companies.

- Stop software companies from being legally 'silly' about what and what features were invented by them and what nots. Imagine if Microsoft is to sue for the copyrights on File Save???.

- Another reason, which is the most important reason, is to encourage advancement in technology. If Microsoft was allowed to be introvert with its Internet Explorer back then, would we have our beloved, though annoying Google Chrome now?

- There is never telling which computer whizkid, working in which computer company would come along with better improvements to a software that helps humanity (remember that random guy - employee of Apple, who came up with the iPod shuffle that propelled Apple to the top?). - There is still a long way to Mars; so, in that respect, in the IT World; it's 'all hands-on deck!'.

Can you buy the Copyright Licence of a Software?

Yes, like when Google bought YouTube; all the legal rights were transferred to Google's name (but it wasn't for small money though).

PART TWO

Portfolio

Portfolio

Portfolios are increasing be required for IT jobs, especially those in Graphic Design. Anyone can claim to be good at this or that, so it's a question of, 'show me what you've done'.

Profile Photo

Nowadays, Profile Photo has become the norm in the career world, so be advised to add one to your portfolio and LinkedIn, etc.

A Profile Photo is not a passport photograph, it should show a relaxed, happy you, with any background or setting, but not indecent. Employers assess you from your Profile Photo; to see the 'fun-loving' you, who would be able to fit in with the team, and not some sour-face person, who would not join them after work to the pub for a drink.

Where to host your Portfolio

You can create a portfolio on any web hosting sites. You can register your name as your domain and host it on a hosting site as your portfolio. The only danger with that is if you fail to renew the domain or the hosting package, all your portfolio items will be deleted.

My recommendation is to host it on a free site, even if the name is nested inside another name. This should not be a problem because in the most, our portfolios are private, until we choose to share the link with others.

There are a few free sites that you can host your portfolio, but the popular one these days is Google Sites.
https://sites.google.com

Go to Google – the link above and sign up for an account.

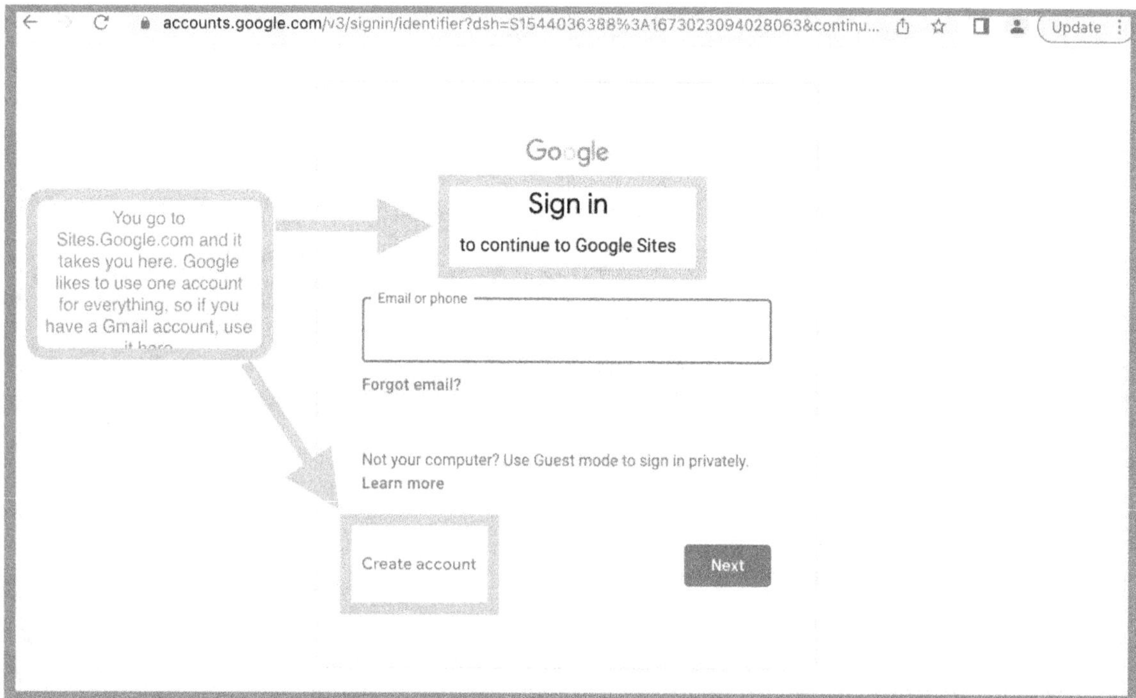

Choose the personal use site.

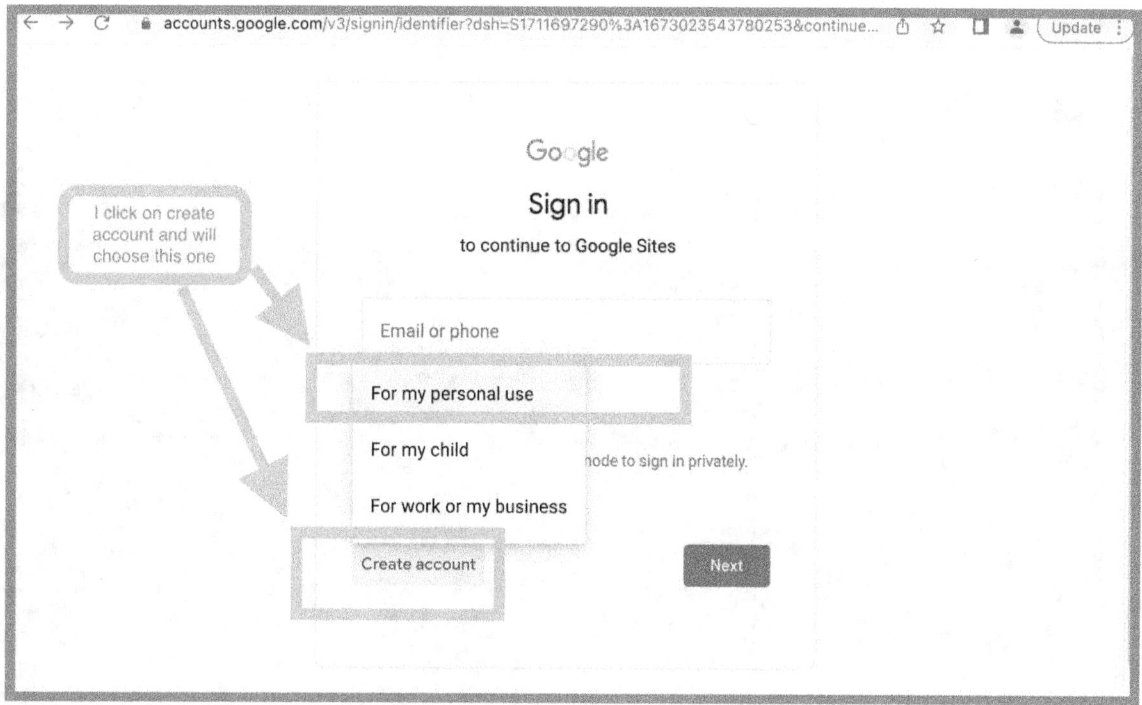

From the templates, choose – Portfolio.

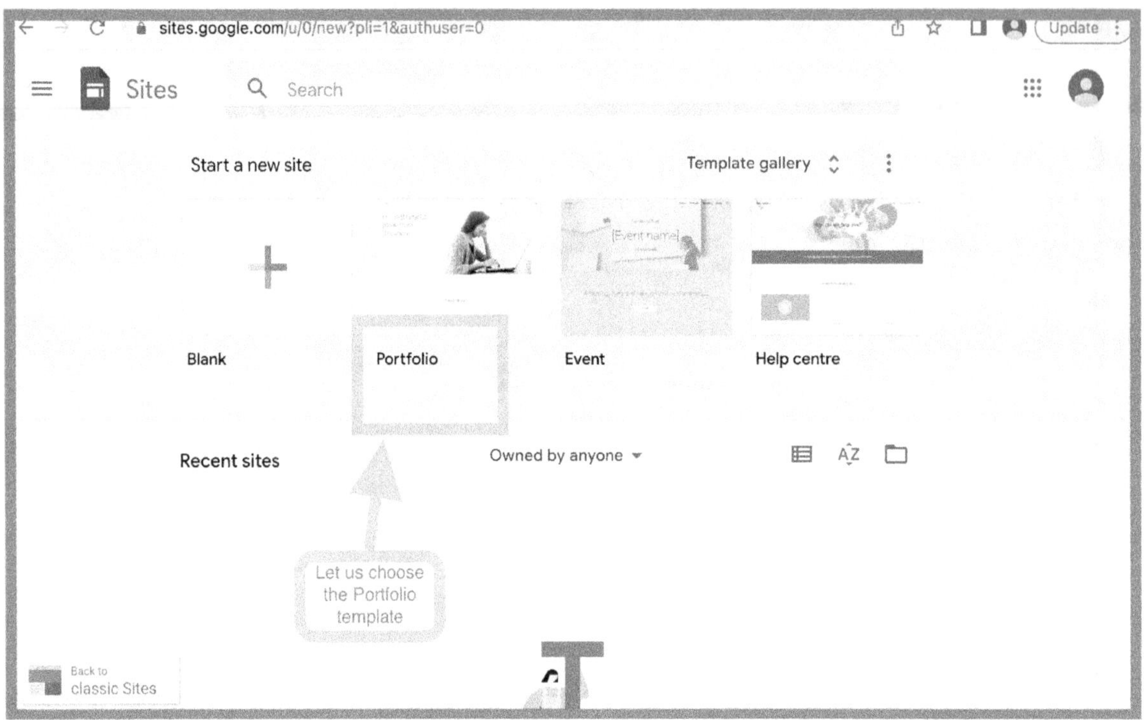

Start customizing.

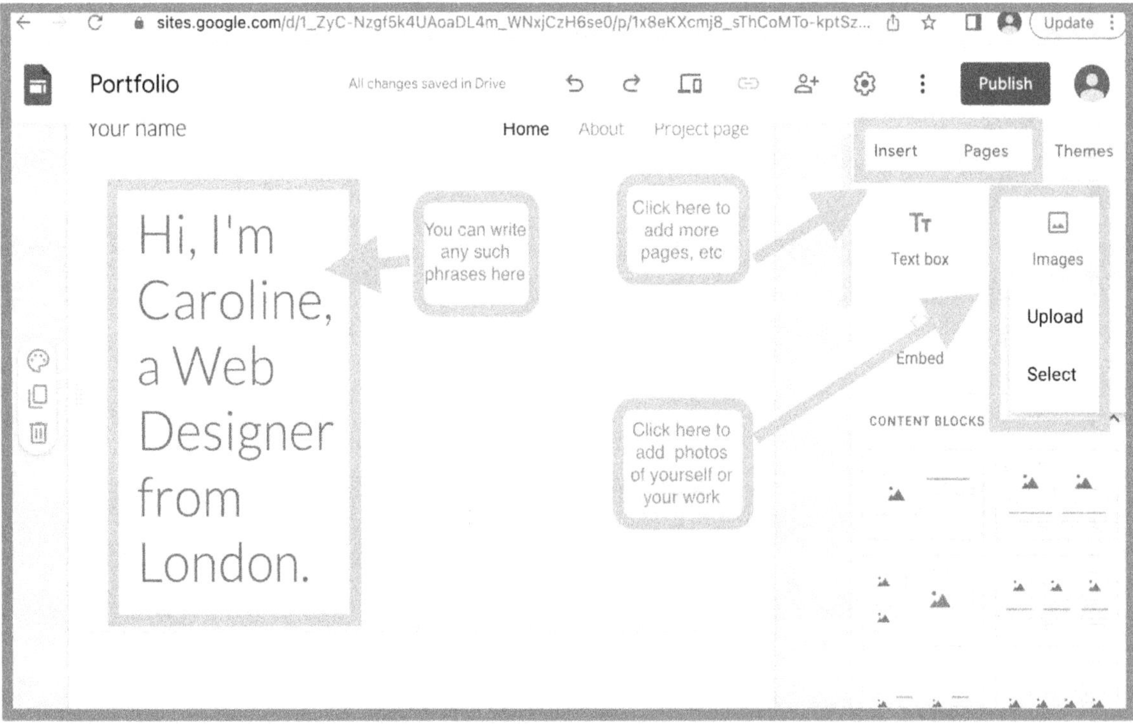

Add your photo and pages

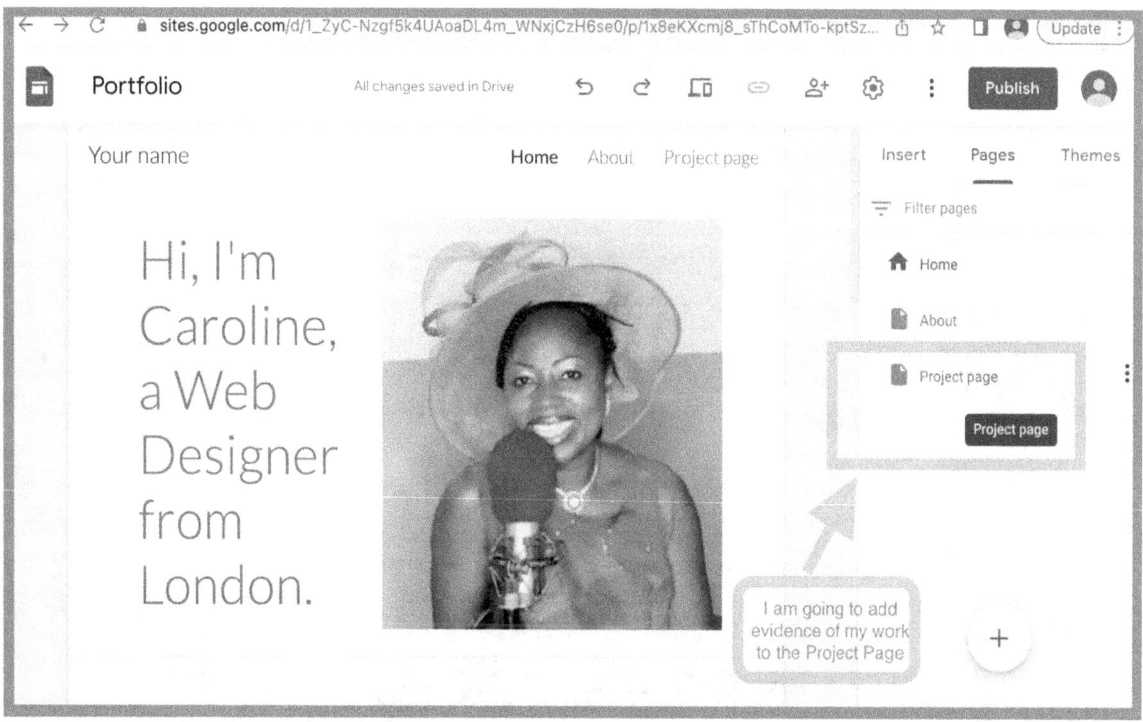

Add some projects for exhibition. Then click on Publish

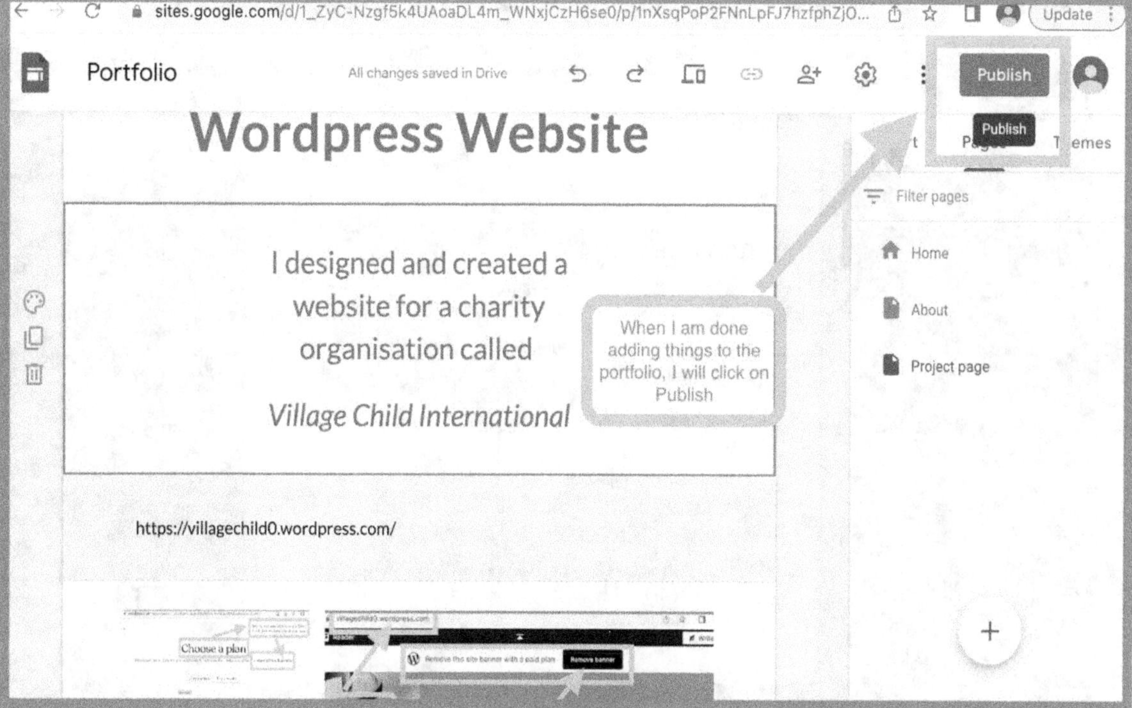

Choose the filter who can view the site – I would choose Anyone

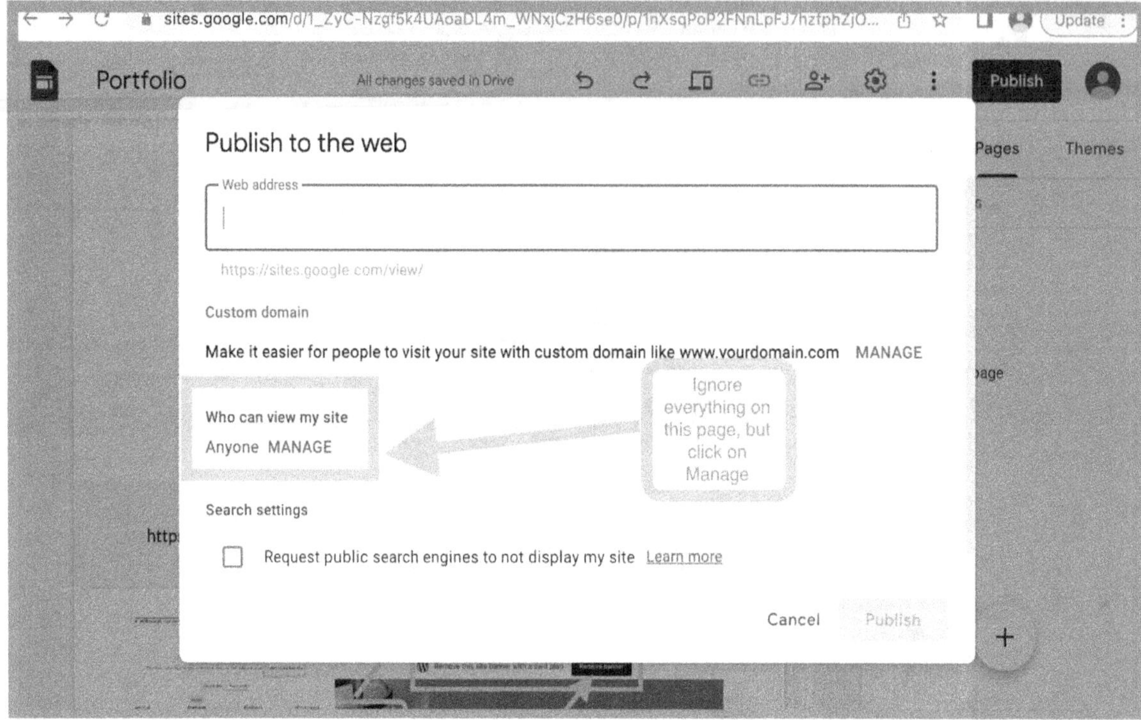

Then choose to make it Public

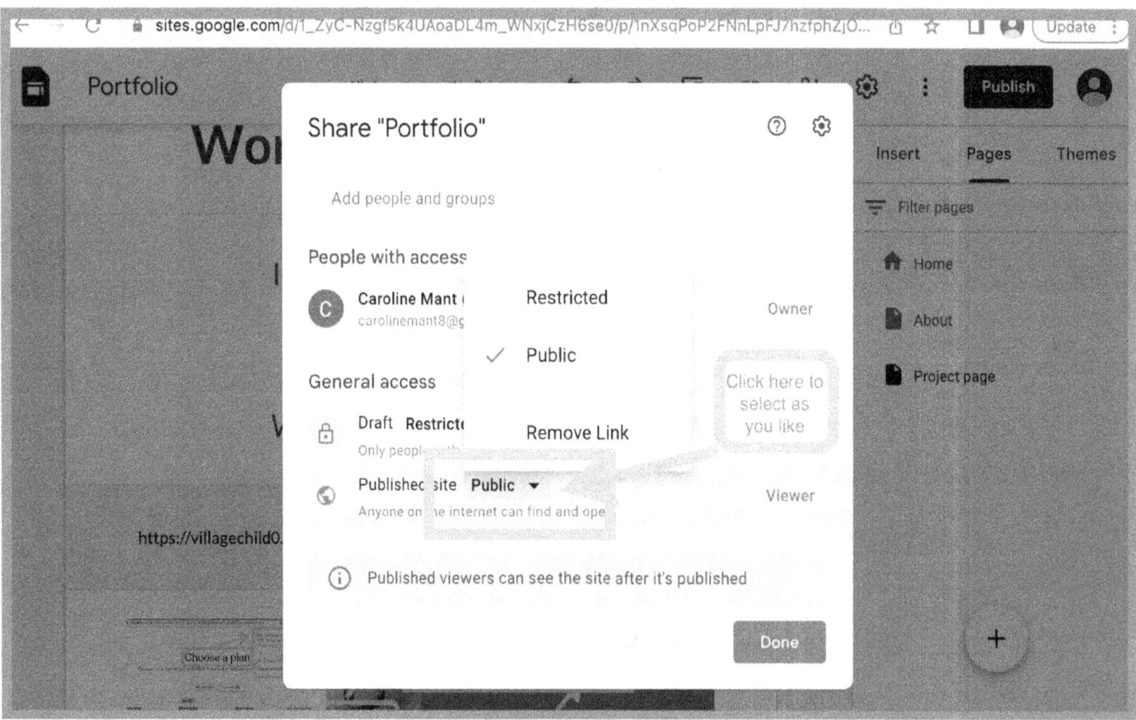

Type in a name that would be used to form your portfolio site address

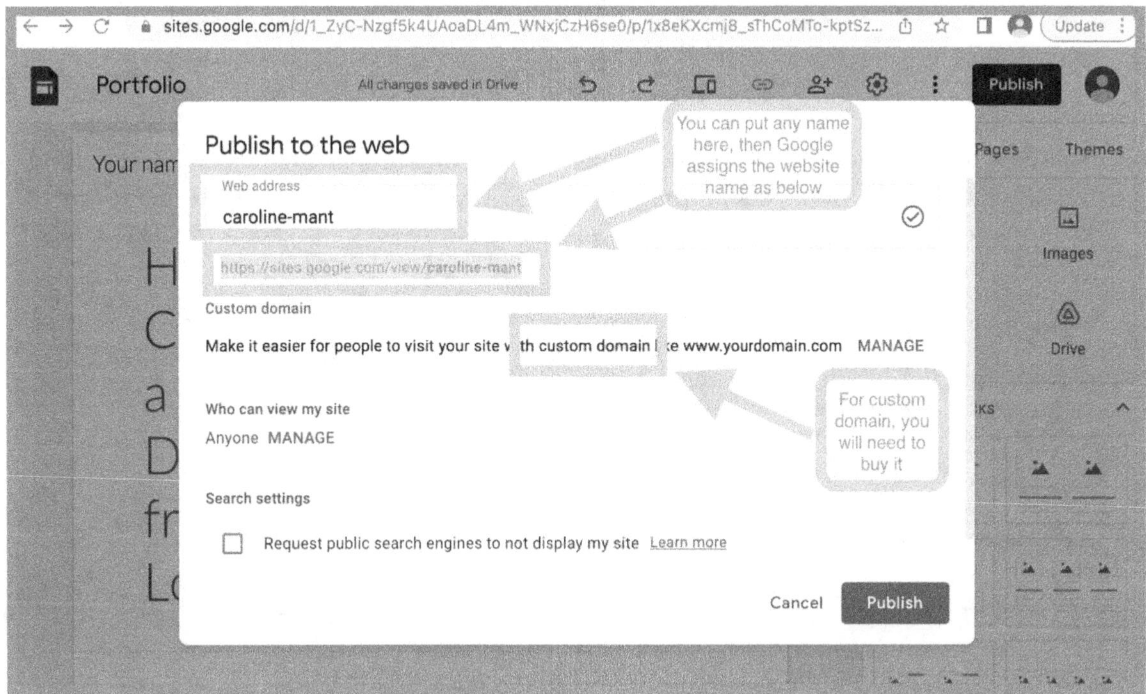

See, my portfolio site address is below. Now copy and paste in the CV or email to employers
https://sites.google.com/view/caroline-mant

LinkedIn

LinkedIn

Since the world has gone social-media crazy, job hunting and hiring can't be left behind. LinkedIn is the professional social media sites in Europe. Employers like to gain a small inside about your life from there, since people like boasting on their social media. https://www.linkedin.com

To create an account, go to their website and click on Join Now.

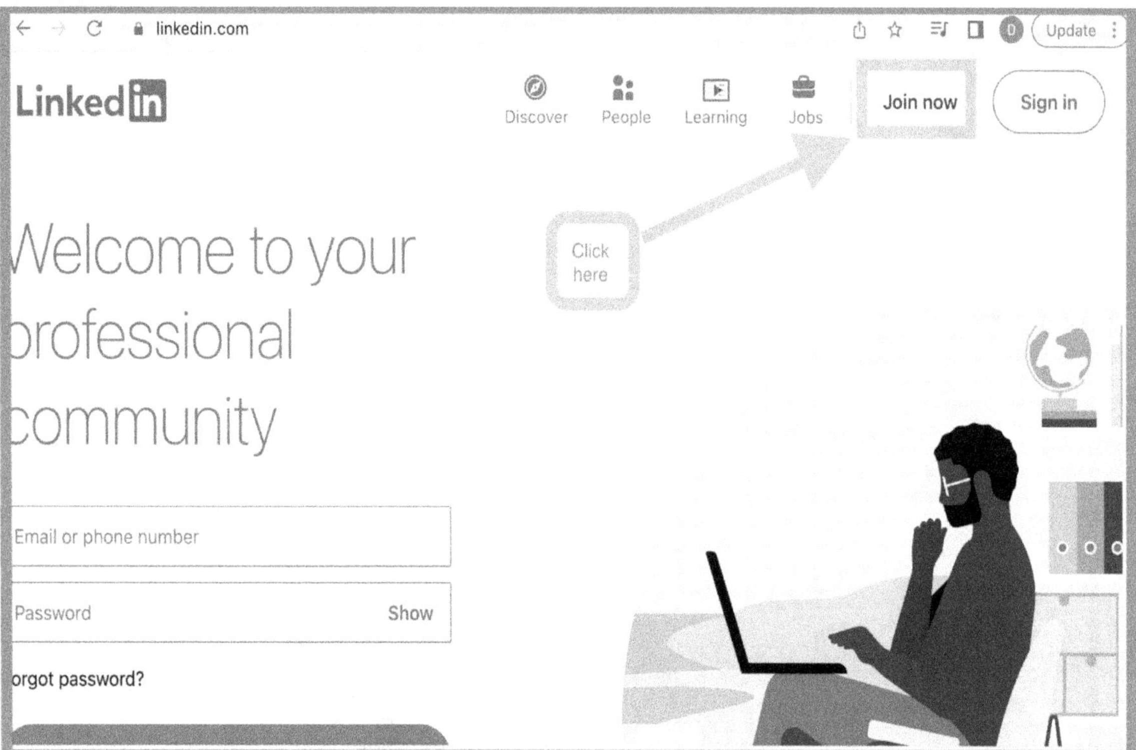

Keep consistent – use your professional email

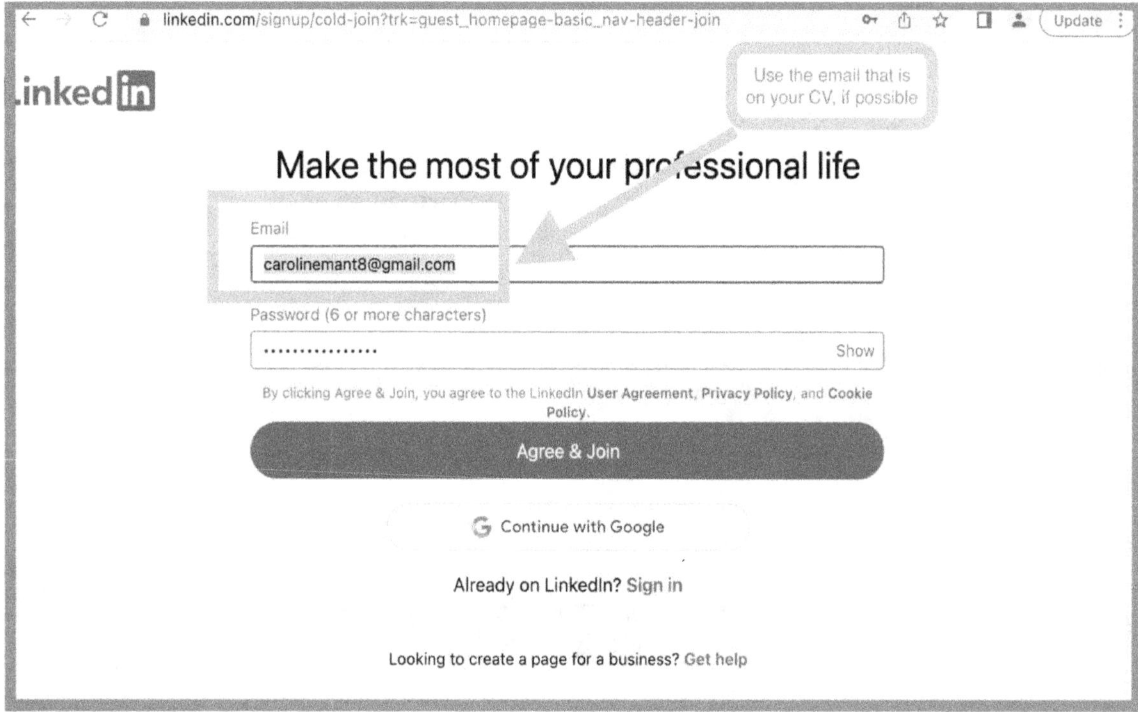

Use the full name on your CV

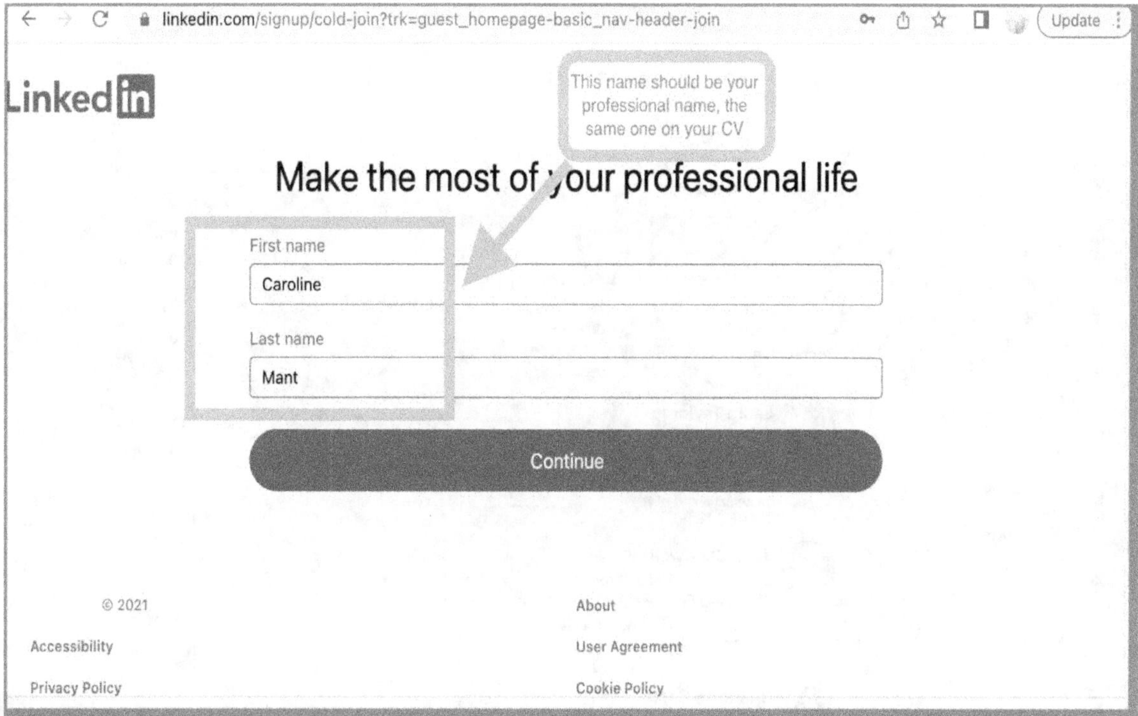

Just fill in anything here to proceed. You can edit it later

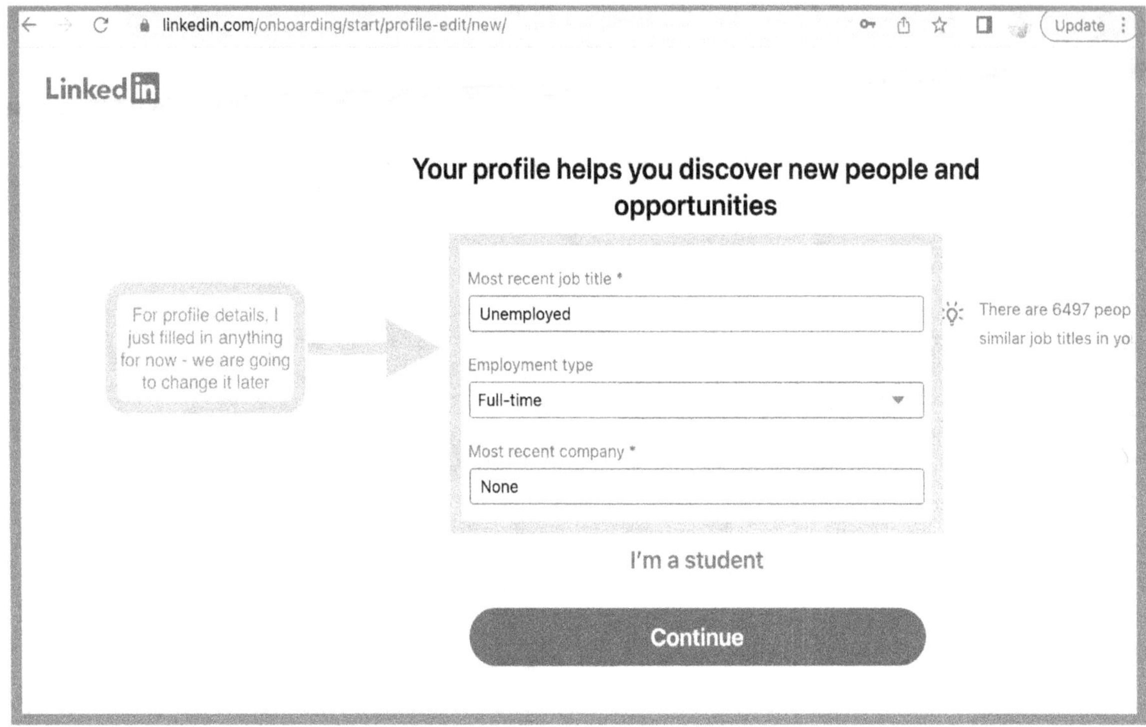

In your Home dashboard, you can add your photo, add or edit info about yourself.

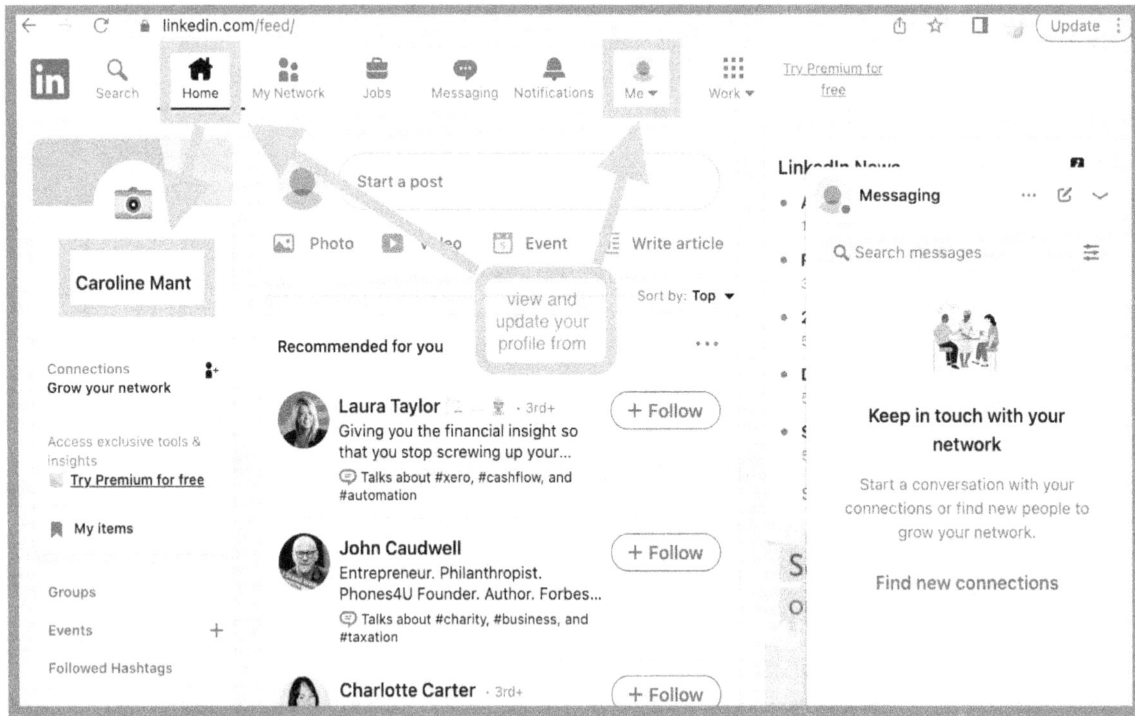

I set my profile to – Open to work. Employers and Agencies do go through profiles here. You can start looking for jobs here. Copy the profile address and paste it on your CV.

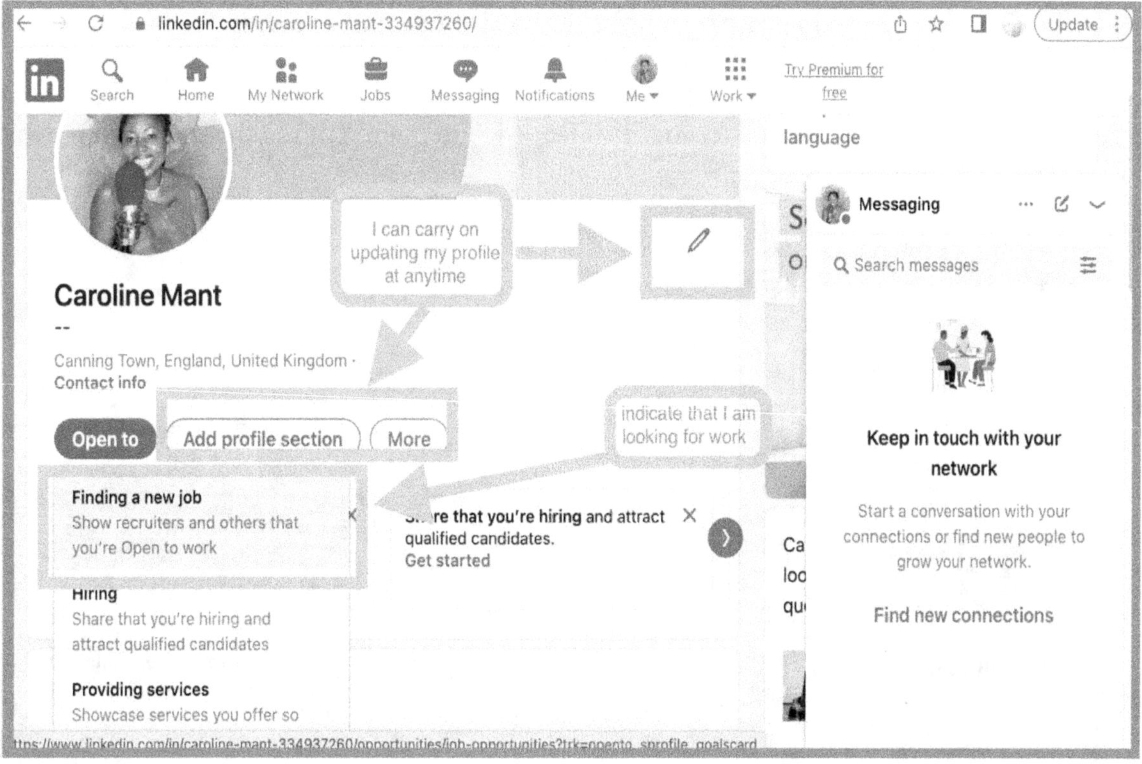

Update our LinkedIn Profile

When you have successfully built a website on WordPress (in Part 3 below) and have also tried building sites on a few other platforms, you can now call yourself – a 'Website Designer'. OK, let's go and update our LinkedIn Profile and start applying for jobs or advertising ourselves as a 'Freelance Website Designer'.

Log into your LinkedIn and go to your Profile or Home, you will see the pencil icon, which is for editing the page.

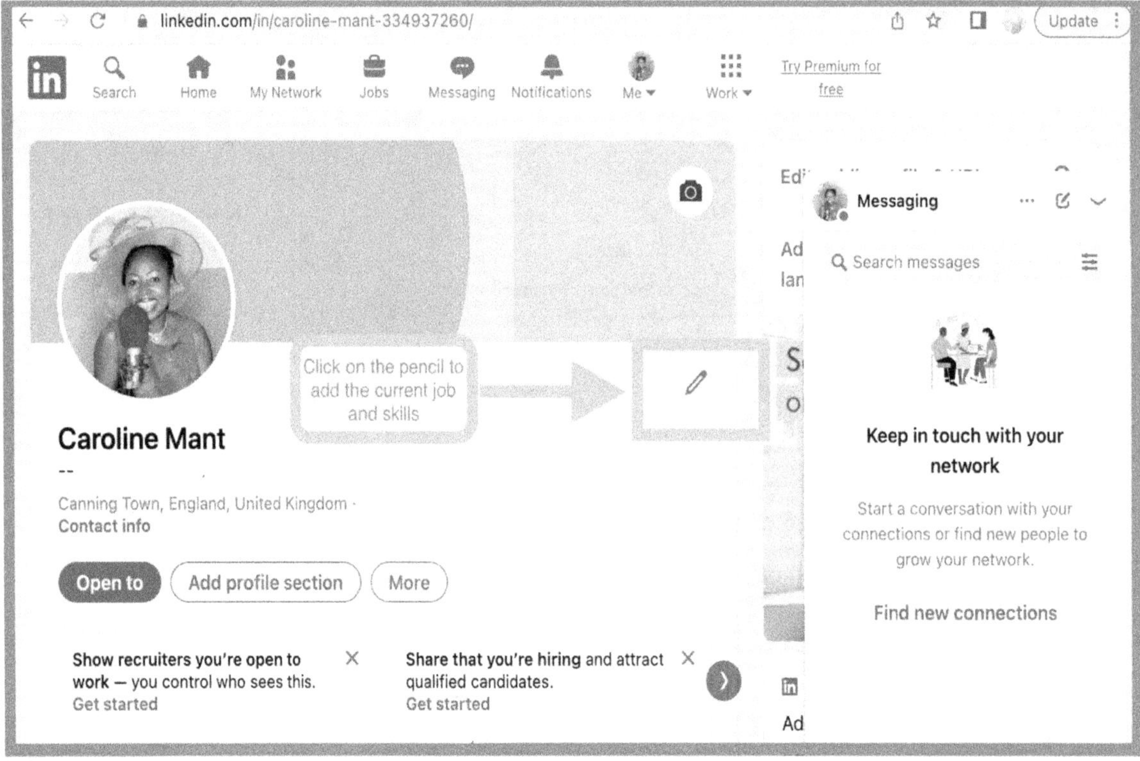

Add as many details as possible

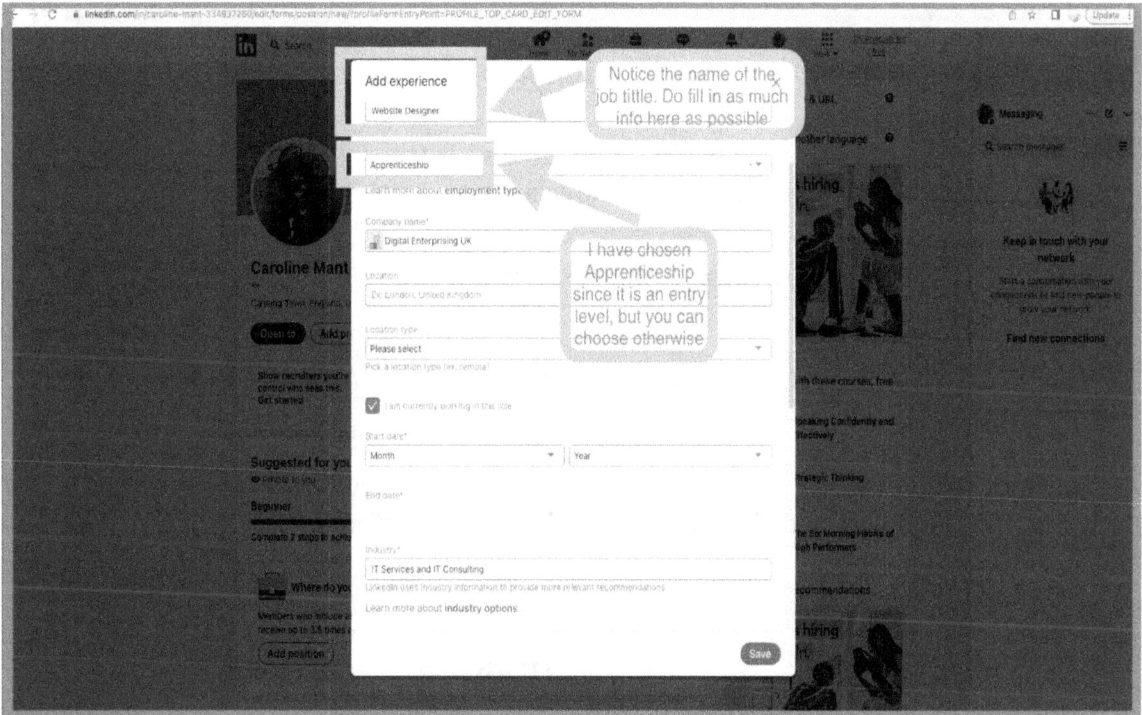

LinkedIn will start marching your profile with suggested jobs similar to Web site Designer

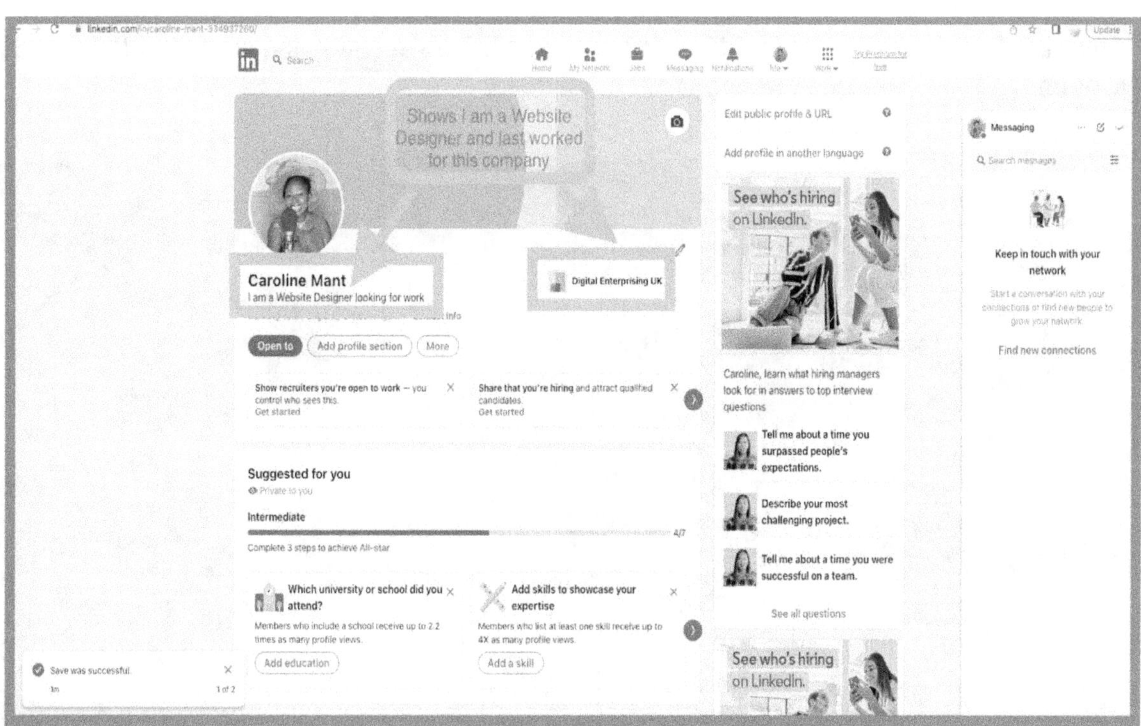

GitHub

GitHub

GitHub, GitLab and Bitbucket

GitHub, GitLab and Bitbucket: All these three are where you can store and share your codes.

GitLab Inc - is a privately owned, fully remote company. You have to pay to use it.
https://gitlab.com

GitHub - is a child company of Microsoft, there is paid plans and a free plan.
https://github.com

Bitbucket - is a Git-based source code repository hosting service owned by Atlassian. Bitbucket offers both commercial plans and free accounts with an unlimited number of private repositories.
https://bitbucket.org

GitHub

Anyone who is anyone among the IT crowd has to have a GitHub account. It is for the show off…. Ok seriously; it is where people store and share codes and collaborate on projects.

Here is a basic step-by-step guide to setting up a GitHub account and starting a Repository Commit.

Go to GitHub and click on Sign up.

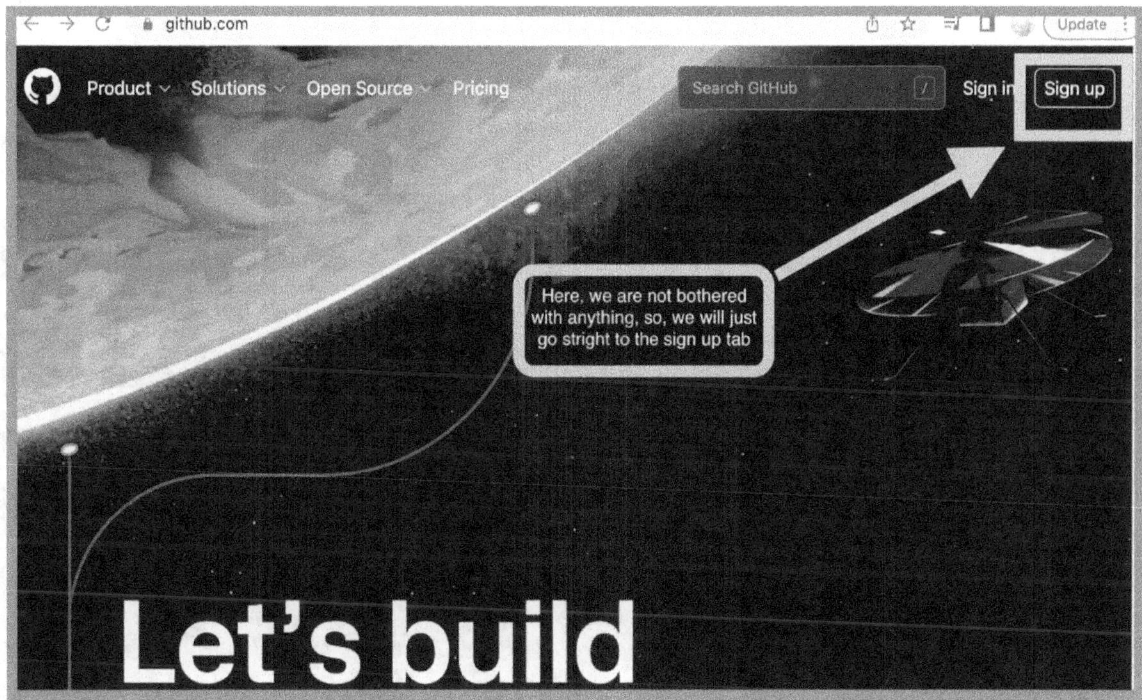

Put your email and continue

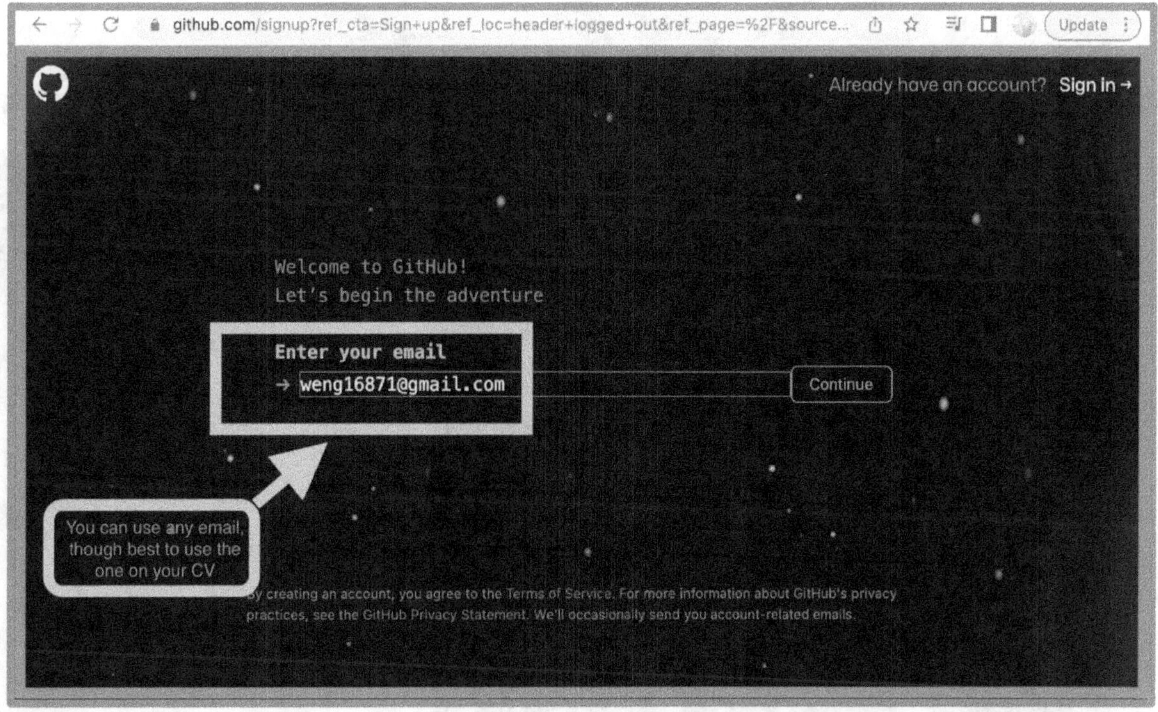

Enter a Username

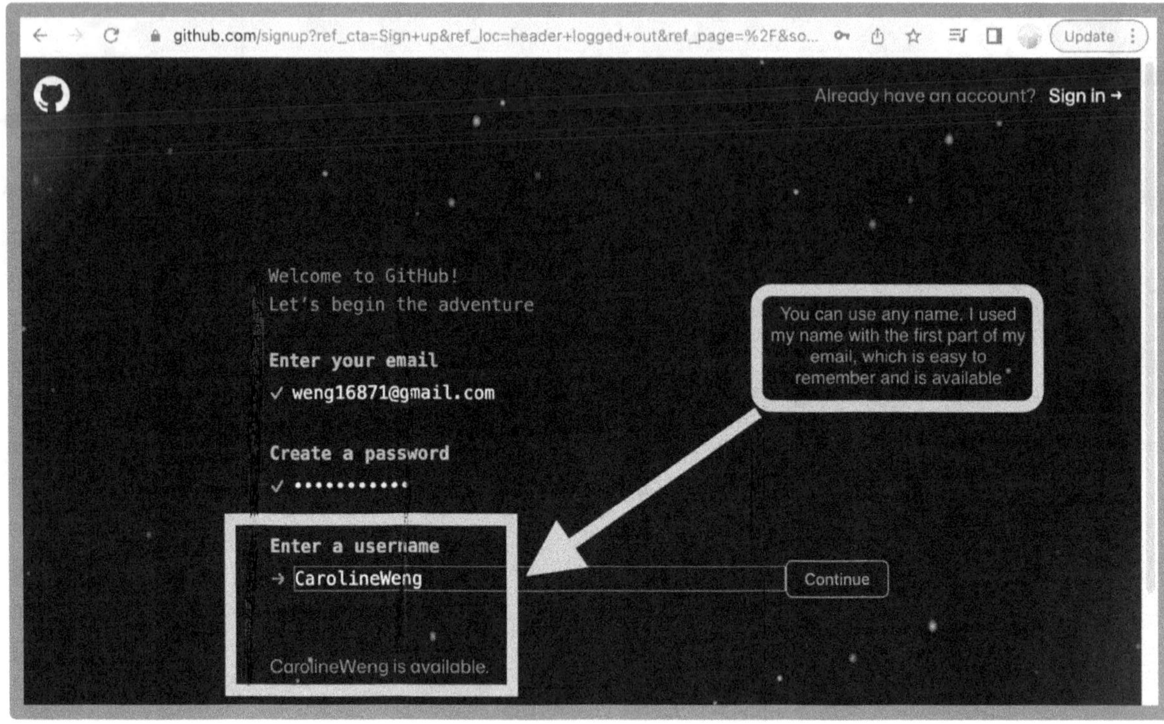

Enter the basic information

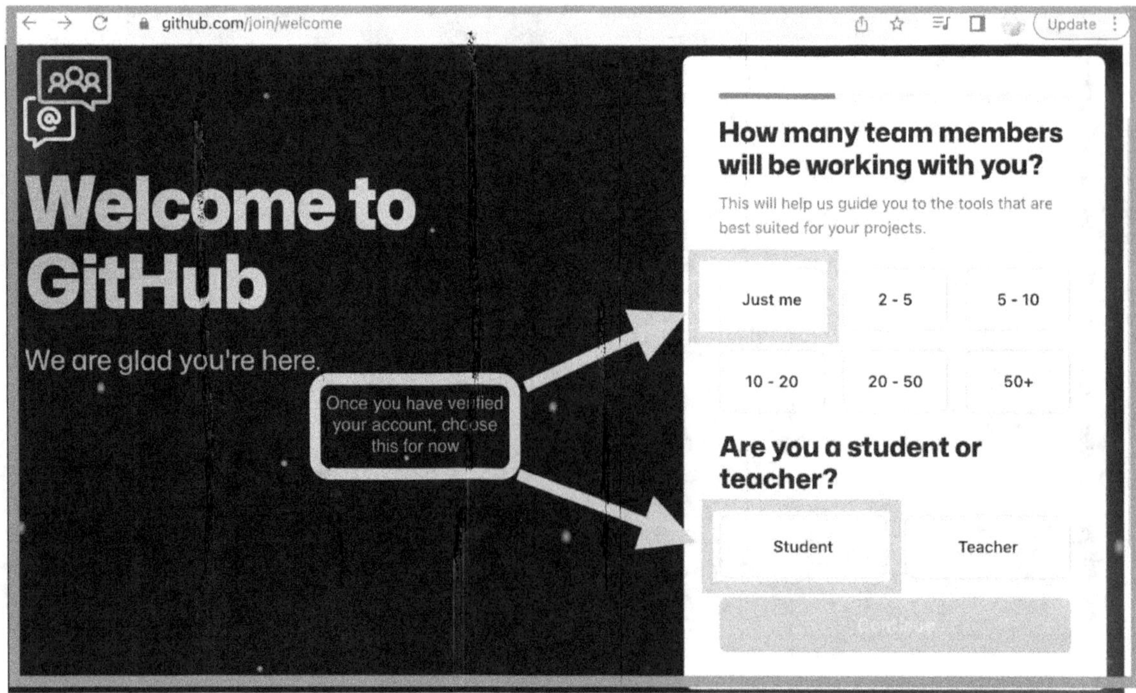

Choose Free Plan

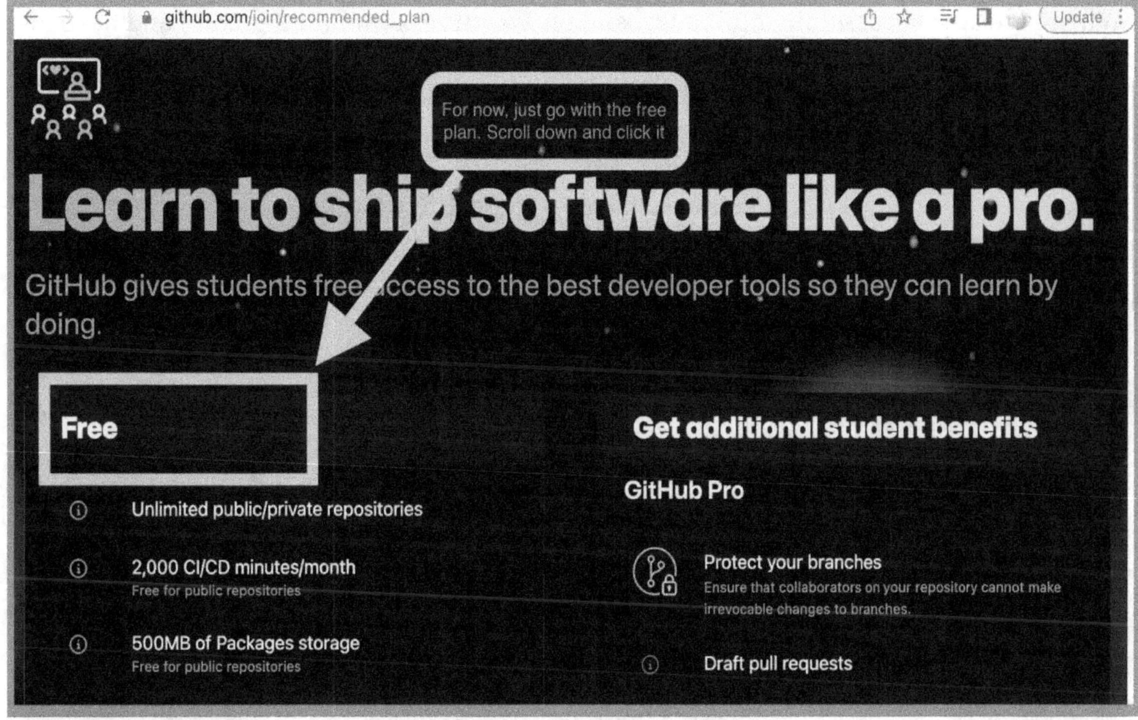

You can edit your profile in your dashboard. Copy your GitHub profile name for your CV

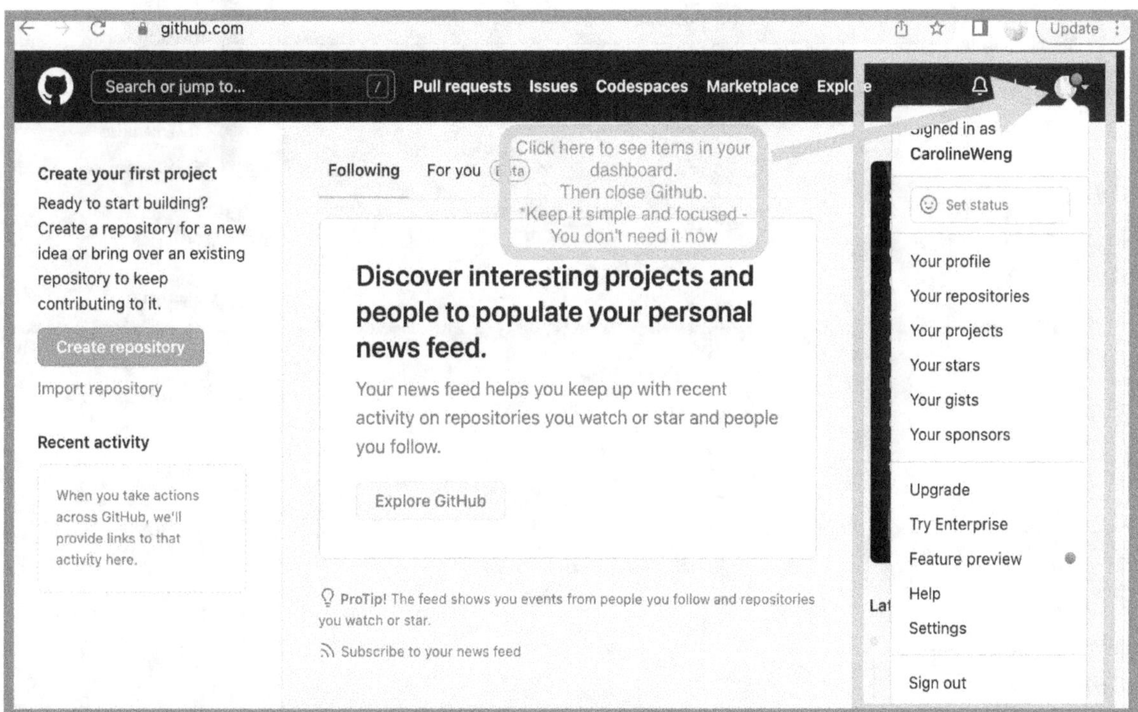

Update our Profile

When you have successfully built a website on WordPress (in Part 3 below) and have also tried building sites on a few other platforms, you can now call yourself – a 'Website Designer'. OK, let's go and update GitHub and start applying for jobs or advertising yourself as a 'Freelance Website Designer'

Update GitHub – Repository Comit

Let's update GitHub and create a new repository for our new project. It will be the First Comit.

Go to the profile page and choose Your Repositories

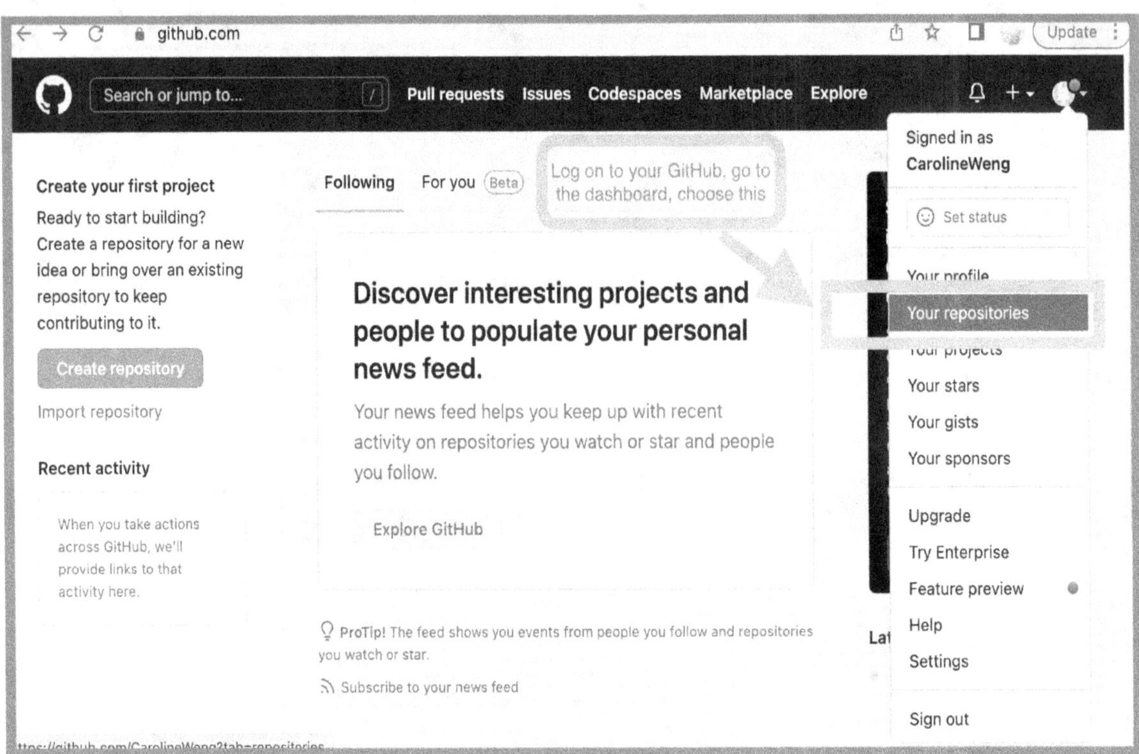

Now choose 'New'.

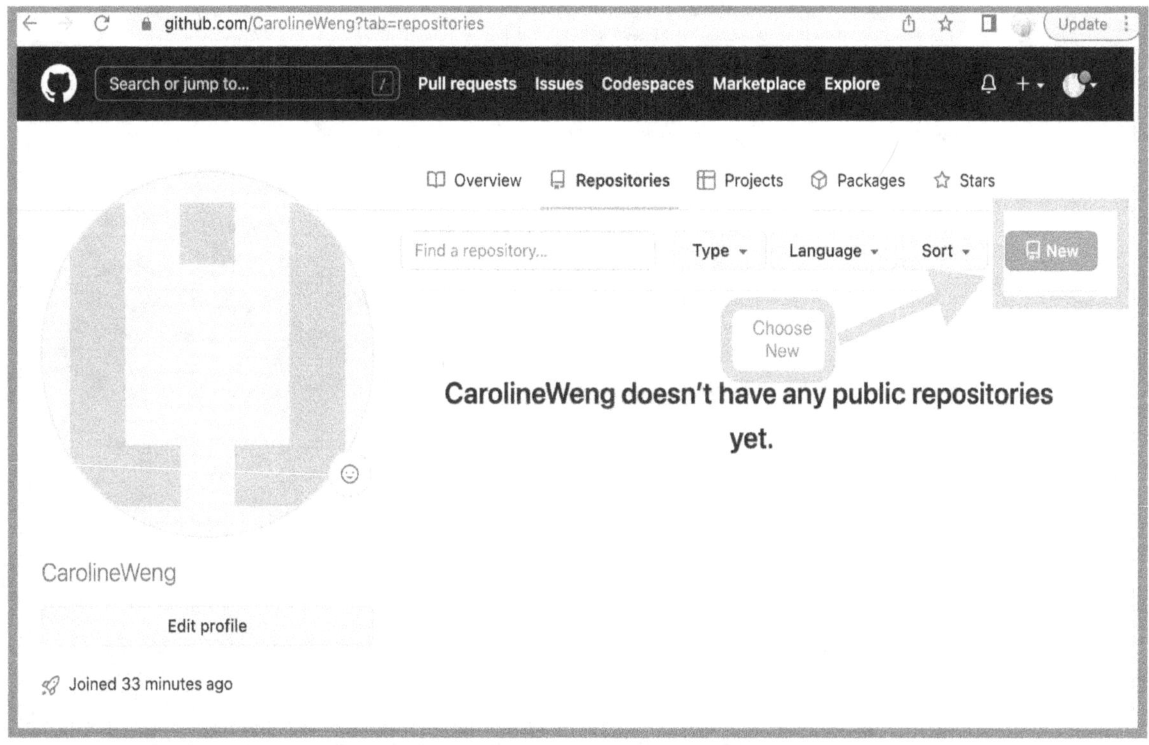

Choose Public if you want others to see your work. If you are using it to find work, then best choose 'Public'. In future, when you are trying to create something and you are not able to put it together, then also choose public, in case someone may see it and contribute to it. The only time people choose 'Private', is if they want to keep it top secret until they have licenced it.

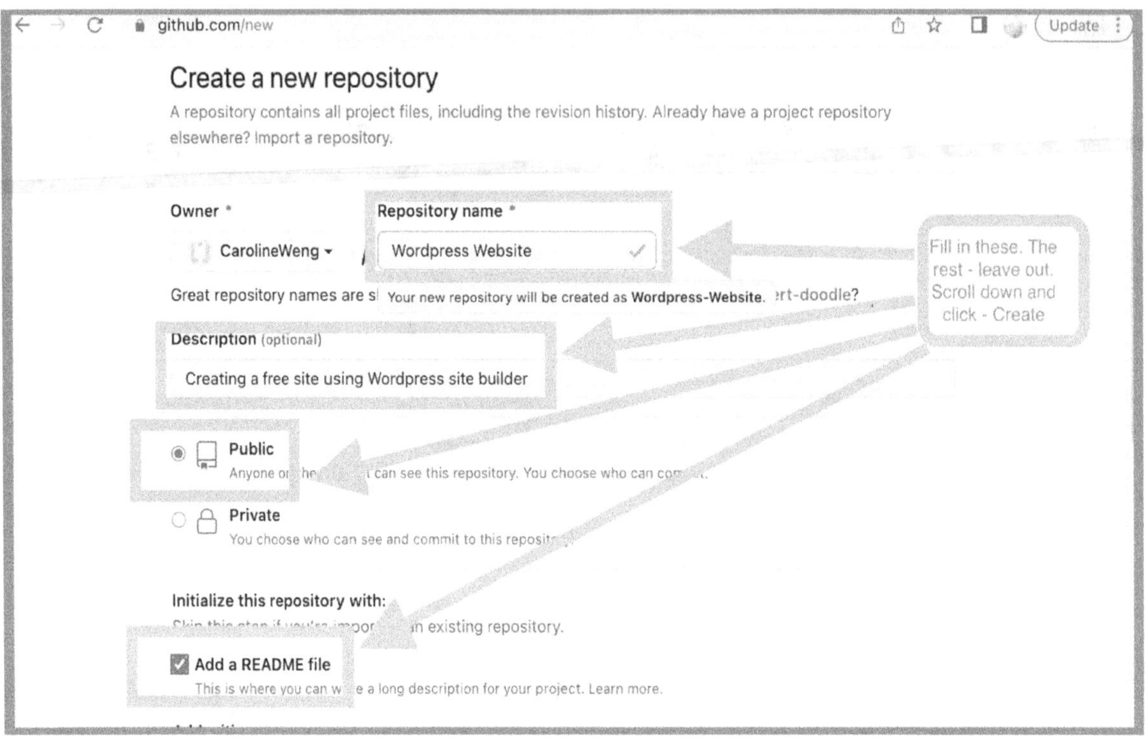

Here is the name of the new project /software that you are currently working on.

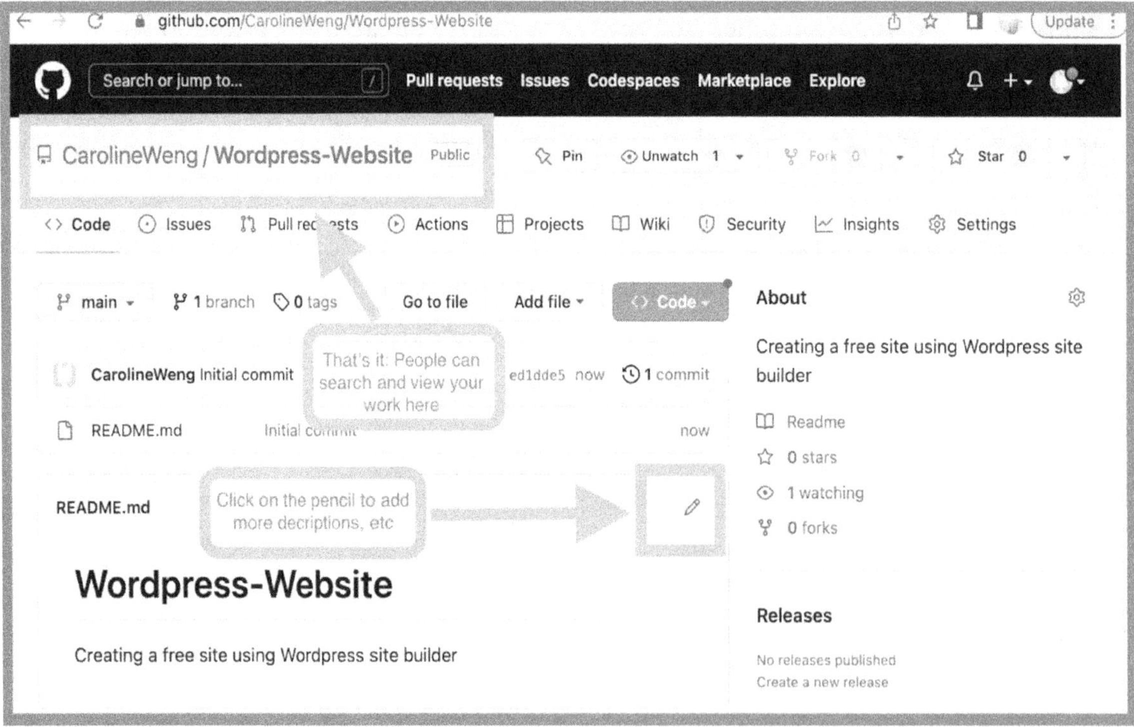

CV

The CV

The general rule about CVs and Resume are.

Keep it sweet and short (3 pages).

Check grammars, phrases, and format (best to use a template).

Make sure that key skills are easily visible.

Make the CV relevant to the job role being applied.

Do I have more than one CVs? – Yes.
Do I modify my CV according to the job am applying? – Absolutely.

Keywords to use on your CV to make you look 'computer-savvy'.
Implementation
Solutions
Teamwork
Contribution
Collaboration
Problem solving
Client's support
Third Party Software
Stakeholders
Tools
Platform
Framework
Ecosystem
Live Environment
SLAs (Service Level Agreement)

Transferable Skills

When you are new to the IT industry, and have no experience in IT, you would have to strongly rely on showing your skillset. Although, you can transfer 'Transferable Skills' from one work sector to another, it is important to rearrange the skills and word them in a way that they are going to serve the new role. For example- If your previous job was as a nurse, and now you are applying for an IT Helpdesk role. Nursing is a highly intelligent role, and you must have gained a lot of useful skills, however, you would have to present these skills as if they were gained in an IT role, like these skillsets thus:

Assessing clients' (patients') needs and providing the right service in real time. (Basically – checking if they are in pain; need medication, and quickly giving it to them).

I usually work as part of a team, which serves our clients efficiently within the agreed SLAs. (I work on a ward with other nurses, doctors, healthcare assistants, cleaners, food service staff, etc, so that the ward runs smoothly, and patients get their food and medication at the correct times).

CV Template

Here are a few CV templates you can review to use or not:

Microsoft Word CV Templates

Open Microsoft Word, go to File -> Open New Template and search for CV. Many different styles would come up.

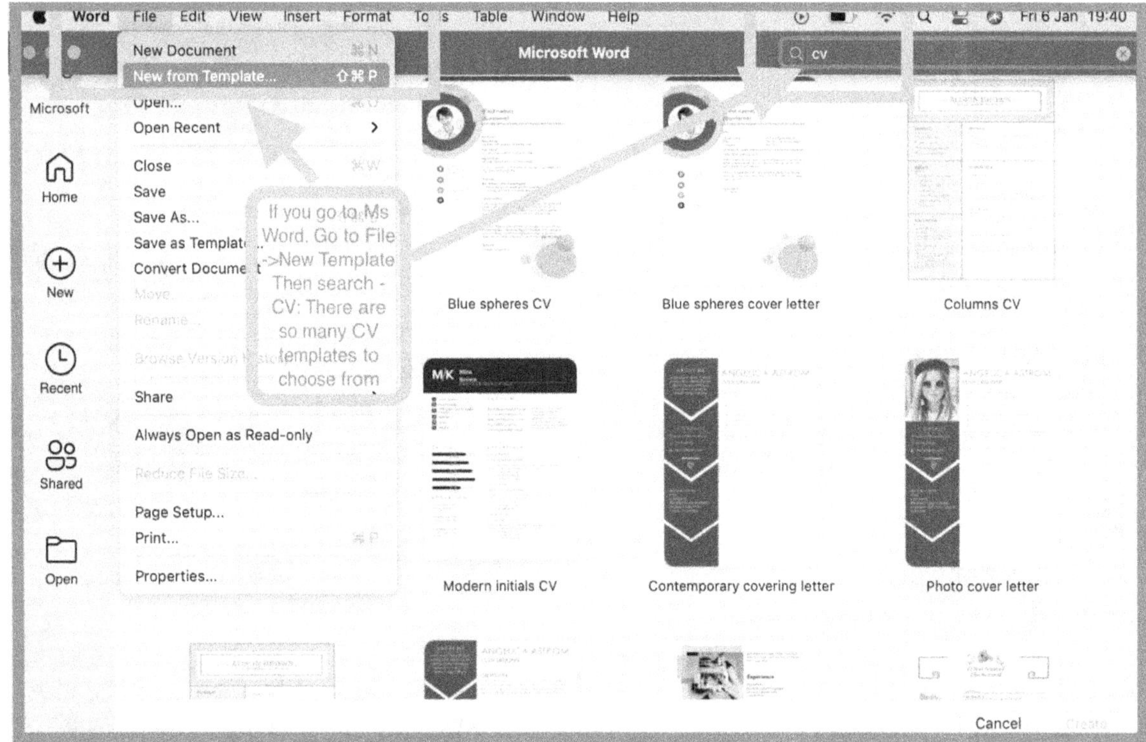

Job Centre CV Template

Here is one of the CV templates that our Local Government Job Centre uses. You can copy it or download from the link provided in Glossary.

CV Information Form

Please complete as much of this form as you can. This information will be used to create a new professional CV for you. Understanding your personality, skills, life and work experiences, means we can create a CV that is unique to you, matches the type of work you are interested in, and will help you get to interview.

Your data: All information provided is confidential between you and C K Futures Ltd. and is only used to help create your new professional CV.

If you have an existing CV, use this form to complete sections not already in your CV.

Name of Recruitment Advisor:

Participant's Number:

Personal Details

Name	
Address	
Telephone Number(s)	
Email Address LinkedIn (if you have one)	

About you

The type of work I am looking for is:	Consider the environment & sectors you see yourself working in e.g. • Outdoors or indoors? In an office? or on the move? • Tasks you enjoy doing • Working on your own or with others? • Managing things / people? • Part time / full time / working from home? / Locations? • Customer facing or behind the scenes? • Sectors you are most interested in working for • Job titles you enter when searching online
I have the	What are you good at doing? For example, Communication / Problem

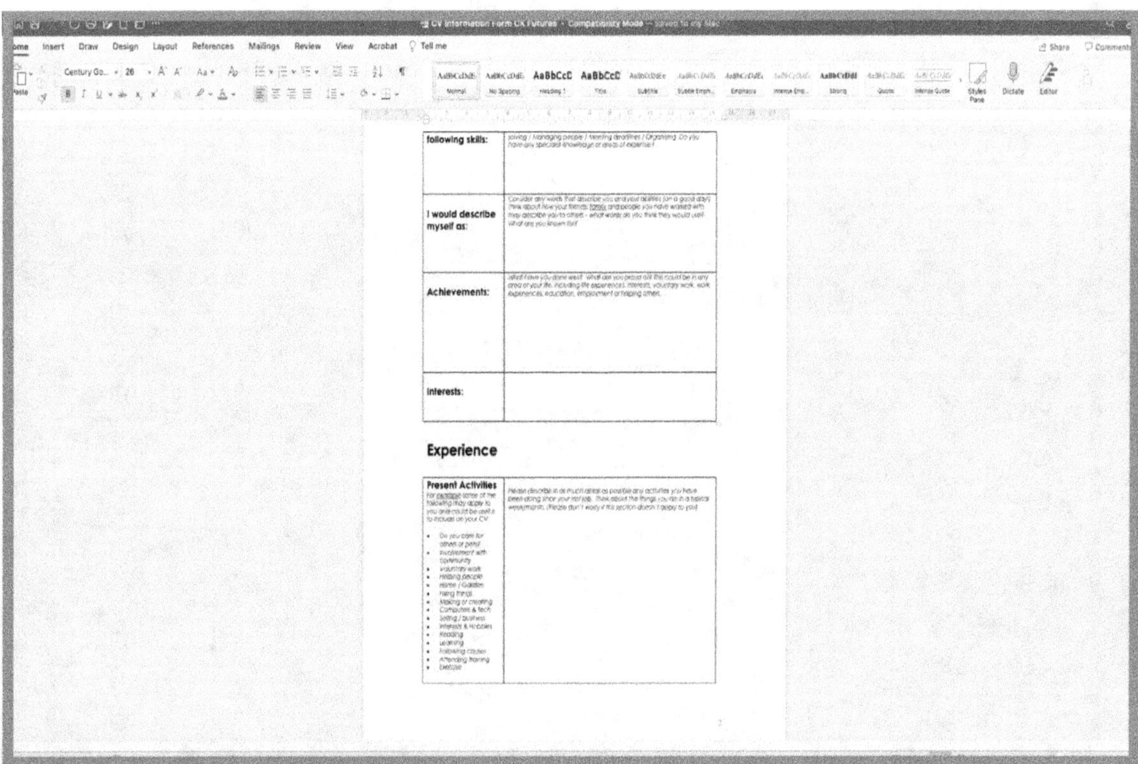

following skills:	solving / Managing people / Meeting deadlines / Organising. Do you have any specialist knowledge or areas of expertise?
I would describe myself as:	Consider any words that describe you and your abilities (on a good day!) Think about how your friends, family and people you have worked with may describe you to others - what words do you think they would use? What are you known for?
Achievements:	What have you done well? What are you proud of? This could be in any area of your life, including life experiences, interests, voluntary work, work experiences, education, employment or helping others.
Interests:	

Experience

Present Activities For example some of the following may apply to you and could be useful to include on your CV • Do you care for others or pets? • Involvement with community • Voluntary work • Helping people • Home / Garden • Fixing things • Making or creating • Computers & tech • Selling / business • Interests & Hobbies • Reading • Learning • Following courses • Attending training • Exercise	Please describe in as much detail as possible any activities you have been doing since your last job. Think about the things you do in a typical week/month. (Please don't worry if this section doesn't apply to you)

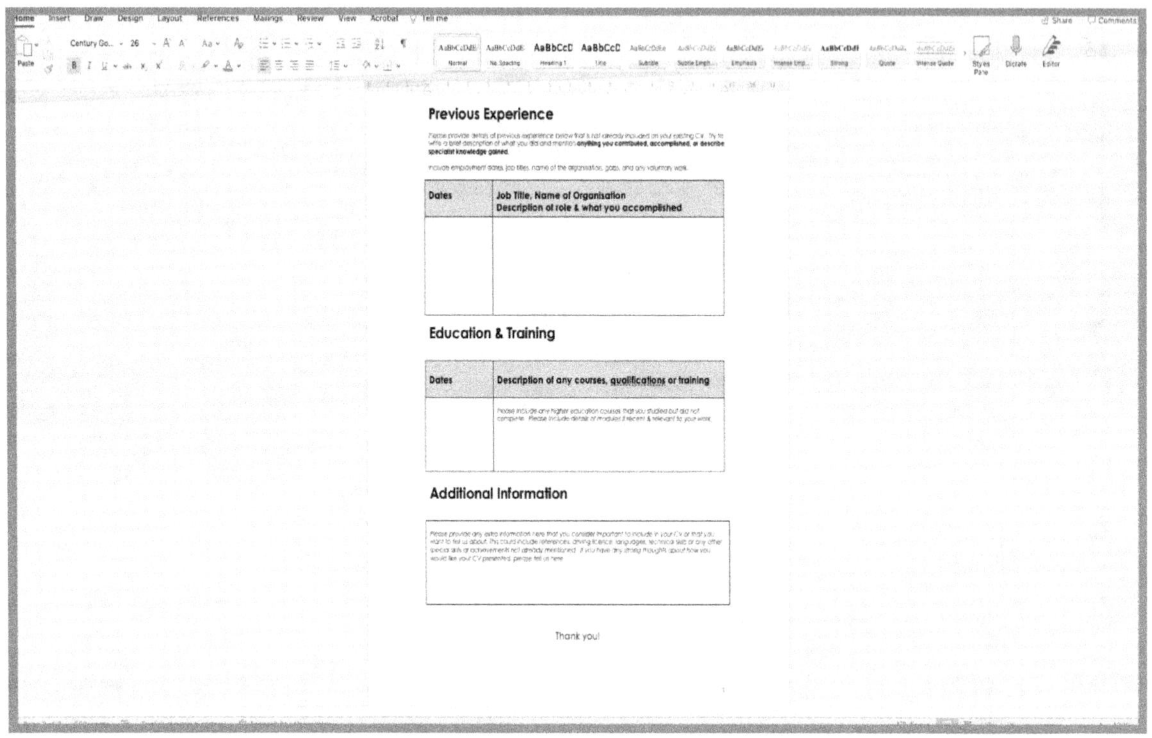

Caroline's CV Template

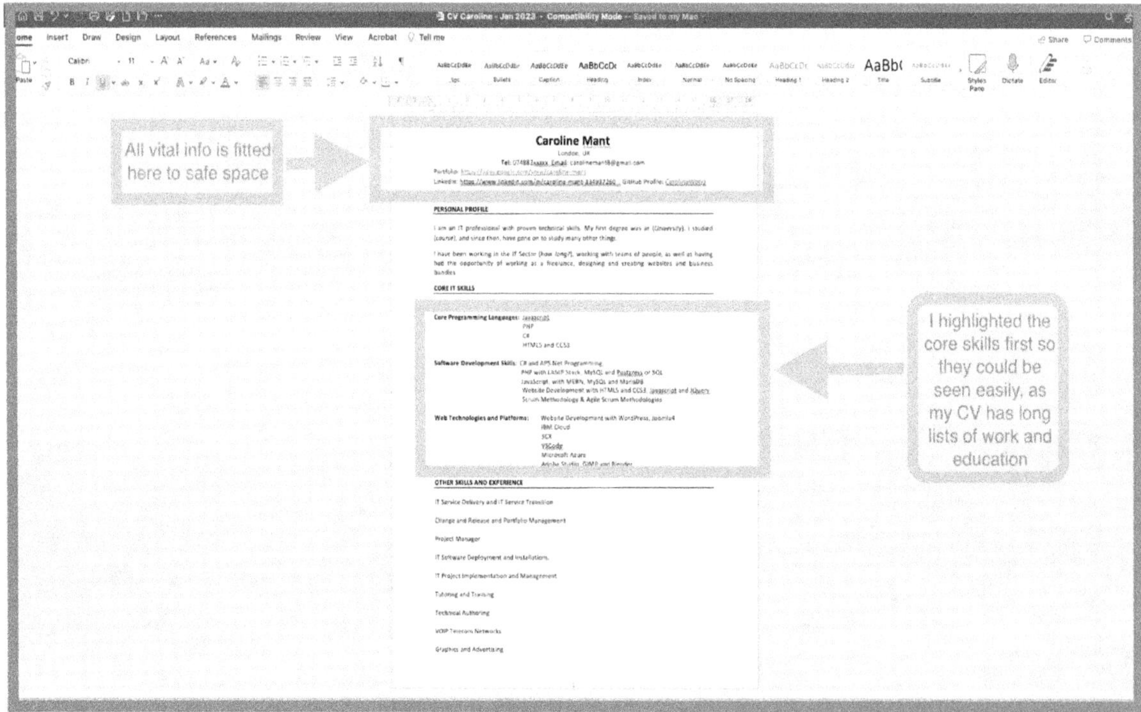

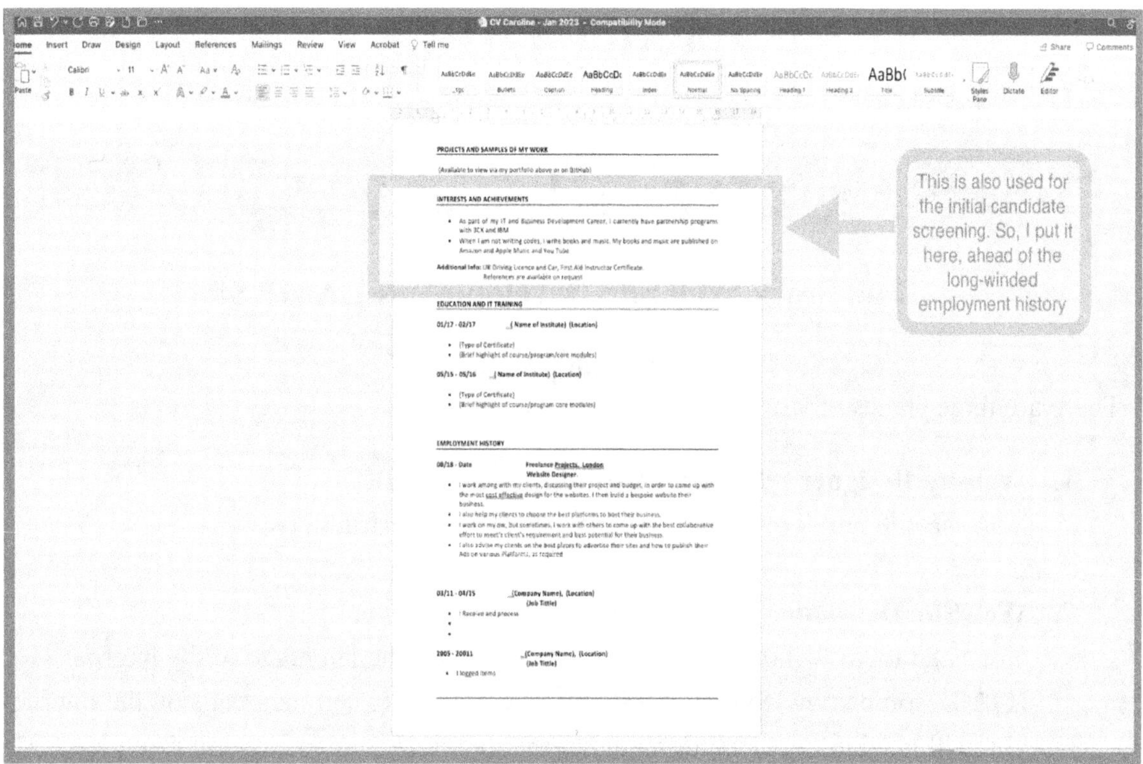

Covering Letter

Some job applications may require you to send a covering letter with your application or CV. Here is a Sample Covering Letter.

Dear Sir / Ma,

I have just viewed your job vacancy for 'Web Designer ' on (name of agency or website), and I would like to be considered for this position.

Please find a copy of my CV attached.

Thank you,
Caroline

PART THREE

Full Stack Web Development: LAMP Stack

Full Stack Web Site Development: LAMP Stack

Building Websites

There are three stages of working as a website's developer.

1. **Website Designer** – Beginner (No coding involved)

   You use site builder wizards with easy-to-follow instructions.

2. **Web Site Developer / Administrator** – Intermediate.

   You need to know how websites are put together, the language of the internet – HTML, some knowledge of CSS. Say, if you want to sell handbags on the internet, you will need to register a domain name, find an ISP, Web Hosting Provider, CMS (content management system), Payment Gateway, etc. You need to know where to find these software and how to put things together.

3. **Web Applications Developer** – Advance.

   For this, you will need to know some programming languages and write your own codes and build the software. This is usually splits into backend developer and frontend developer, and Full Stack Developer. Once you've built software, then put things together. For example, if Tesco wants a website to sell their goods, you will have to write a custom software that fits their needs. The same with Uber, etc. Usually, it would be a team of people, each working on one part or section of the project.

Full-stack Web Site Developer

When it comes to web site development, we are not going to use a wizard to build the web site, rather we are going to manually build the web site from the ground up to finish using different applications and software. We will need to decide on the front-end matter, and on the back-end matter, and the technologies needed to build a full stack web site.

A full stack web developer is someone who can build a complete web site architecture that includes both the back end and front-end applications. Also, that include the integration of web services and interfaces, version control, and web hosting platform and any other necessary third-party software and extensions needed for the smooth operation on the business' web services. The front end, that is the client site would normally need HTML and CSS, JavaScript, jQuery, Angular, or Vue. While the back end would be in server technologies such as PHP, Java, ASP, Python, or Node. The full stack web developing uses a combination of these programming languages and technologies, along with the database type and hosting web server to make up a stack, and depending on which set is being used, it could be; MEAN, LAMP, MERN, or .NET.

MEAN = MongoDB, Express, Angular, Node. js
LAMP = Linux, Apache, MySQL, PHP
MERN = MongoDB, Express, React, and Node.js
.NET = JavaScript, Java, SQL, CSS, Python, PHP, ASP.NET and DevOps.

In this tutorial we are going to be working with the LAMP Stack (Linux, Apache, MySQL, PHP), a full-stack technology.
The operating system - Linux
The web server - Apache
The database server - MySQL
The programming language - PHP

The LAMP Stack is one of the most popular Stacks for both hosted servers and cloud applications. This stack has been around for longer than some stacks, all the items on the stack are free, open-source ware, with a great community and lots of applications and software for integration available out there.

Here is our stack information for this tutorial. I bought this plan from the web hosting provider

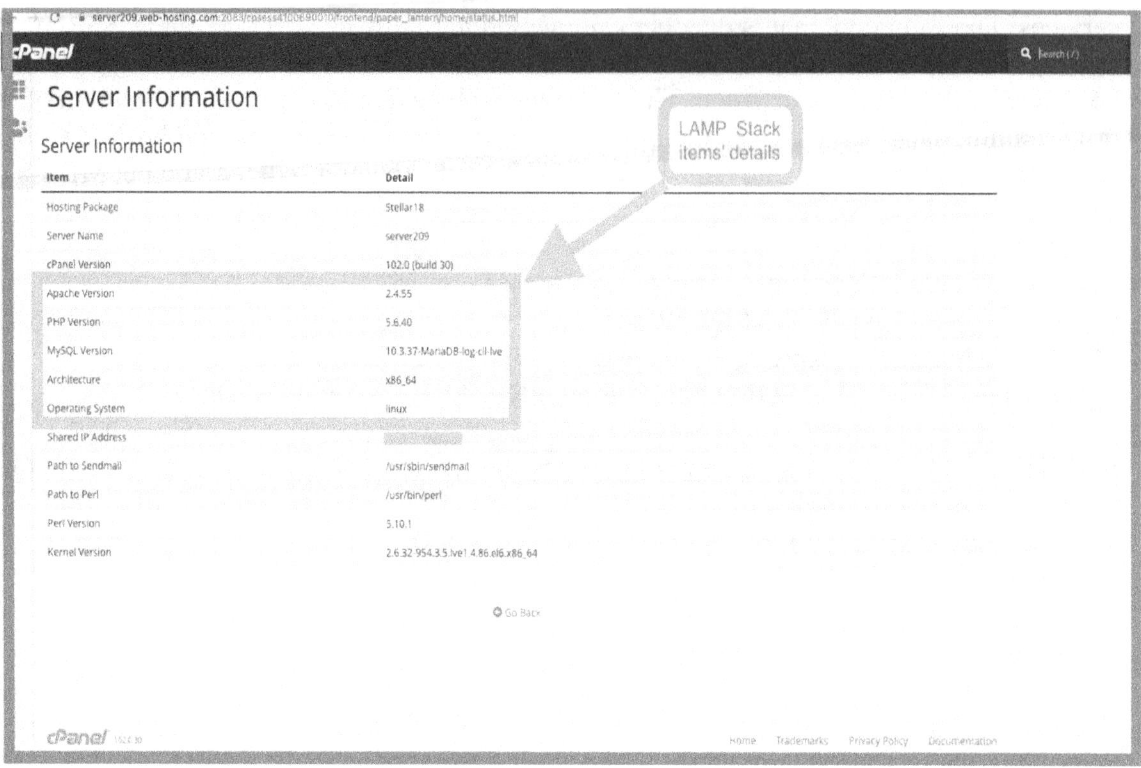

We are not going to build new applications from scratch - that is more advance-level software development, usually needed for big companies needing highly customised web applications. For example, it was rumoured to have cost around $150,000 to build Uber App, by a team of many developers.

We will be following this Full-stack technology to build our web sites, using available software and applications. Here are stages and steps that we are going to take in this tutorial.

1. Basic Programming: HTML, CSS, JavaScript
2. Templates - Responsive HTML, CSS
3. Responsive Web Technologies and Frameworks
4. Register A Domain Name
5. Buy A Web Hosting Space for Your Domain
6. Internet Web Server
7. Content Management Systems
8. Joomla! Web Site with New Template
9. Magento Ecommerce Site with PayPal Payment
10. PrestaShop Ecommerce Site with Stripe Payment
11. Database, MySQL and PhpMyAdmin
12. Local Development Server - Localhost

Programming Languages: HTLM, CSS, JavaScript

Programming Languages: HTLM, CSS, JavaScript

HTML

HTML is the programming language that the browser recognises, to display contents on the internet. Even if an application or software has been written in other programming languages, in order for it to be seen on the web, it still has to be encapsulated in HTML.

HTML documents are displayed on the internet as pages, similar to the pages of a book, say; first page, second page, third page.... The first page to be seen on the internet is the 'Index' page, then followed by other pages, which can be navigated from the index page. The index page is usually renamed as the 'Home' page or other, while the other pages can be renamed to something like, 'About', 'Contact', etc. The index page is like the 'doorway' into the site, so when writing HTML codes, the first page to write is the index page and every other page radiates from it.

Inspect

We can view a web site index page by using the 'Inspect' command. E.g., to go Google: https://www.google.com. On Google home page, right-click and choose -> Inspect.

Here is the Index page, showing the HTML codes in the middle and the CSS layout on the right. The index page has been renamed to 'Google' (on the right) and been represented with the google logo.

Here is the Index page, showing the HTML codes in the middle and the CSS layout on the right. The index page has been renamed to 'Google' (on the right) and been represented with the google logo.

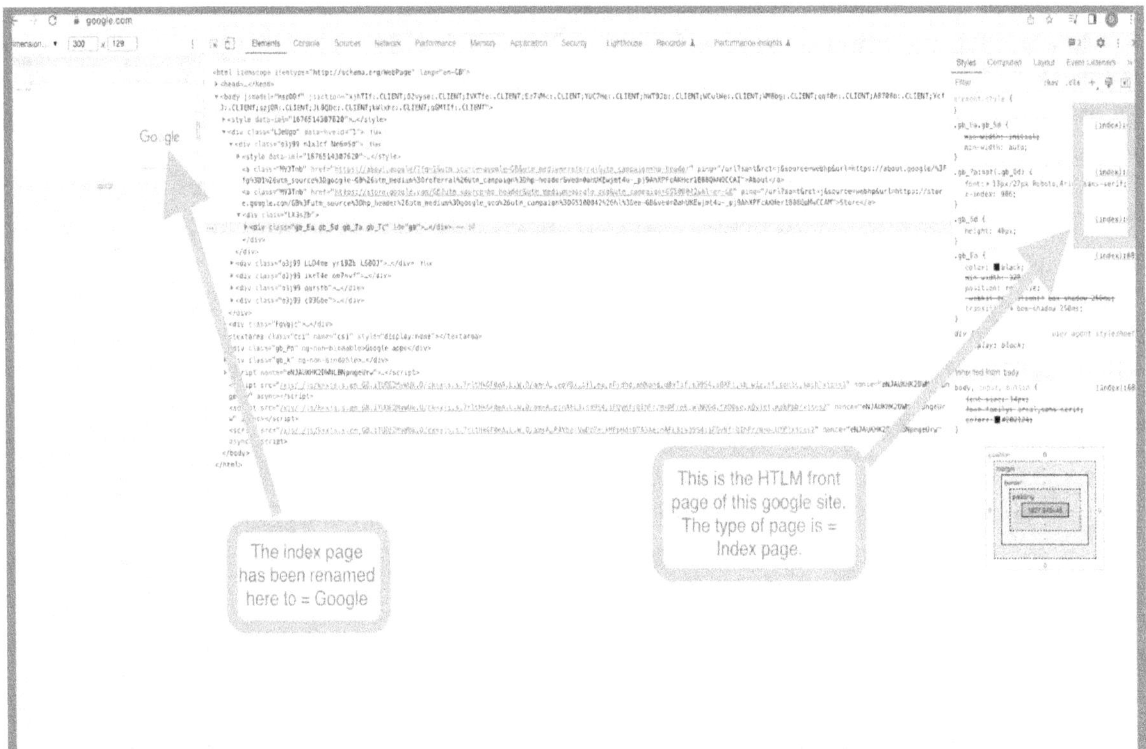

Text Editor

HTML codes are written as HTML documents in a text editor like Notepad (on Windows) or TextEdit (on Mac), then simply saved as a file with the '. HTM' extension. There are other specialised or advance text editors like Sublime, Visual Studio, etc.

TextEdit HTML File.

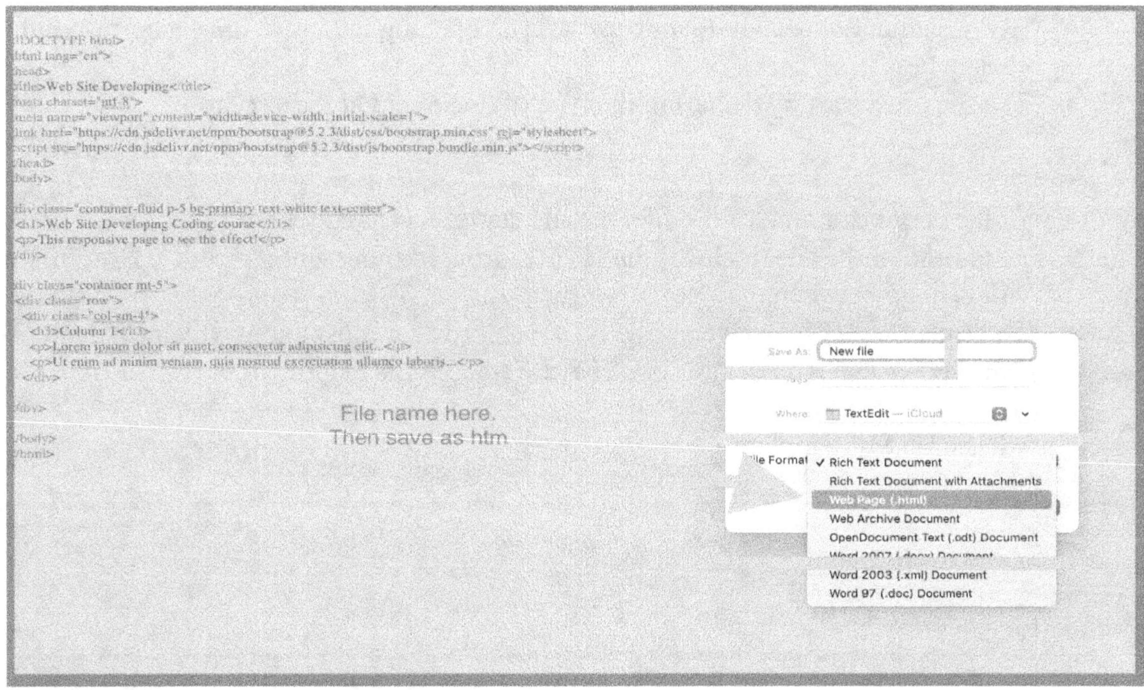

HTML codes can also be written in Word, although Word is a bit too bulky writing that.

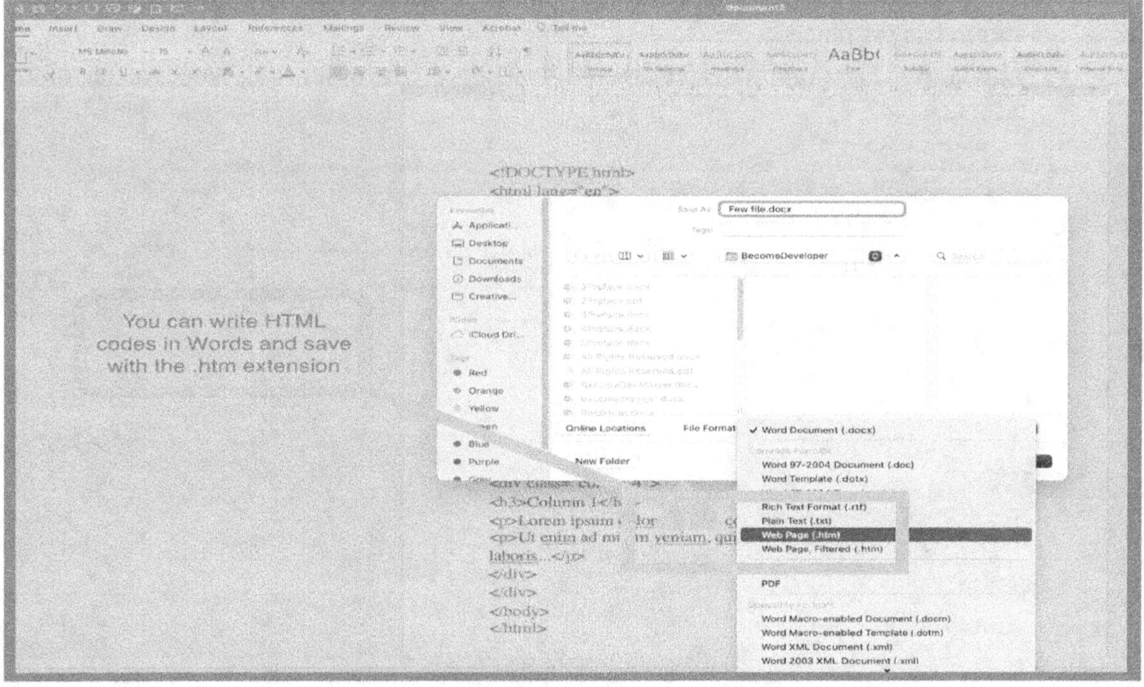

HTML Files

All HTML files must take a set format:
- They must have opening tags and closing tags for all elements: < >
- Every element or section that opens with an opening tag, must have a corresponding closing tag
- The file must start by declaring the type of document at the very top: <!DOCTYPE html>.

-
- At the very beginning of the file, the file starts as HTML with: <html>
- At the end of the file, it closes the HTML programming with: </html>. Everything will then go between the <html></html> tags.
- To display an HTML page correctly, a web browser must know which Character set (Charset) to use. The default is UTF8, ISO-8859-1 standard, <charset="utf-8">.

Here is a basic HTML template -

```
<!DOCTYPE html>
<html>

</html>
```

The HTML file is divided into three main parts:
- The Declaration - The very top - tells the browser what type of document.
- The head - Tells browser about the file itself, and what to do with it, how to present it to the world. This information is for behind the scenes use only. The 'metadata' (data about data) is placed.
- The body - The core material that is shown by the browser, i.e., what we see on the internet.

```
<!DOCTYPE html>
<html lang="en">


<head>
<title></title>
<meta charset="utf-8">
<meta>
<link>
<script> </script>
</head>
```

```
<body>

<div>
   <h1>This is a header</h1>
</div>

<div>
   <p>This is a paragraph with small writing within it!</p>
</div>

</body>


</html>
```

Notice with the above, if we publish it, the only thing that we will see on the internet is the two sentences written in black, in the middle of the screen, with a white background with no layout.

Ordinarily, the normal layout of web page looks like this:

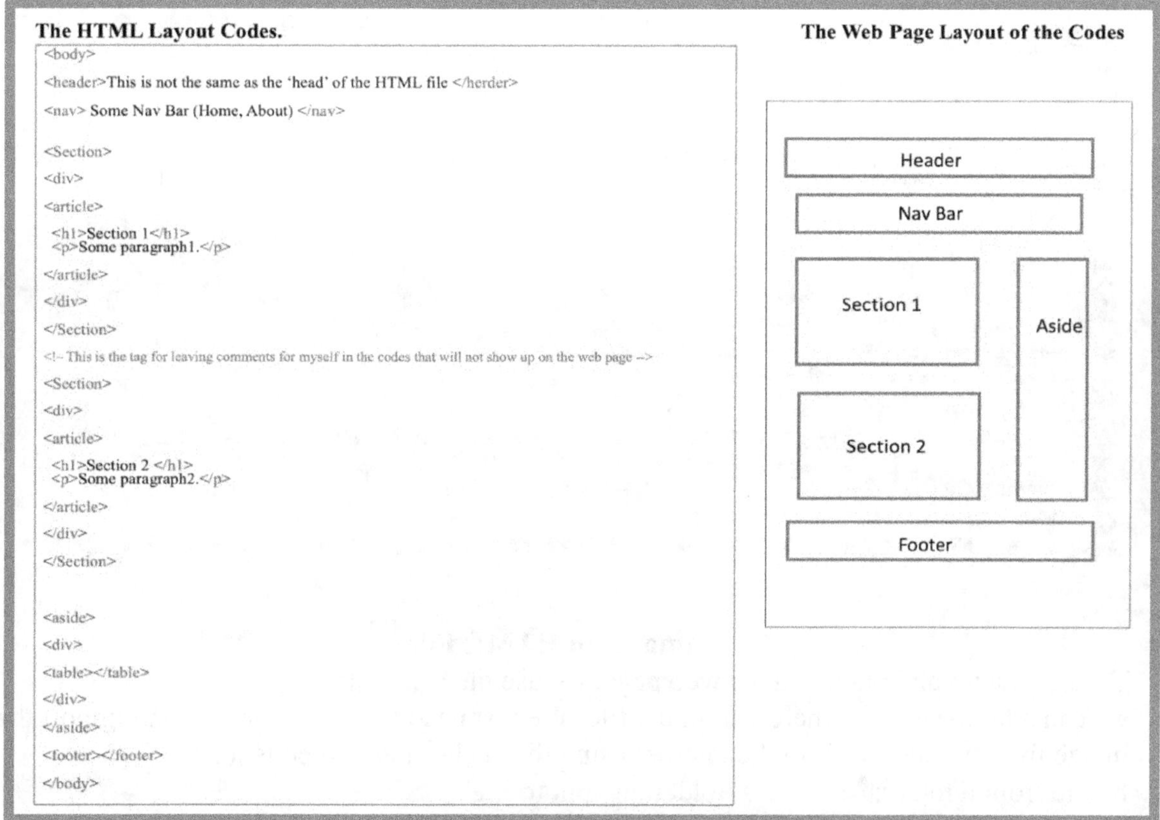

The HTML Layout Codes.

```
<body>

<header>This is not the same as the 'head' of the HTML file </herder>

<nav> Some Nav Bar (Home, About) </nav>

<Section>

<div>

<article>
   <h1>Section 1</h1>
   <p>Some paragraph1.</p>
</article>

</div>

</Section>

<!-- This is the tag for leaving comments for myself in the codes that will not show up on the web page -->

<Section>

<div>

<article>
   <h1>Section 2 </h1>
   <p>Some paragraph2.</p>
</article>

</div>

</Section>


<aside>

<div>

<table></table>

</div>

</aside>

<footer></footer>

</body>
```

The Web Page Layout of the Codes

The above layout codes did not show the 'heads', which would normally have a clear instruction of what method is being used so that the layout will appear as it did above.

Here is Google index page codes. This is the HTLM front page. If you look at the type of page = Index page. The index page has been renamed to 'Google'. Under the 'head' section are lots of instructions for the styling to the body.

```
html itemscon        :ype="http://schema.org/WebPage" lang="en-GB">
 <head>                                                      Head starts here
    <meta chars.      F-8">                                   & ends here
    <meta content="u igin" name="referrer">
    <meta content="/images/branding/googleg/1x/googleg_standard
    <link href="/manifest?pwa=webhp" crossorigin="use-crede    ts" rel= manifest >
    <title>Google</title>
    <script src="https://apis.google.com/ /scs/abc-     ic/ /js/k=gapi.gapi.en.3R2S2.../sv=1/d=1/ed=1/r
  ▶ <script nonce="NcKkD_ivlqsYr1pNjtrC4g">…</sc    .>
  ▶ <script nonce="NcKkD_ivlqsYr1pNjtrC4g">.     ript>
  ▶ <script nonce="NcKkD_ivlqsYr1pNjtrC4    </script>
    <script defer src="/xjs/ /js/k=x    .en GB.JrGUmecObSg.O/am=AAFkEK4AOAAABAAAAJCAAAAAAABAA...g=2/br
  ▶ <script nonce="NcKkD_ivlqsYr1    rC4g">…</script>
  ▶ <style data-iml="167665081   u5">…</style>
    <script async type="t   ,javascript" charset="UTF-8" src="https://www.gstatic.com/og/ /js/k=og.g
    ivlqsYr1pN;  C4g"    ript>
    <link typ         ss" rel="stylesheet" href="https://www.gstatic.com/og/ /ss/k=og.qtm.bSgZOT-aZX
  ▶ <style t       t/css" data-late-css>…</style>
    <scrip           t/javascript" charset="UTF-8" src="//www.google.com/js/bq/1ltCRSOx5k-1I0D0UILHF
 </head>
 <body i          DDf" jsaction="xjhTIf:.CLIENT;O2vyse:.CLIENT;IVKTfe:.CLIENT;Ez7VMc:.CLIENT;YUC7H
    c:.CLIEN           .CLIENT;qGMTIf:.CLIENT">
  ▶ <style da          '50827366">…</style>
  ▼ <div class=  .eUgb" data       "1">  flex
    ▶ <div class="o3j99 n1xJcf Ne6nsu       iv>  flex
    ▶ <div class="o3j99 LLD4me yr19Zb LS8OJ">…       flex  == 50
    ▶ <div class="o3j99 ikrT4e om7nvf">…</div>
    ▶ <div class="o3j99 qarstb">…</div>
    ▶ <div class="o3j99 c93Gbe">…</div>           Body starts here
    </div>                                          & ends here
  ▶ <div class="Fgvgjc">…</div>
    <textarea class="csi" name="csi" style="display:n-     extarea>
    <div class="gb_Pd" ng-non-bindable>Google a       iv>
  ▶ <div class="gb_k" ng-non-bindable>…</
  ▶ <script nonce="NcKkD_ivlqsYr1         g">…</script>
    <script src=" xjs/ /js         s.en GB.JrGUmecObSg.O/ck=xjs.s.K6GO2ZJRHMI.L.W.O/am=A...,epYOx,ifl,mu
    <script s            /k=xjs.s.en GB.JrGUmecObSg.O/ck=xjs.s.K6GO2ZJRHMI.L.W.O/am=A...e;nAFL3:s39S4
    <script         s/ /js/k=xjs.s.en GB.JrGUmecObSg.O/ck=xjs.s.K6GO2ZJRHMI.L.W.O/am=A...P4Vbe:VwDzFe;
 </body>
```

Images in HTML Files

To add images and photos to the web page, we use the <img> tag.
we can add images anywhere within the file. We just need to create our 'div' and import the image from a folder or from the internet using the anchor tag, which is this: <a> (anchor).
Image from a folder: <img src="folder/any photo.jpg">

Image on the internet <a href="https://www.someimagesite.com/any photo.jpg"> Any Photo</a>

href = HTML reference of the image, that is the image's URL.

CSS

With HTML files, we need CSS to add colours and styles to the page. CSS is invoked by the use of the keyword 'style', along with the type of style attribute. We can add CSS style to each element individually, that is - 'Inline' (works on a very small piece of code). Or we can put it at top, that is 'Internal', in the 'head' section, which then tells the rest of the codes what to do.

```
<html>
<head>

<style>
.all-browsers {
  margin: 0;
  padding: 5px;
  background-color: lightgray;
}
.all-browsers > h1, .browser {
  margin: 10px;
  padding: 5px;
}
.browser {
  background: white;
}
.browser > h2, p {
  margin: 4px;
  font-size: 90%;
}
</style>

</head>
<body>
<article class="all-browsers">
  <h1>Most Popular Browsers</h1>
  <article class="browser">
    <h2>Google Chrome</h2>
    <p>Google Chrome is a web browser developed by Google, released
in 2008. Chrome is the world's most popular web browser today!</p>
```

```
  </article>
  <article class="browser">
    <h2>Mozilla Firefox</h2>
    <p>Mozilla Firefox is an open-source web browser developed by
Mozilla. Firefox has been the second most popular web browser since
January, 2018.</p>
  </article>
</article>
</body>
</html>
```

In the above HTML document, the CSS styling instructions is specified in the section - <style>...</style>, which is withing the ' head '. A set of styles withing the brackets is given a 'Class' name. Then down in the 'body' section, elements are assigned the class name, so they can follow that specified style. This is better than re-writing the same style for each element.

Here are how the articles used the same styles specified in the 'head'

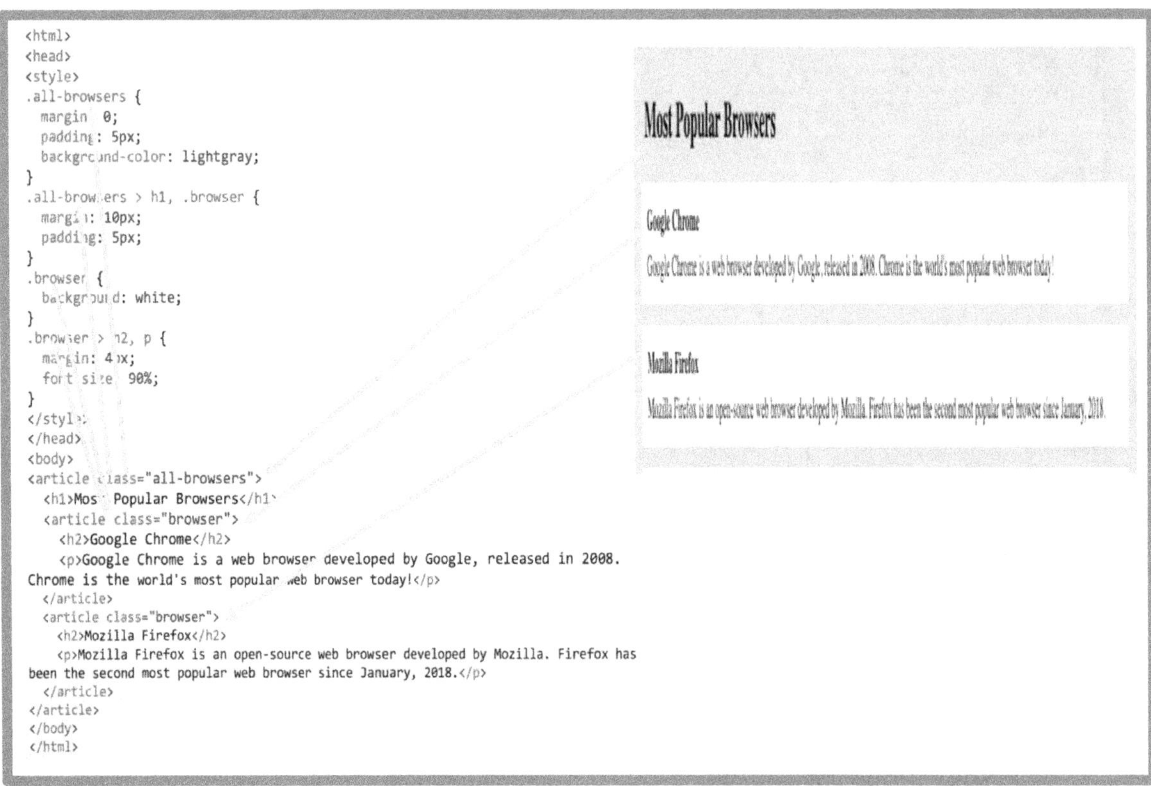

Responsive HTML and CSS Documents Web Design - Frameworks

Using the above method is good, but what is even better, is to use an external framework out there on the internet that other people have already put together. The two popular frameworks for CSS are W3Schools and Bootstrap 5.

Responsive Web Pages

Responsive means that the web page will scale to the screen size of any device. It uses the keyword 'Viewport'. This is achieved by setting the initial 'Viewpoint' scale in the HTML document, and then using the external dynamic styling frameworks to maintain its fluidity.

W3School CSS framework.
https://www.w3schools.com/w3css/4/w3.css

Here is the CSS framework for W3School. I can tell you; it did not take them just a few hours to put it together. It has been a team of people's many hours or days' works.

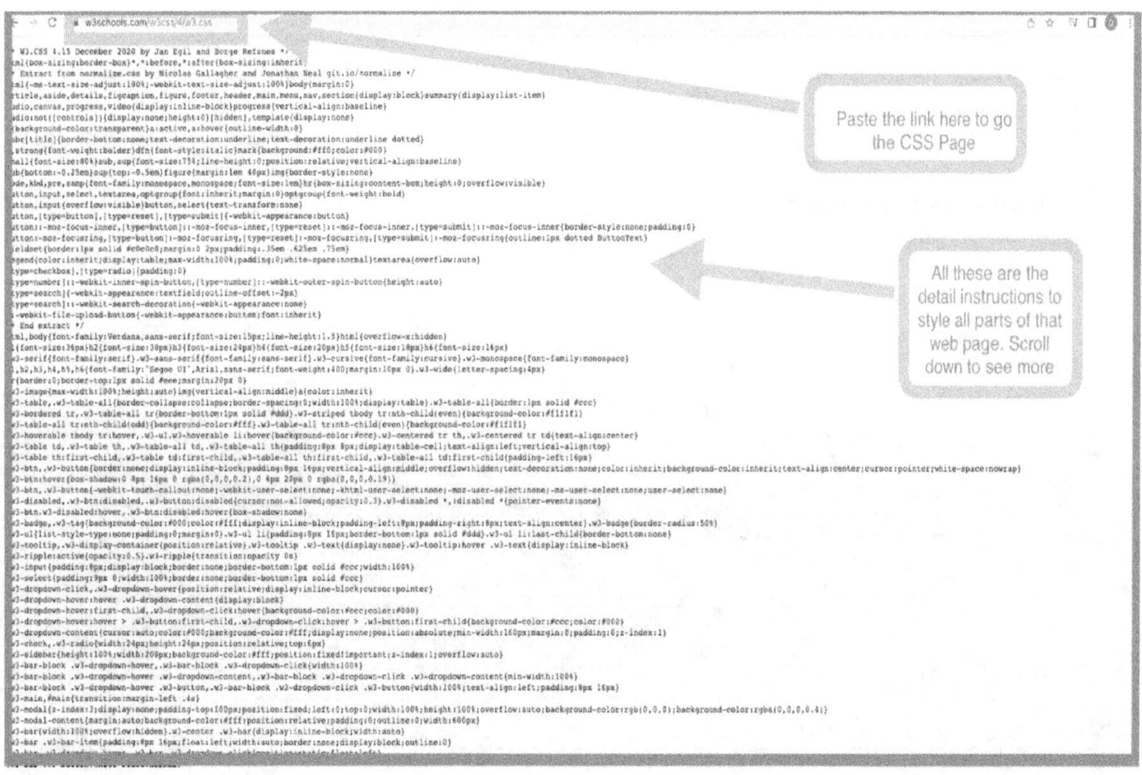

Here is a close-up, so you can see some of the styles. Have a look at it and forget about it.

```
/* W3.CSS 4.15 December 2020 by Jan Egil and Borge Refsnes */
html{box-sizing:border-box}*,*:before,*:after{box-sizing:inherit}
/* Extract from normalize.css by Nicolas Gallagher and Jonathan Neal git.io/normalize */
html{-ms-text-size-adjust:100%;-webkit-text-size-adjust:100%}body{margin:0}
article,aside,details,figcaption,figure,footer,header,main,menu,nav,section{display:block}summ[...]
audio,canvas,progress,video{display:inline-block}progress{vertical-align:baseline}
audio:not([controls]){display:none;height:0}[hidden],template{display:none}
a{background-color:transparent}a:active,a:hover{outline-width:0}
abbr[title]{border-bottom:none;text-decoration:underline;text-decoration:underline dotted}
b,strong{font-weight:bolder}dfn{font-style:italic}mark{background:#ff0;color:#000}
small{font-size:80%}sub,sup{font-size:75%;line-height:0;position:relative;vertical-align:base[...]
sub{bottom:-0.25em}sup{top:-0.5em}figure{margin:1em 40px}img{border-style:none}
code,kbd,pre,samp{font-family:monospace,monospace;font-size:1em}hr{box-sizing:content-box;height:0;overflow:visible}
button,input,select,textarea,optgroup{font:inherit;margin:0}optgroup{font-weight:bold}
button,input{overflow:visible}button,select{text-transform:none}
button,[type=button],[type=reset],[type=submit]{-webkit-appearance:button}
button::-moz-focus-inner,[type=button]::-moz-focus-inner,[type=reset]::-moz-focus-inner,[type=submit]::-moz-focus-inner{border-
style:none;padding:0}
button:-moz-focusring,[type=button]:-moz-focusring,[type=reset]:-moz-focusring,[type=submit]:-moz-focusring{outline:1px dotted
ButtonText}
fieldset{border:1px solid #c0c0c0;margin:0 2px;padding:.35em .625em .75em}
legend{color:inherit;display:table;max-width:100%;padding:0;white-space:normal}textarea{overflow:auto}
[type=checkbox],[type=radio]{padding:0}
[type=number]::-webkit-inner-spin-button,[type=number]::-webkit-outer-spin-button{height:auto}
[type=search]{-webkit-appearance:textfield;outline-offset:-2px}
[type=search]::-webkit-search-decoration{-webkit-appearance:none}
::-webkit-file-upload-button{-webkit-appearance:button;font:inherit}
/* End extract */
html,body{font-family:Verdana,sans-serif;font-size:15px;line-height:1.5}html{overflow-x:hidden}
h1{font-size:36px}h2{font-size:30px}h3{font-size:24px}h4{font-size:20px}h5{font-size:18px}h6{font-size:16px}
.w3-serif{font-family:serif}.w3-sans-serif{font-family:sans-serif}.w3-cursive{font-family:cursive}.w3-monospace{font-
family:monospace}
h1,h2,h3,h4,h5,h6{font-family:"Segoe UI",Arial,sans-serif;font-weight:400;margin:10px 0}.w3-wide{letter-spacing:4px}
hr{border:0;border-top:1px solid #eee;margin:20px 0}
.w3-image{max-width:100%;height:auto}img{vertical-align:middle}a{color:inherit}
.w3-table,.w3-table-all{border-collapse:collapse;border-spacing:0;width:100%;display:table}.w3-table-all{border:1px solid #ccc}
```


Bootstrap CSS framework

https://cdn.jsdelivr.net/npm/bootstrap@5.2.3/dist/css/bootstrap.min.css

These frameworks are detailed and can be used to style different HTML documents. They are also used to create responsive Apps designs.

The external styling frameworks from the internet are imported into the HTML file by using the link tag, which is this: <link>.

```
<link rel="stylesheet" href="https://www.somestylesheetsite.com/stylesheet.css">
```

href = HTML reference of the CSS file; that is the File's URL

Here is a file with a link for a stylesheet on W3School website.

```html
<!DOCTYPE html>
<html>
<meta name="viewport" content="width=device-width, initial-scale=1">
<link rel="stylesheet" href="https://www.w3schools.com/w3css/4/w3.css
">
<body>

<div class="w3-container w3-blue">
  <h1>W3Schools Demo</h1>
  <p>Resize this responsive page!</p>
</div>

<div class="w3-row-padding">
  <div class="w3-third">
    <h2>London</h2>
    <p>London is the capital city of England.</p>
    <p>It is the most populous city in the United Kingdom,
    with a metropolitan area of over 13 million inhabitants.</p>
  </div>

  <div class="w3-third">
    <h2>Paris</h2>
    <p>Paris is the capital of France.</p>
    <p>The Paris area is one of the largest population centres in Eu-
rope,
    with more than 12 million inhabitants.</p>
  </div>

  <div class="w3-third">
    <h2>Tokyo</h2>
    <p>Tokyo is the capital of Japan.</p>
```

```html
    <p>It is the centre of the Greater Tokyo Area,
    and the most populous metropolitan area in the world.</p>
  </div>
</div>


</body>
</html>
```

The above is styled as below on the right using the linked stylesheet

HTML and CSS Codes

```html
<!DOCTYPE html>
<html>
<meta name="viewport" content="width=device-width, initial-scale=1">
<link rel="stylesheet" href="https://www.w3schools.com/w3css/4/w3.css">
<body>

<div class="w3-container w3-blue">
  <h1>W3Schools Demo</h1>
  <p>Resize this responsive page!</p>
</div>

<div class="w3-row-padding">
  <div class="w3-third">
    <h2>London</h2>
    <p>London is the capital city of England.</p>
    <p>It is the most populous city in the United Kingdom,
    with a metropolitan area of over 13 million
inhabitants.</p>
  </div>

  <div class="w3-third">
    <h2>Paris</h2>
    <p>Paris is the capital of France.</p>
    <p>The Paris area is one of the largest population centers
in Europe,
    with more than 12 million inhabitants.</p>
  </div>

  </div>

</body>
</html>
```

Web Page of the Codes

Here is another example, using Bootstrap 5.

```html
<!DOCTYPE html>
<html lang="en">
<head>
<title>Bootstrap 5 Example</title>
<meta charset="utf-8">
<meta name="viewport" content="width=device-width, initial-scale=1">
<link href="https://cdn.jsdelivr.net/npm/boot-
strap@5.2.3/dist/css/bootstrap.min.css" rel="stylesheet">
<script src="https://cdn.jsdelivr.net/npm/boot-
strap@5.2.3/dist/js/bootstrap.bundle.min.js"></script>
</head>
<body>

<div class="container-fluid p-5 bg-primary text-white text-centre">
  <h1>My First Bootstrap Page</h1>
  <p>Resize this responsive page to see the effect!</p>
</div>

<div class="container mt-5">
  <div class="row">
    <div class="col-sm-4">
      <h3>Column 1</h3>
      <p>Lorem ipsum dolor sit amet, consectetur adipisicing
elit...</p>
      <p>Ut enim ad minim veniam, quis nostrud exercitation ullamco
laboris...</p>
    </div>
    <div class="col-sm-4">
      <h3>Column 2</h3>
      <p>Lorem ipsum dolor sit amet, consectetur adipisicing
elit...</p>
      <p>Ut enim ad minim veniam, quis nostrud exercitation ullamco
laboris...</p>
    </div>

</div>

</body>
</html>
```

The above is styled as below on the right

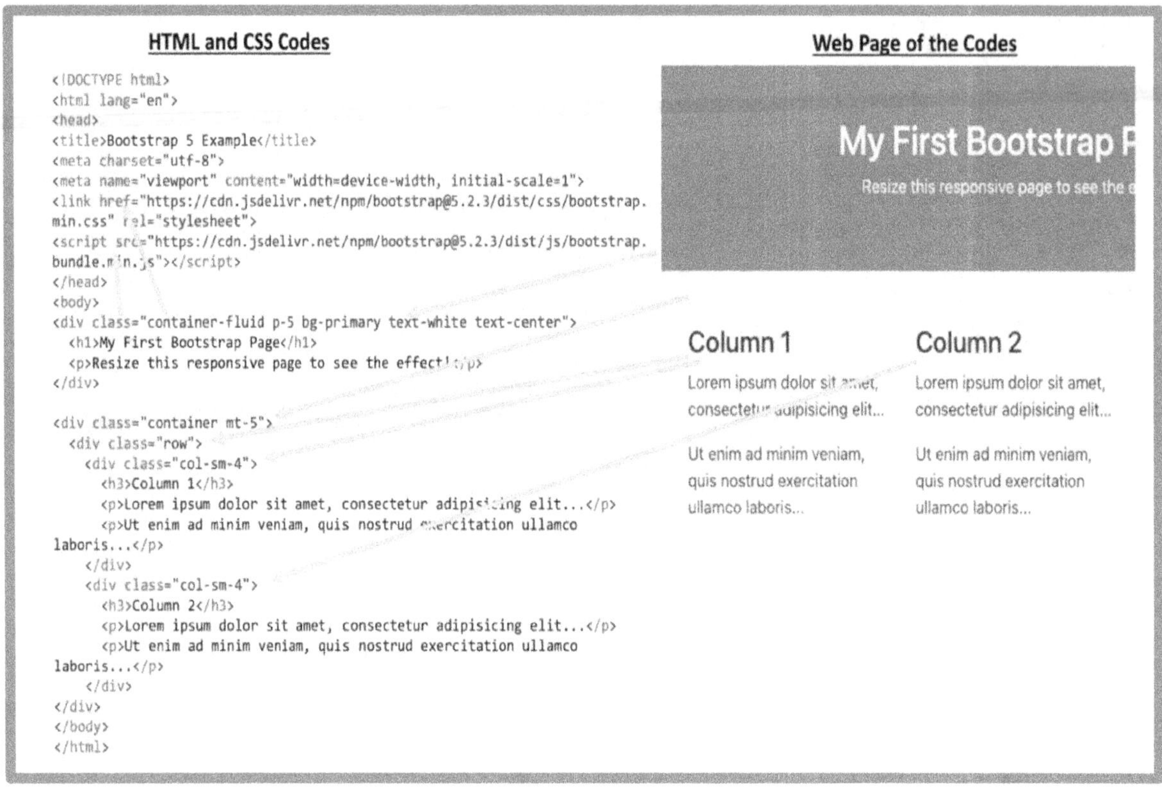


```
<!DOCTYPE html>
<html lang="en">
<head>
<title>Bootstrap 5 Example</title>
<meta charset="utf-8">
<meta name="viewport" content="width=device-width, initial-scale=1">
<link href="https://cdn.jsdelivr.net/npm/bootstrap@5.2.3/dist/css/bootstrap.
min.css" rel="stylesheet">
<script src="https://cdn.jsdelivr.net/npm/bootstrap@5.2.3/dist/js/bootstrap.
bundle.min.js"></script>
</head>
<body>
<div class="container-fluid p-5 bg-primary text-white text-center">
  <h1>My First Bootstrap Page</h1>
  <p>Resize this responsive page to see the effect!</p>
</div>

<div class="container mt-5">
  <div class="row">
    <div class="col-sm-4">
      <h3>Column 1</h3>
      <p>Lorem ipsum dolor sit amet, consectetur adipisicing elit...</p>
      <p>Ut enim ad minim veniam, quis nostrud exercitation ullamco
laboris...</p>
    </div>
    <div class="col-sm-4">
      <h3>Column 2</h3>
      <p>Lorem ipsum dolor sit amet, consectetur adipisicing elit...</p>
      <p>Ut enim ad minim veniam, quis nostrud exercitation ullamco
laboris...</p>
    </div>
  </div>
</div>
</body>
</html>
```

JavaScript Framework

Notice the above responsive web page is also set to use an external scripts framework, which is JavaScript from the internet, and it is imported into the HTML file by using the script keyword, which is this: <script>.

<script src="https://www.somejavascriptsite.com/anyjavascriptfile.js">

src = The source code file of the JavaScript.

Bootstrap JavaScript Framework

The Bootstrap framework used above is here.
https://cdn.jsdelivr.net/npm/bootstrap@5.2.3/dist/js/bootstrap.bundle.min.js.

Have a look and forget about it.

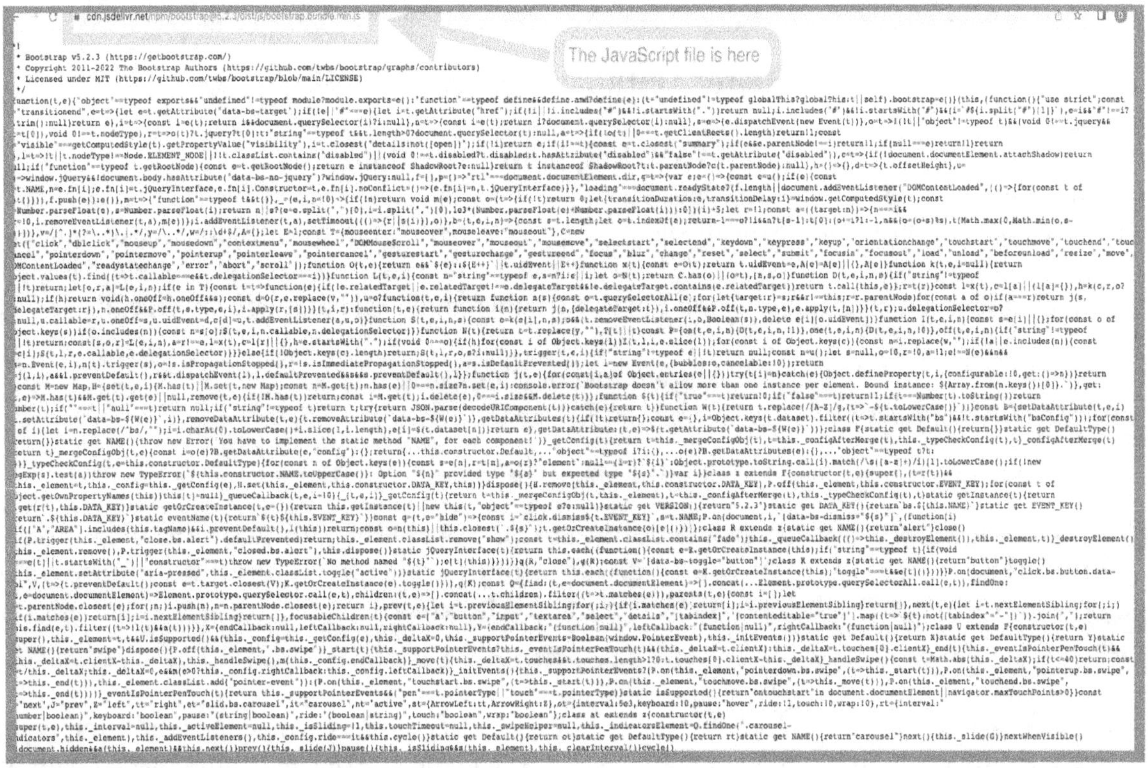
cdn.jsdelivr.net
The JavaScript file is here
/*!
* Bootstrap v5.2.3 (https://getbootstrap.com/)
* Copyright 2011-2022 The Bootstrap Authors (https://github.com/twbs/bootstrap/graphs/contributors)
* Licensed under MIT (https://github.com/twbs/bootstrap/blob/main/LICENSE)
*/

Templates With Responsive HTML, CSS

Templates With Responsive HTML, CSS

HTML Responsive Templates

Understanding HTLM, CSS and JavaScript and how to create responsive HTML document is a basic place to start from. Now, instead of trying to build your own responsive template to use for your webpage, it is worthwhile to look at the thousands of responsive templates that have already been created out there. Some are paid templates, but many are free.

Lorem ipsum Block of Text

What is **Lorem ipsum?**

> **Lorem ipsum dolor sit amet, consectetur adipiscing elit, sed do eiusmod tempor incididunt ut labore et dolore magna aliqua. Ut enim ad minim veniam, quis nostrud exercitation ullamco laboris....**

'Lorem ipsum' - Is just a block of text that programmers use as a 'place holder', simply to save them time when creating templates. The text can then be deleted and replaced with whatever you like.

Free Responsive Templates

Free Responsive Templates are all over the place these, and without much effort you can easily find one that fits your purpose. Here are a few sites that have lots of them:

https://www.free-css.com/template-categories/responsive

https://html5up.net

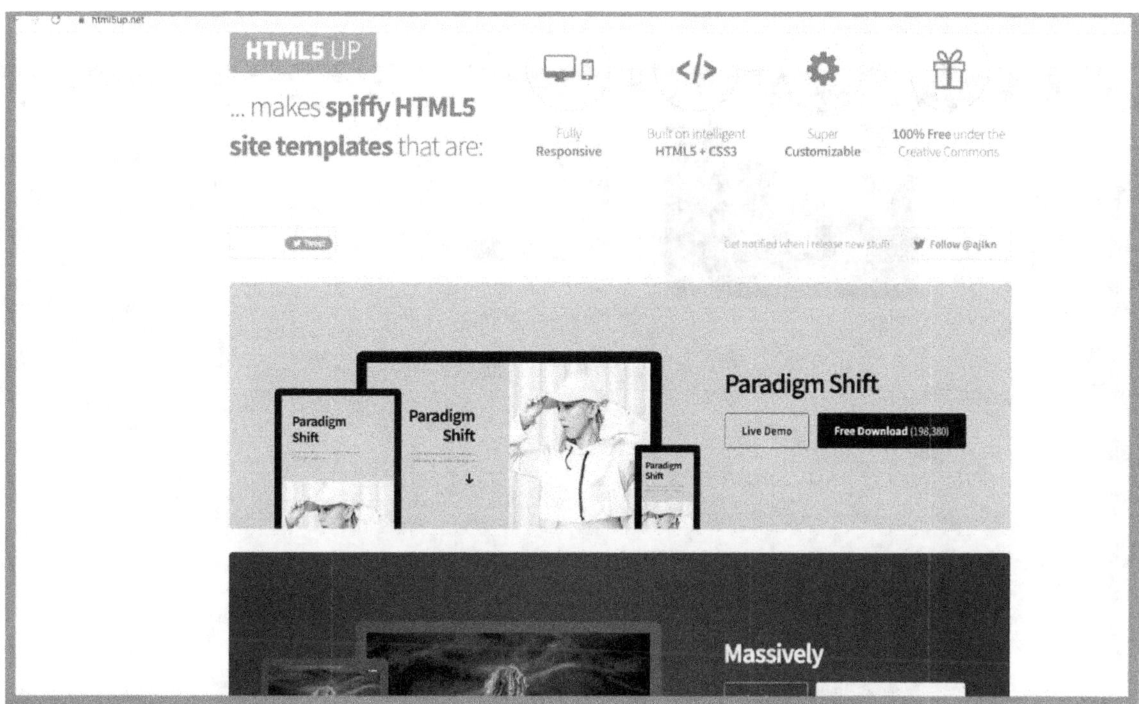

https://webflow.com/free-website-templates

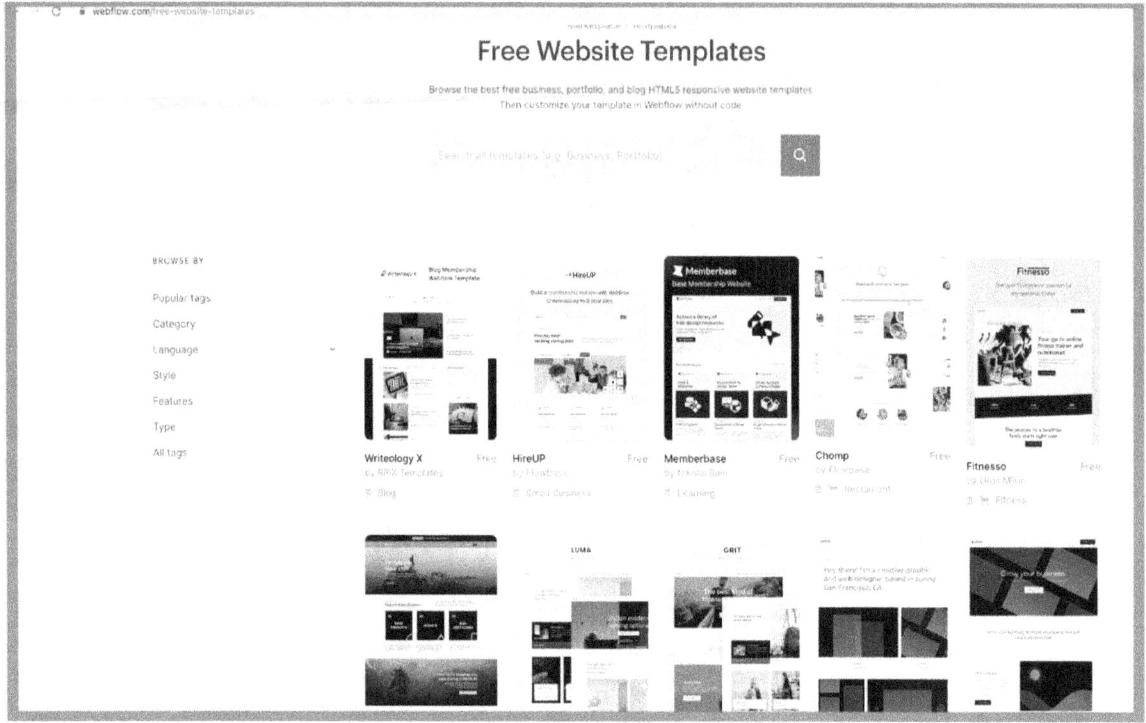

https://bootstrapmade.com

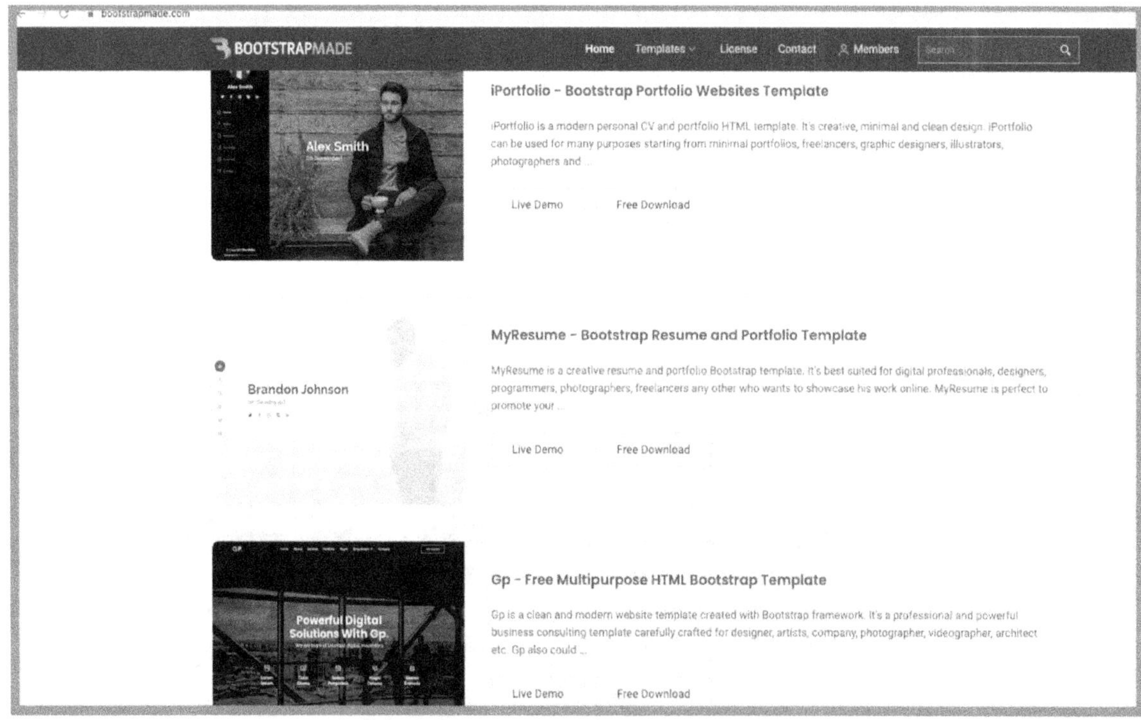

https://github.com/topics/website-template

Keep it Real - Pls Note   Please note that at the time of writing this book, the author, editors, or anyone linked with the publishing of this book have not received any paid endorsement from any of the companies and products' providers mentioned here.

Responsive Web Technologies and Frameworks

Responsive Web Technologies and Frameworks

Better than using responsive templates, use a Responsive HTML / CSS framework.
There are many free CSS Frameworks that offer Responsive Designs. With these frameworks, there are already completed HTML pages, which has classes and IDs built-in for common website elements to set up a web page - the footer, slider, navigation bar, hamburger menu, column-based layouts, etc. The HTML pages have already been linked to CSS stylesheets to give them structure.

These frameworks are built on HTML, CSS and one or more other programming languages, so mastering them would require some knowledge of those programming languages as well. And that ventures into software development. Also, some of these are on various platforms.

Web application frameworks

Bootstrap

https://getbootstrap.com

Bootstrap is a free and open-source CSS framework established in 2013 and has a large community support. This framework is built in HTML, SASS, and JavaScript. The framework works on two technologies, WebGL and Canvas. CSS and JavaScript-based design templates for typography, forms, buttons, navigation, and other interface components. It is a front-end/UI development framework that supports interactive video games on both mobile and desktop browsers.

Vue 2

https://vuejs.org

Vue.js is a UI component libraries tools and frameworks, originally created as an early fork of Angular by engineers at Google, it well organised and easy to understand for web building using HTML, CSS, JavaScript.

Angular

https://angular.io

Angular is a TypeScript-based, free and open-source web application framework led by the Angular Team at Google and by a community of individuals and corporations. Angular is a complete rewrite from the same team that built AngularJS.

Flask
https://flask.palletsprojects.com

Flask is a micro web framework written in HTML and Python. It is classified as a micro-framework because it does not require particular tools or libraries. It has no database abstraction layer, form validation, or any other components where pre-existing third-party libraries provide common functions.

ASP.NET
https://dotnet.microsoft.com

ASP.NET is an open-source, server-side web-application framework designed for web development to produce dynamic web pages. It was developed by Microsoft to allow programmers to build dynamic web sites, applications and services. The name stands for Active Server Pages Network Enabled Technologies.

Blazor is a feature of ASP.NET for building interactive web UIs using C# instead of JavaScript. Blazor gives you real .NET running in the browser.
ASP.NET is used by Microsoft, Xbox.com, Stack Overflow, and many others.

Laravel
https://laravel.com

Laravel is a free and open-source PHP web framework, created by Taylor Otwell and intended for the development of web applications following the model–view–controller architectural pattern. It has expressive, elegant syntax, and already inbuild some common tasks.

jQuery
https://jquery.com

jQuery is a fast, small, and feature-rich JavaScript library, designed to simplify HTML DOM tree traversal and manipulation, as well as event handling, CSS animation, and Ajax. It is free, open-source software using the permissive MIT License

Alpine.js
https://alpinejs.dev

Alpine.js is a new, lightweight, JavaScript framework built on HTML.

Register A Domain Name

Register a Domain Name

Web Hosting Provider

We need a Web Hosting Provider to register our domain. We look can through on the internet to find some. There are some listed in Part 1 of this book.

Here is a Web Hosting Provider, what to look for before deciding.

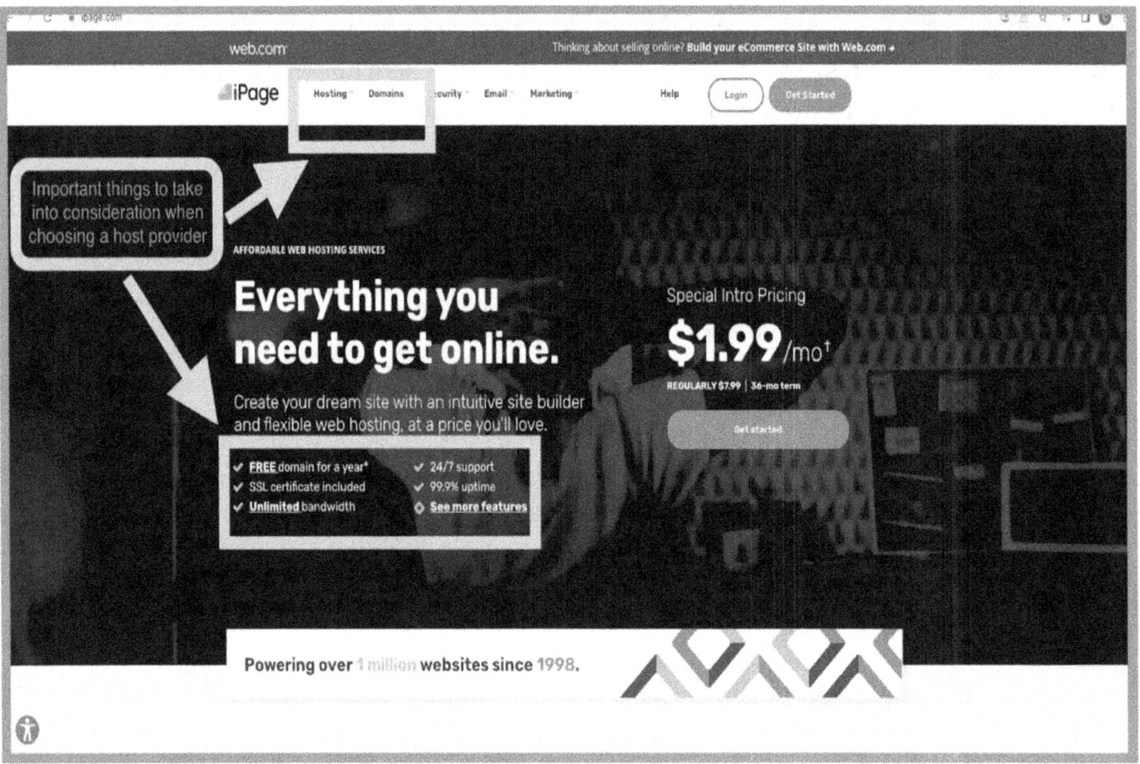

Keep it Real - Pls Note   Here is another Web Hosting Provider. We can register a domain, without needing to take up web hosting with them. We can easily transfer the domain to another web hosting provider later.

Here is a domain that was registered, but not being hosted anywhere at the moment.

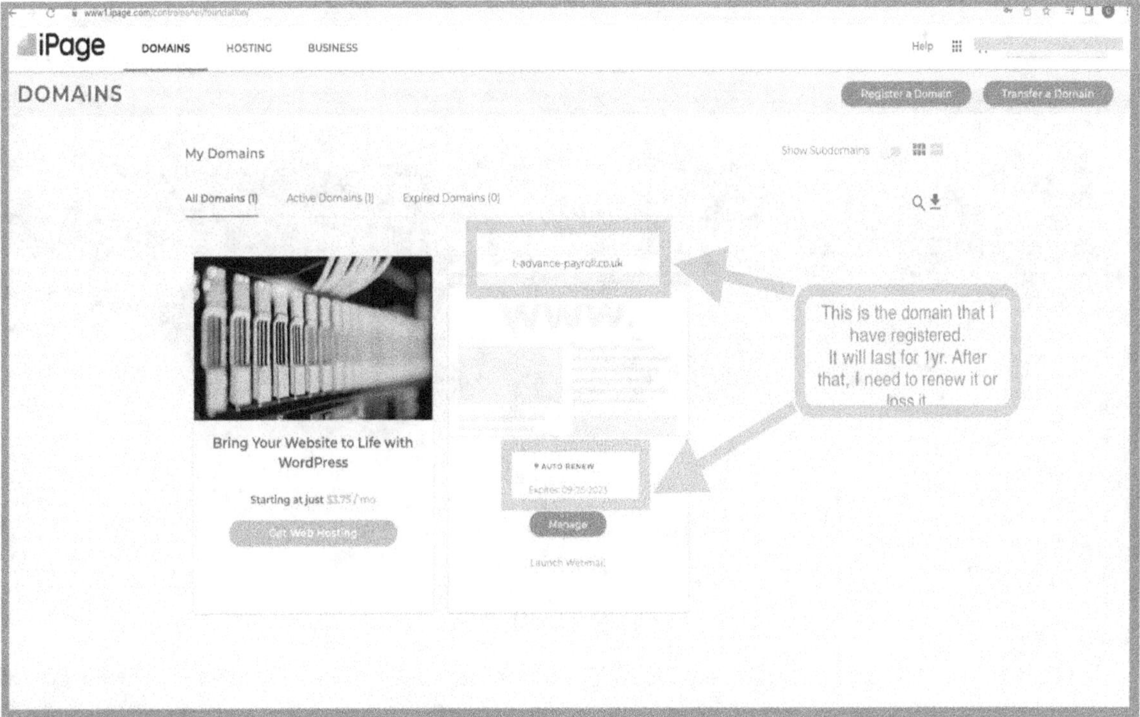

It has no website address, since it not hosted yet.

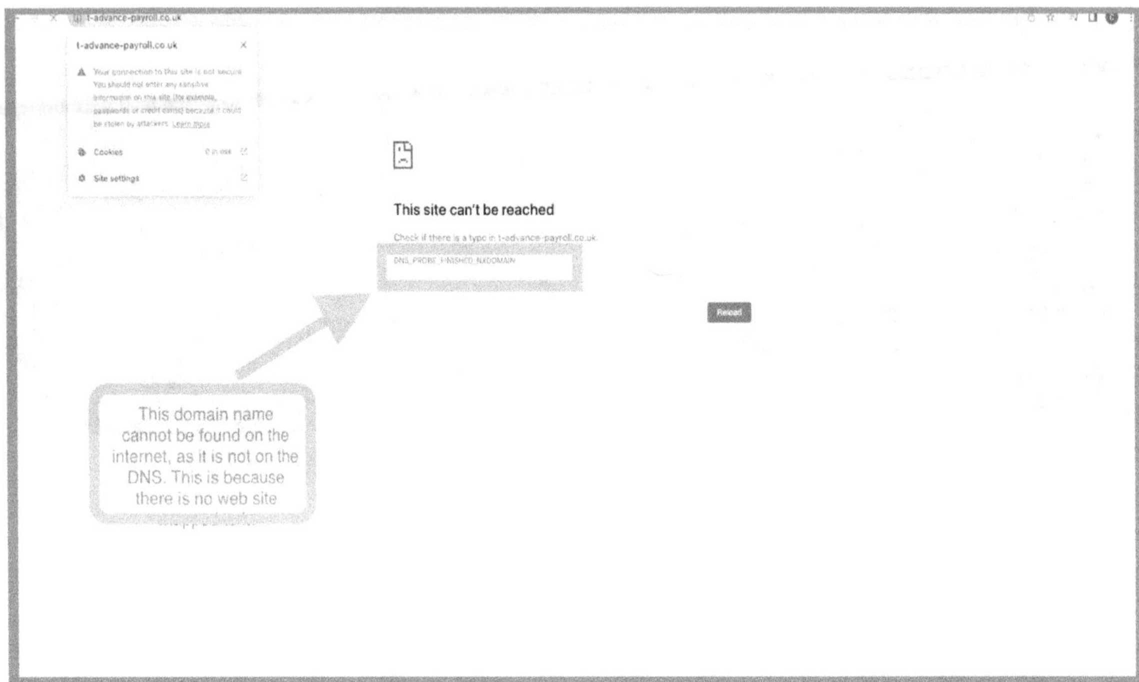

To register a new domain, click on Domains

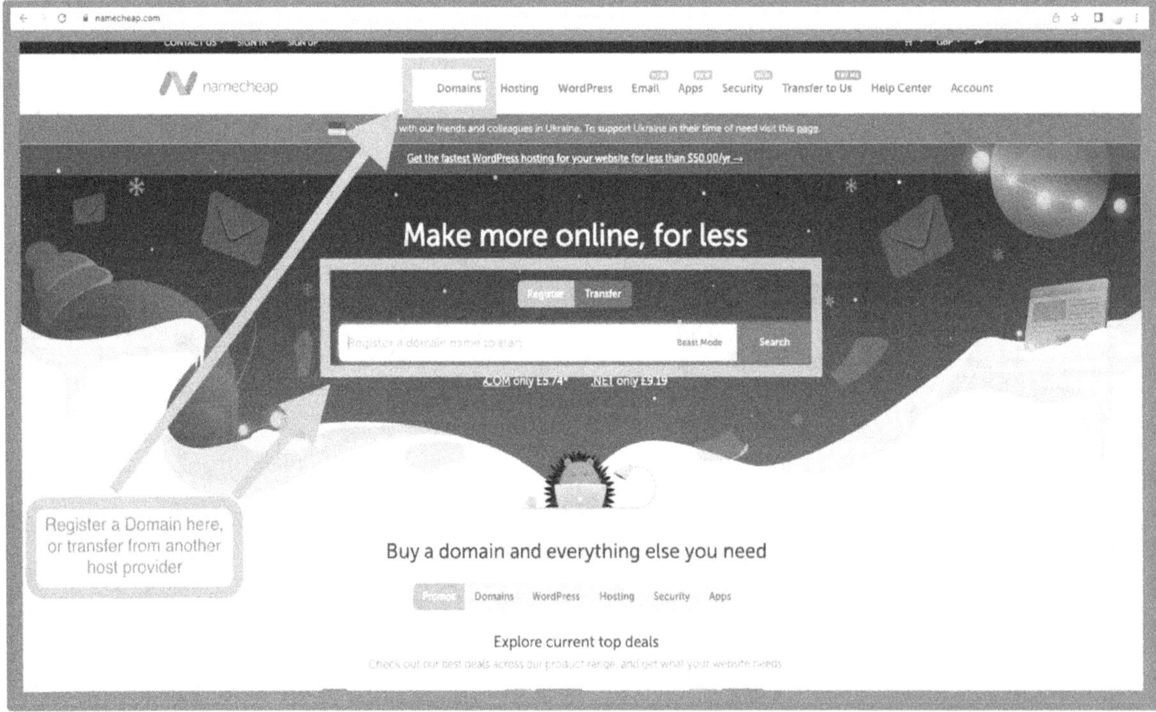

Here, I have chosen this domain and it is available.

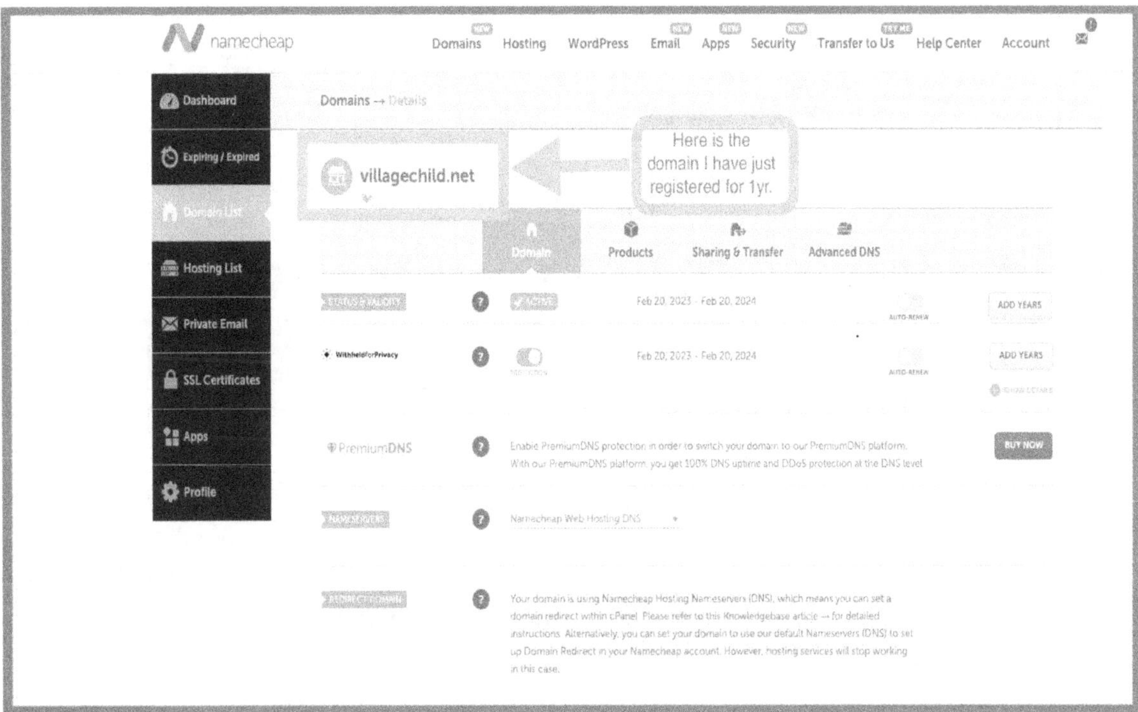

This is the Dashboard with some details of the domain.

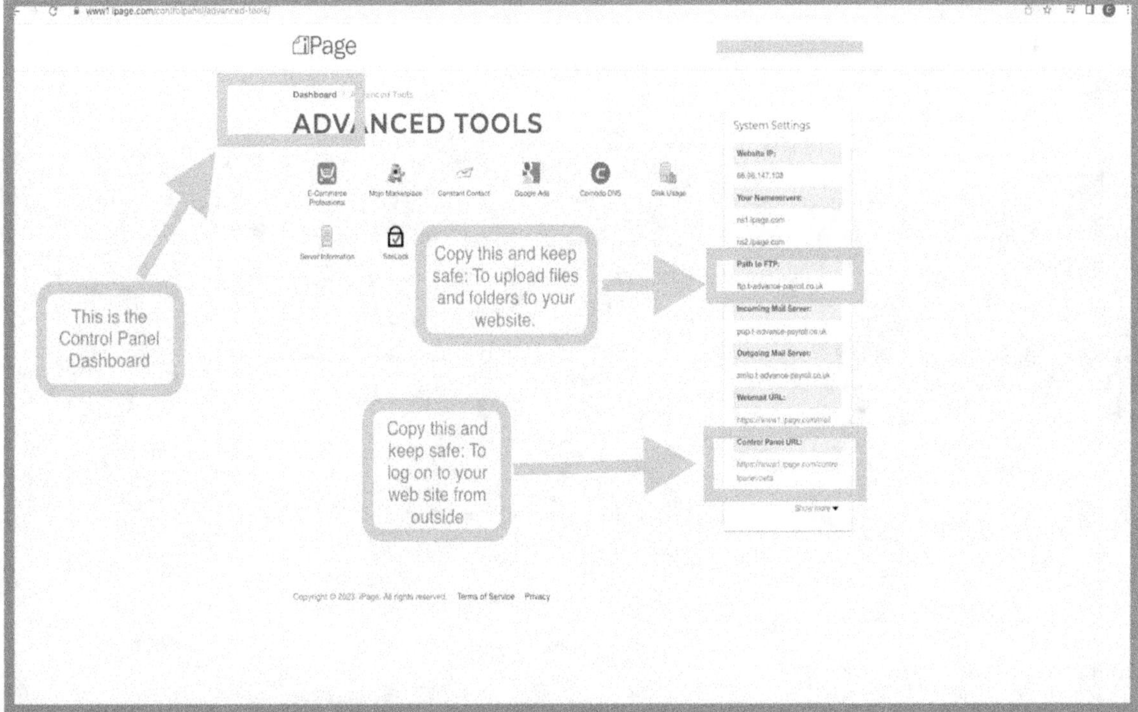

Note these and keep safe.

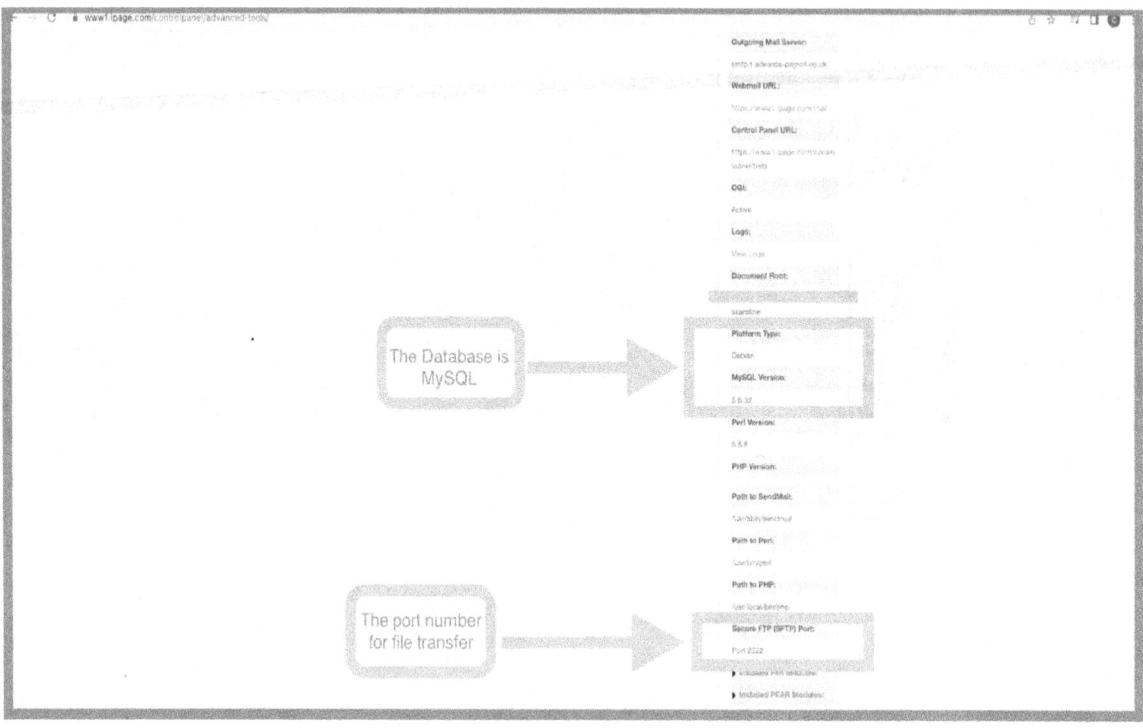

Note the DNS server names, and the SSL Certificate and when it will expire.

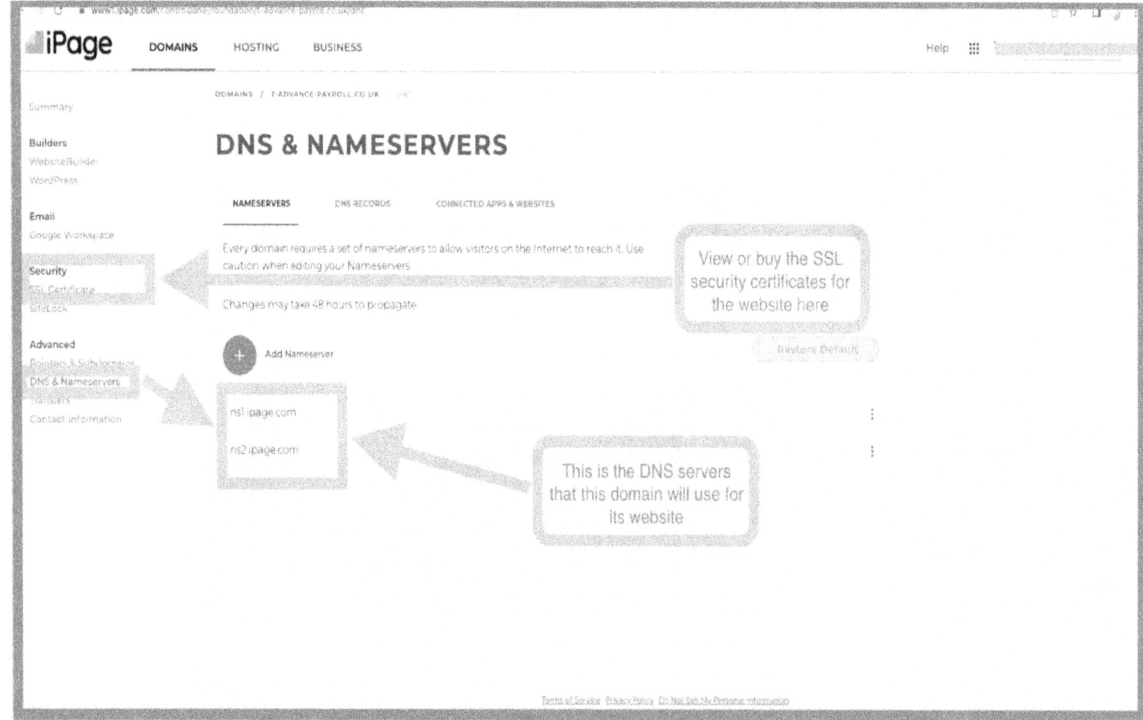

Subdomain: We can create a subdomain under the main domain

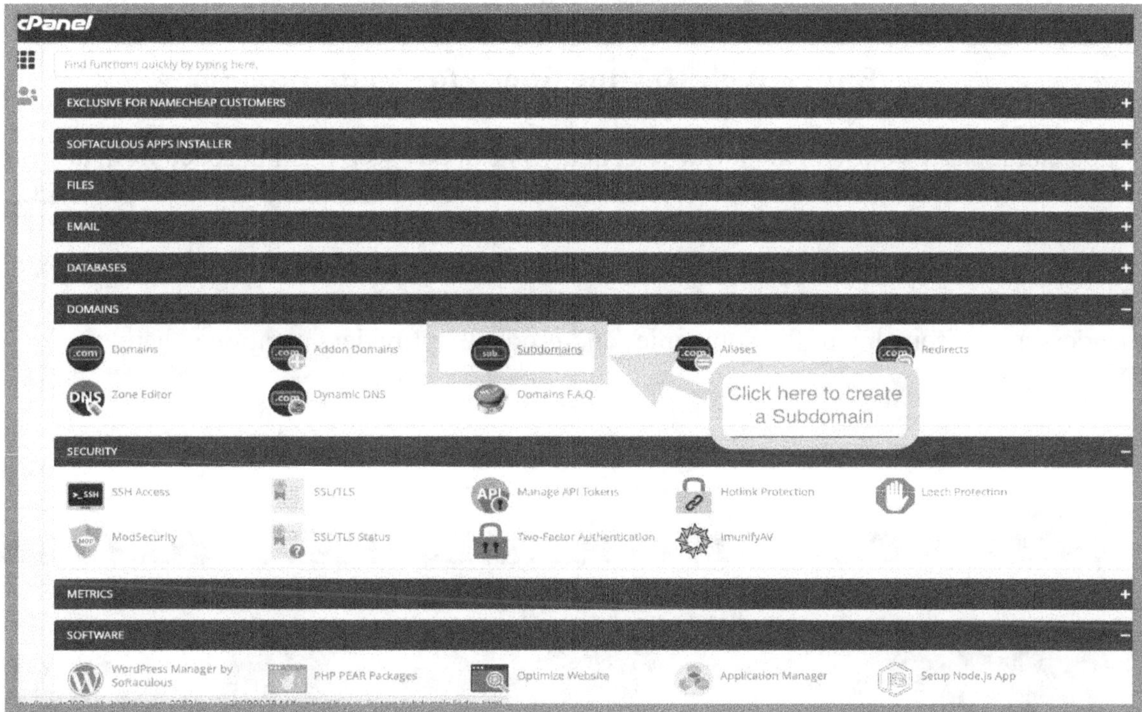

I have now created two new subdomains as below.

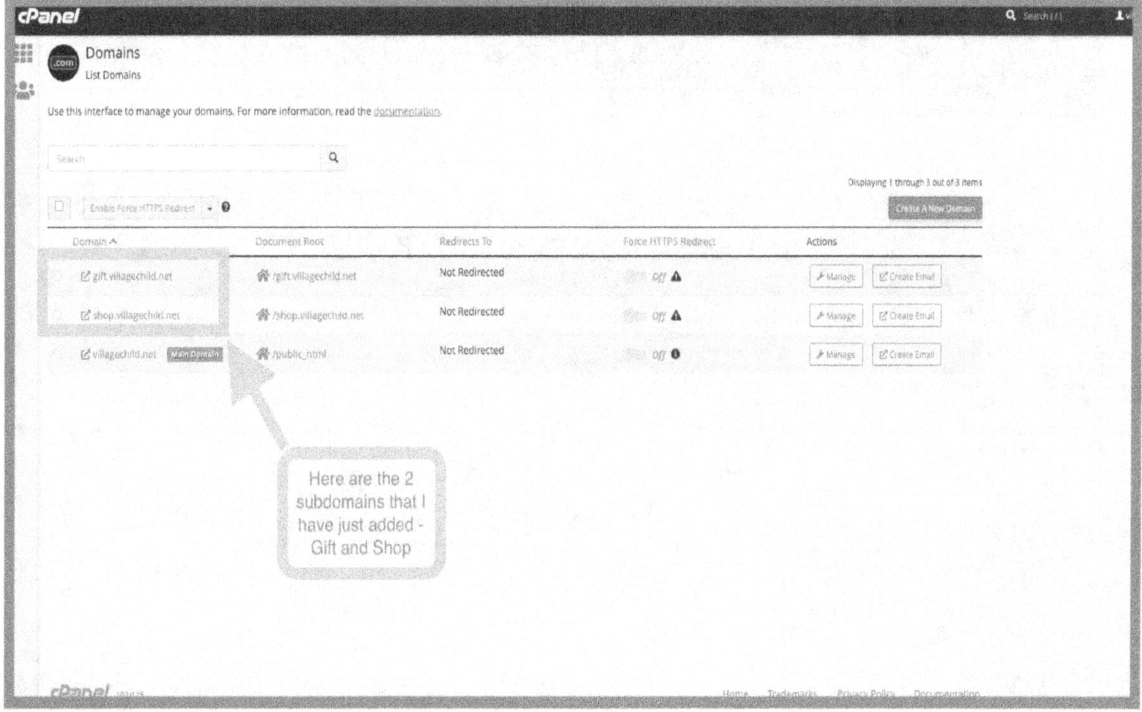

Buy A Web Hosting Space for Your Domain

Buy A Web Hosting Space for Your Domain

You can register your domain anywhere, and you can buy web hosting space from any provider. If you find that, is it a good offer, then you can have them with the same provider.

Keep it Real - Pls Note   Please note that at the time of writing this book, the author, editors, or anyone linked with the publishing of this book have not received any paid endorsement from any of the companies and products' providers mentioned here.

To buy hosting space, click on 'Hosting'.

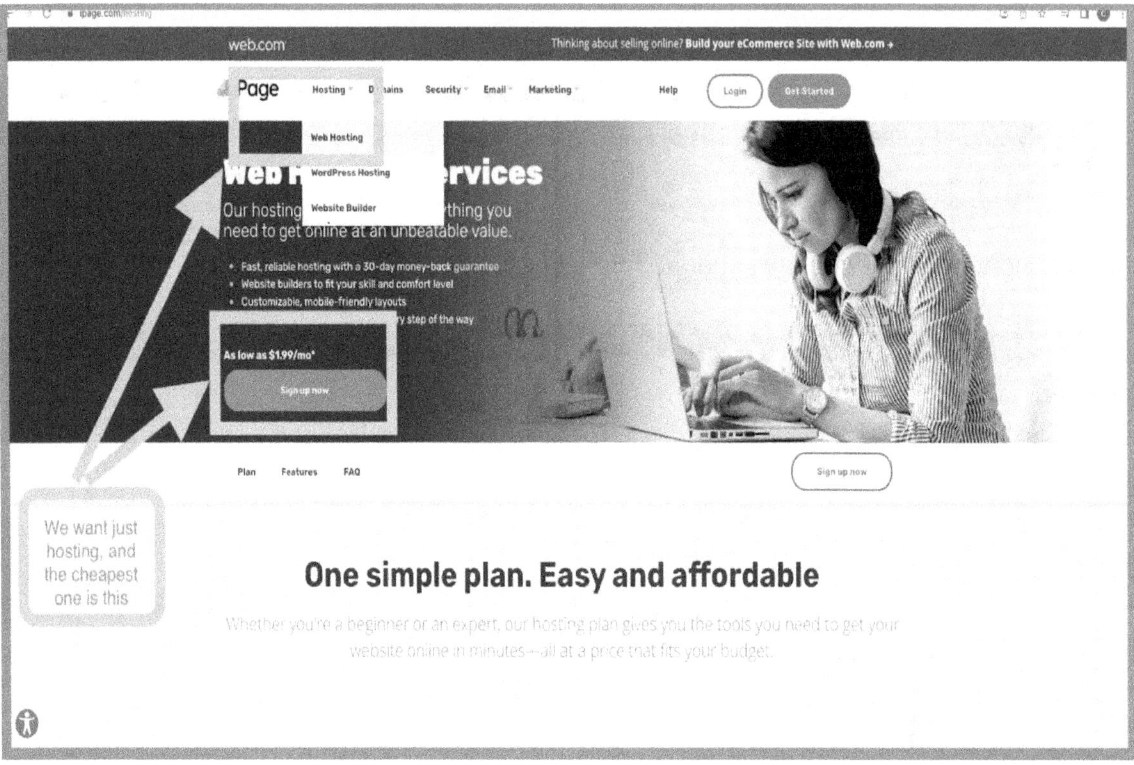

Then look to see the best and cheapest plans that meet your needs.

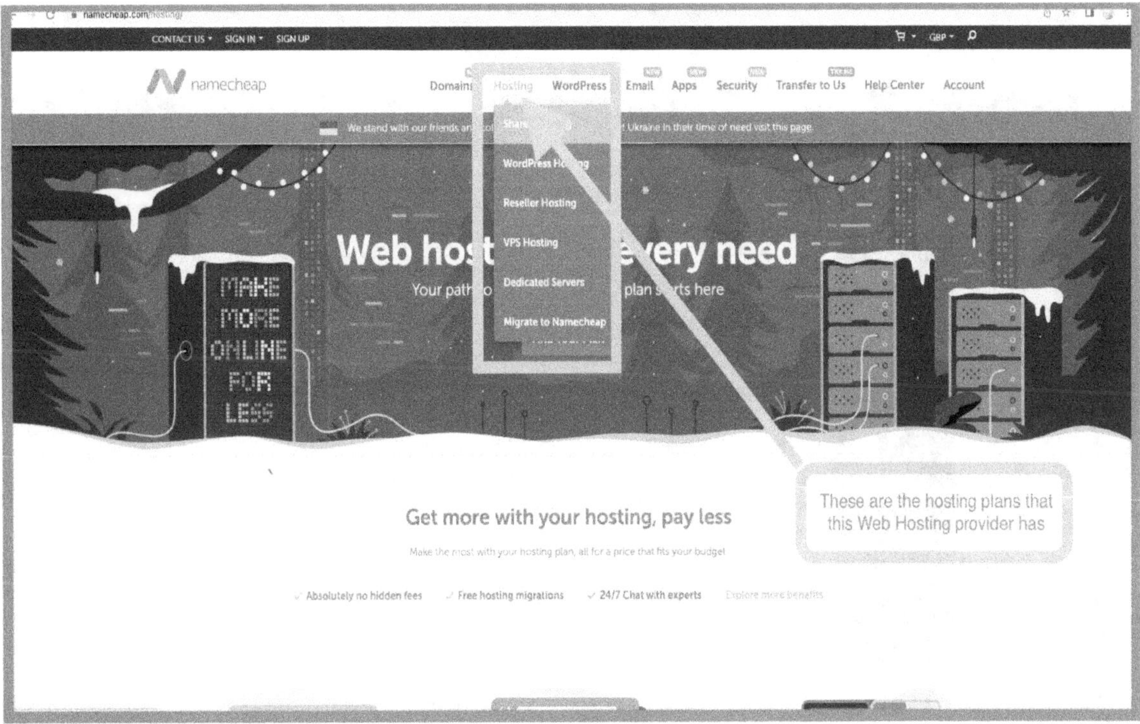

For now, I will choose the cheapest one.

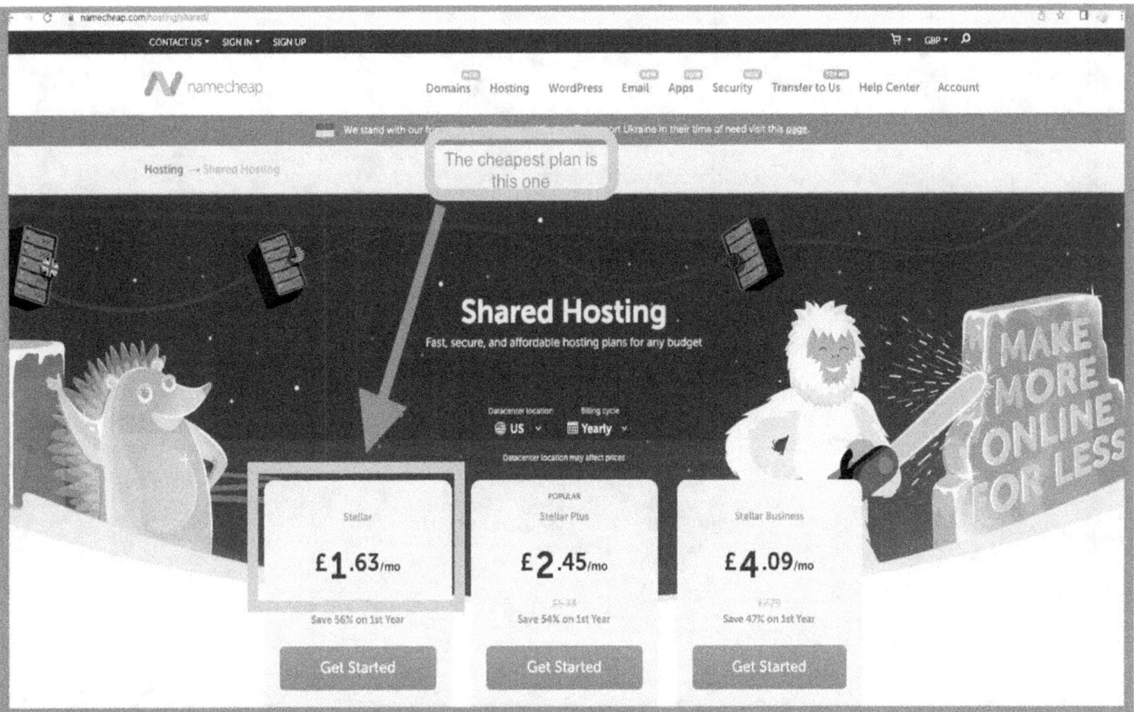

Here is the Web Hosting Dashboard

Once the website is in place, you can view it on the internet, but you will need to build it.

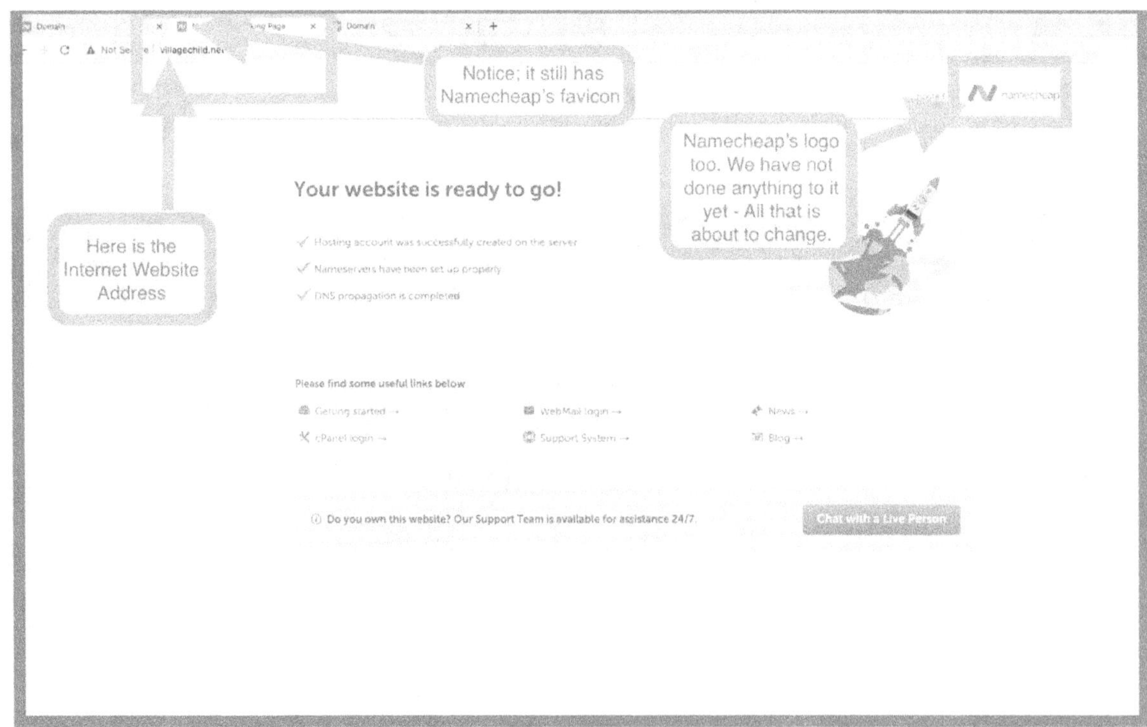

Internet Web Server

Internet Web Server

Now that we have paid for a hosting plan, the hosting provider will allow us access to use a shared part of their internet Web Server.

A web server is computer software that accepts requests via HTTP (Hypertext Transfer Protocol) or its secure variant HTTPS. This software is installed on a hardware computer - any computer, but the more powerful and high specs, the better. Our web site files, that is the HTML documents, CSS stylesheets, JavaScript files, images and all that is needed to run our web site would be stored on it. The web server connects to the internet on one hand and to the database on the other, so that all requests for files, items, coming from the internet are processed through the web server and the results for these requests are then sent back from there. It acts as a data interchange between a client computer and a database server. The requested information can then be viewed on the client web browser (Edge, Chrome, Firefox).

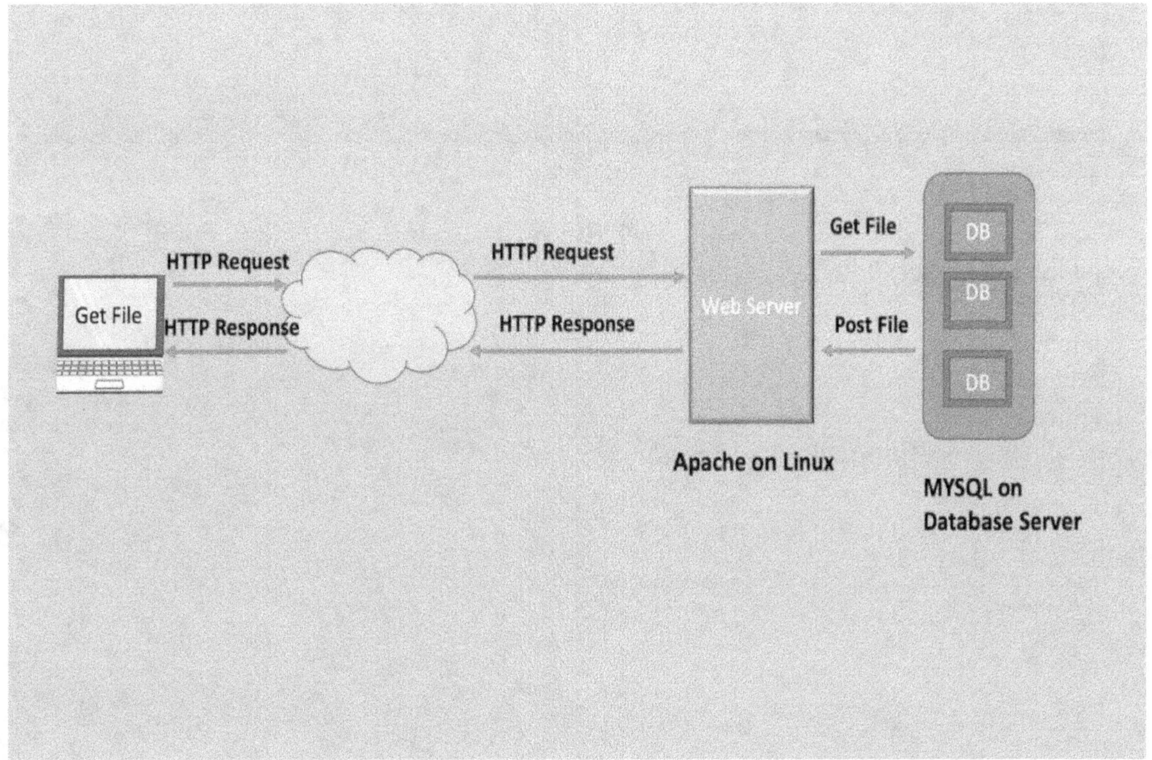

Here is the web server that we are hiring out for our web site.

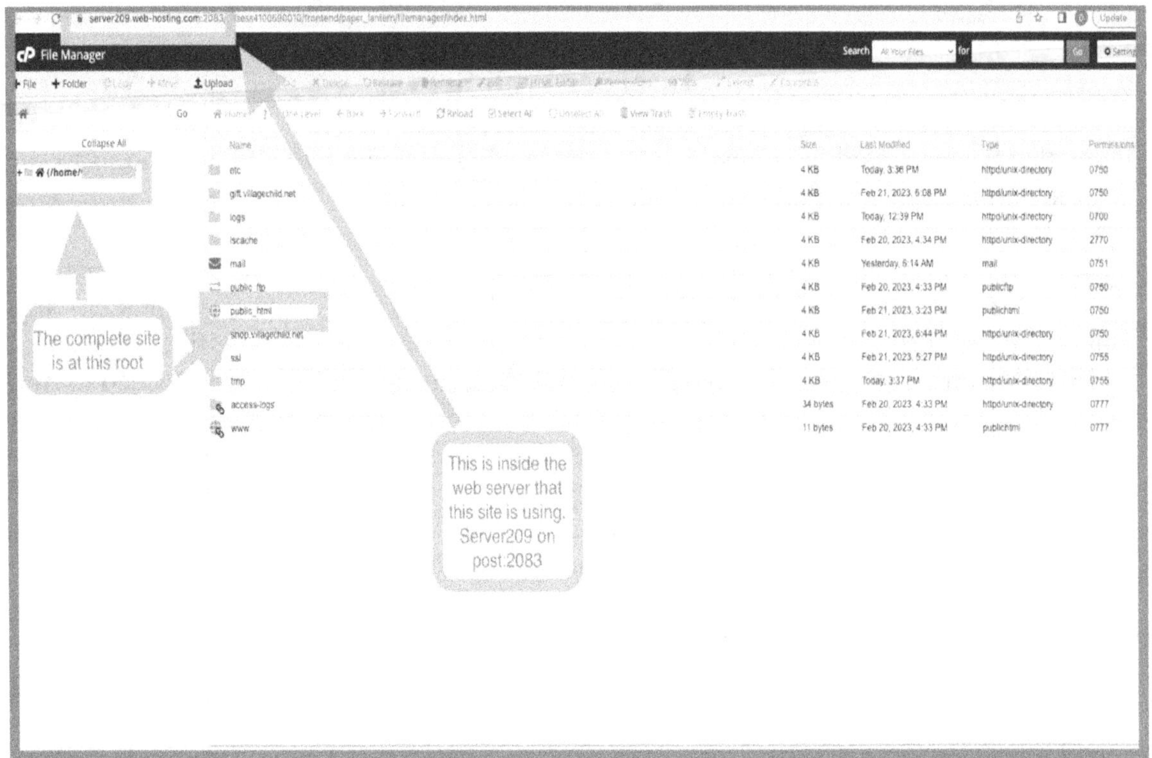

Web Server Brands

Apache HTTP Server.
NGINX
Apache Tomcat
Node.js
Lighttpd
Ms IIS (Internet Information Services)

Content Management Systems

Content Management Systems

A content management system (CMS) is computer software or platform that is used to manage the contents on a website. Sort of like a 'pop-up store, with shelves, so you can arrange things in an orderly manner. The content management system makes it easier to create and manage contents on the site.

You can customise CMS built-in functionalities, although you may have to use extensions, which may come at an additional cost and may require extensive development work. If possible, look for a CMS solution that meets all of your requirements out of the box.

Content management system types

There are many different types of content management system out there, so when choosing a CMS for your business, it is important to look for one that best merges the business model and would provide the best features and functions needed.
CMS can Open-source, Proprietary and Software-as-a-Service CMS on the cloud.

Proprietary CMS

Proprietary or commercial CMS software is built and managed by a single company. You would need to buy a licence or subscribes it to use. The cost depends on company, the core and extended parts of CMS you need, and any technical support or training they offer.

Examples of popular CMS solutions include:
Kentico
Microsoft SharePoint
IBM Enterprise Content Management
Pulse CMS
Sitecore
Shopify

Software as a Service (SaaS) CMS

SaaS CMS are a cloud computing solution, where the CMS may be included with the web content management software, web hosting, bandwidth, data storage, and technical support that a user can then pay a subscription to use as a service package. With the SaaS CMS, more than one user from different locations can be working on it.

Open-source CMS

There are so many open-source CMS software that you can download and use on your web site. Almost all have great communities that maintain them and offer free upgrades, but you may not get technical help during installation and customisation. The licence for these CMS would normally allow for onward sell or the finished products. Modifications can be done by means of extensions, templates and plugins.

Examples of the open-source CMS platforms include:
WordPress
Joomla
Drupal
Magento (e-commerce)
PrestaShop (e-commerce)

WordPress

https://wordpress.com

WordPress a popular website builder as well as Content Management System. It was originally intended for blogging, but now you can build any kind of website using it.

WordPress Market Place:
https://wordpress.org/plugins/tags/marketplace

Joomla!

https://www.joomla.org

Joomla, also spelled Joomla! is a free and open-source Content Management System (CMS) which enables you to build websites and powerful online applications. It was built for journalists to publish news on to websites, but it is used to build other web content applications, include discussion forums, photo galleries, e-Commerce and user communities and numerous other web-based applications. It was released on 22 September 2005 by the community base company, Open Source Matters, Inc, and it still maintained by them.

Joomla! Market Place:
https://extensions.joomla.org

Drupal

https://www.drupal.org

Drupal is a free and open-source web content management system written in PHP and distributed under the GNU General Public License. It was released on 15 January 2001 by developers; Drupal Association, Dries Buytaert, Daniel Kudwien.
Drupal 10 comes with even more features that Drupal developers and users love, including incredible tools to help build the versatile, structured content.

Drupal Market Place:
https://www.drupal.org/drupal-services

Magento

https://business.adobe.com/products/magento/magento-commerce.html

Adobe's acquisition of Magento was complete 2018. Magento Open Source is a powerful, but simple ecommerce CMS that comes complete with shop storefront, shopping cart and payment gateways.

Magento Market Place:
https://marketplace.magento.com

PrestaShop

https://www.prestashop.com
PrestaShop is a freemium, open-source e-commerce platform. The software is published under the Open Software License. It is written in the PHP programming language with support for the MySQL database management system. PrestaShop offers a highly flexible and scalable ecommerce platform to launch an online business that include a shop storefront, product boxes, shopping basket and payment gateway.

PrestaShop Market Place:
https://addons.prestashop.com/en/2-modules-prestashop

In this tutorial, we are going to be setting up our web sites using Joomla!, Magento and PrestaShop.

Joomla! Web Site with a New Template

Joomla! Web Site with a New Template

Setting up A Joomla! Web Site

Go to the Control Panel (cPanel) on the Web server of the Web Hosting Provider and go to Softaculous Installer. Look for Magento and install it on the main domain - villagechild.net.

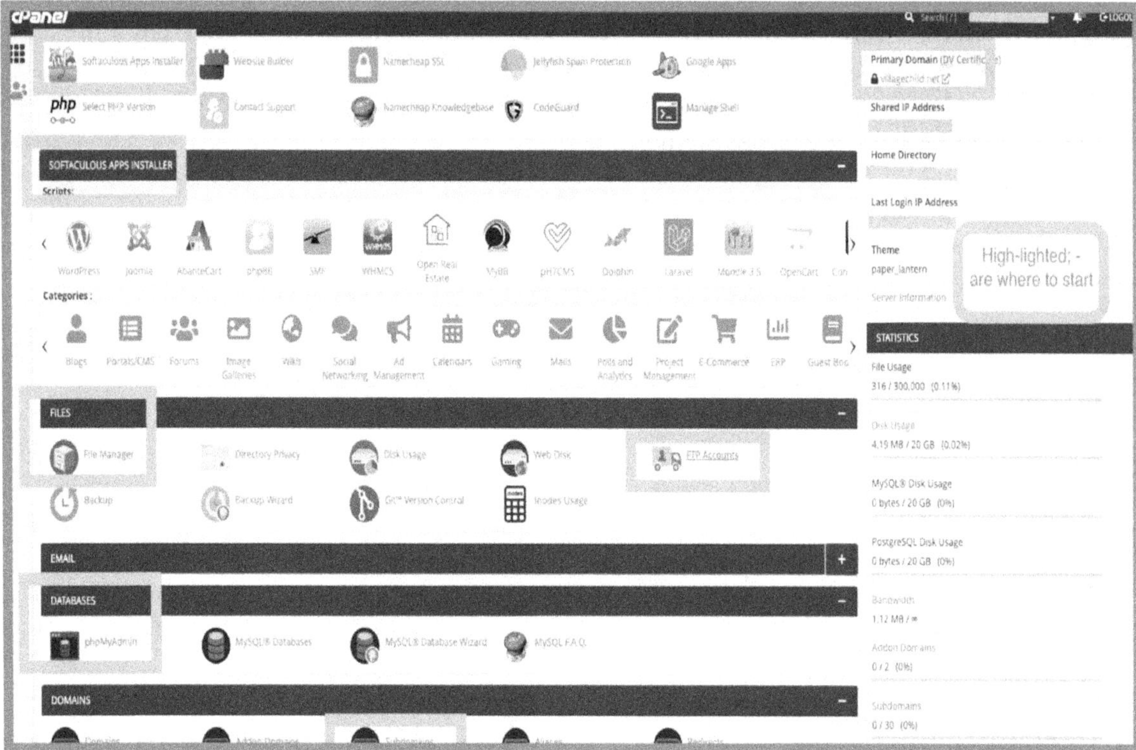

Look for Joomla, view it, watch the Demo and if happy, click on Install.

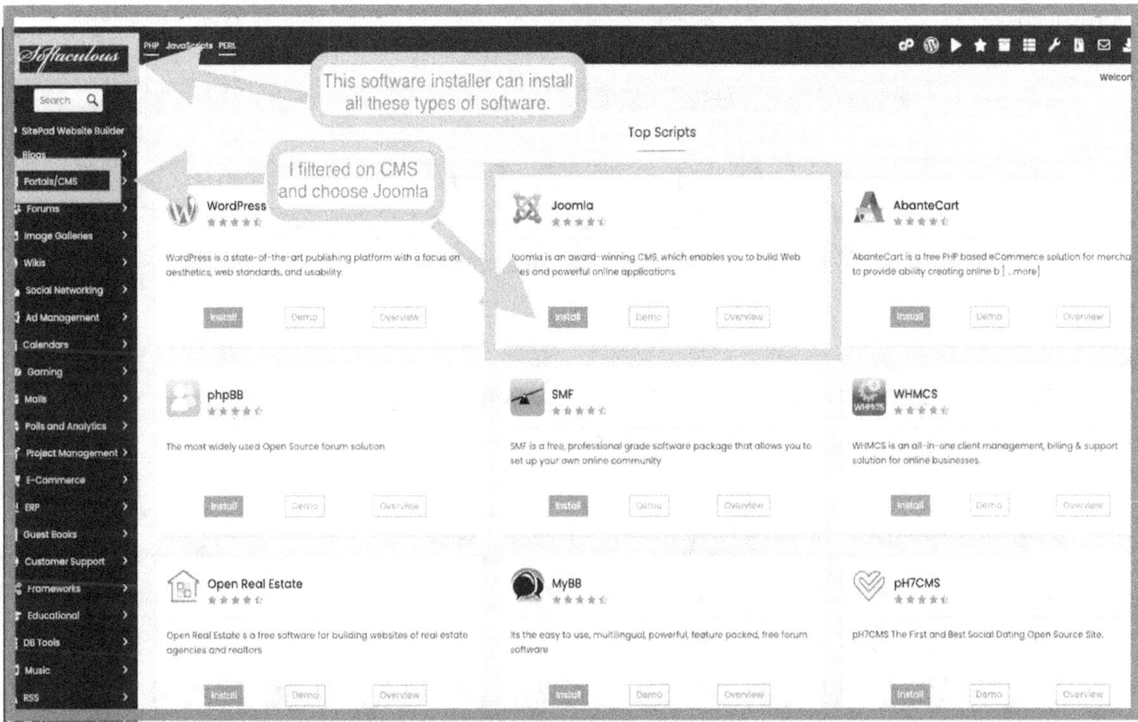

Here are the installation details, please copy and keep safe. Also need an email address.

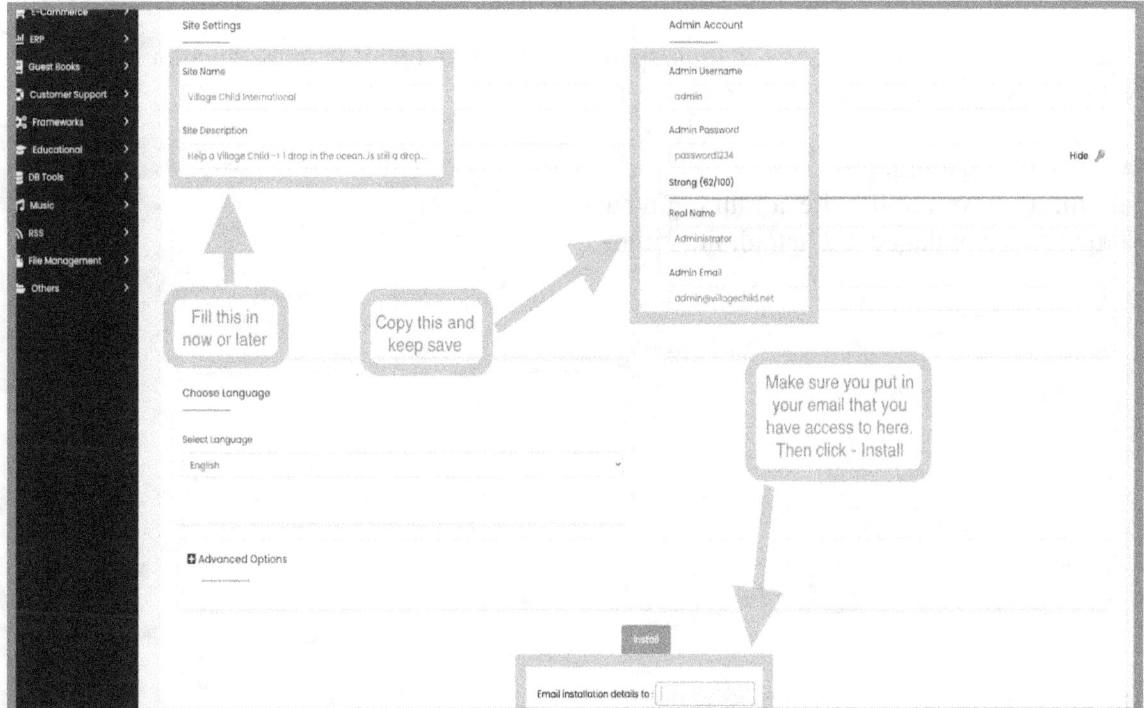

All the installed files will be placed in the File Manager box. It installed on the main domain, which is Public.htm folder. To transfer some more files and folders to the site, we would use Public.ftp.

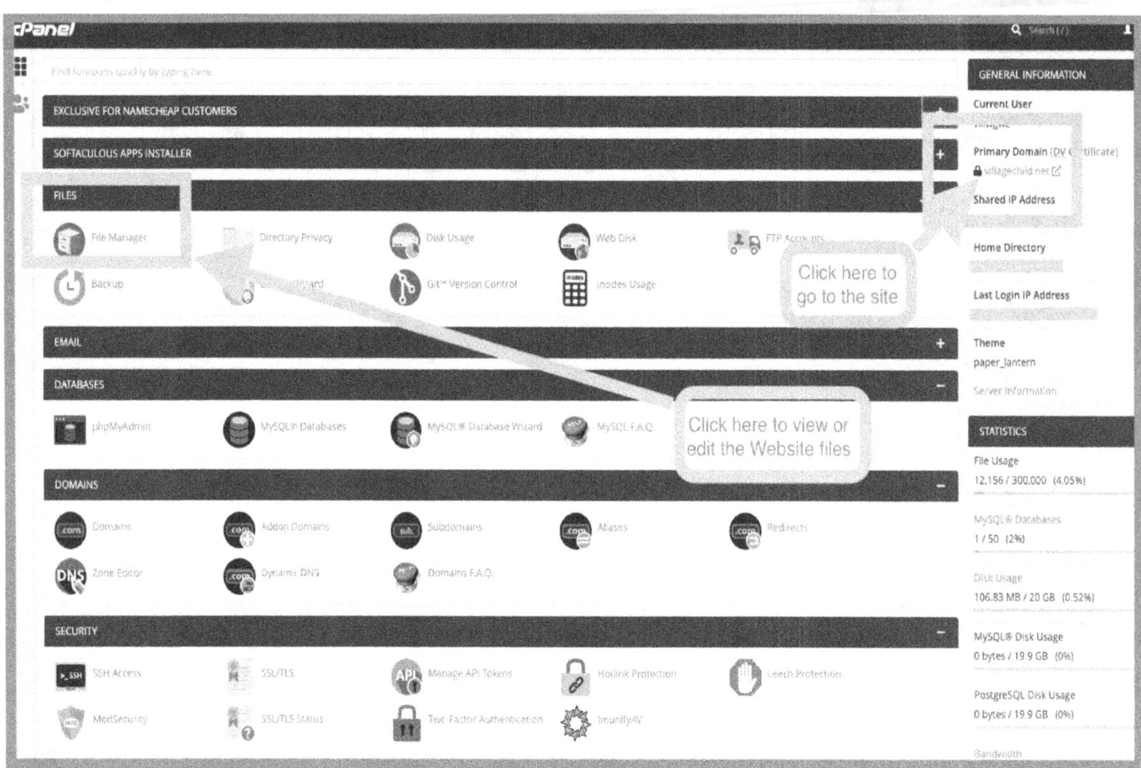

Now go to your email inbox (or Junk/spam), look for an email from Softaculous - with the subject: New Installation of Joomla.

Click on the Admin URL link
It will bring you to the site admin login page.
https://www.villagechild.net/administrator

Here is the web site on the internet. Joomla has set up some basics for us.

Here is the Admin login, to customise the site.

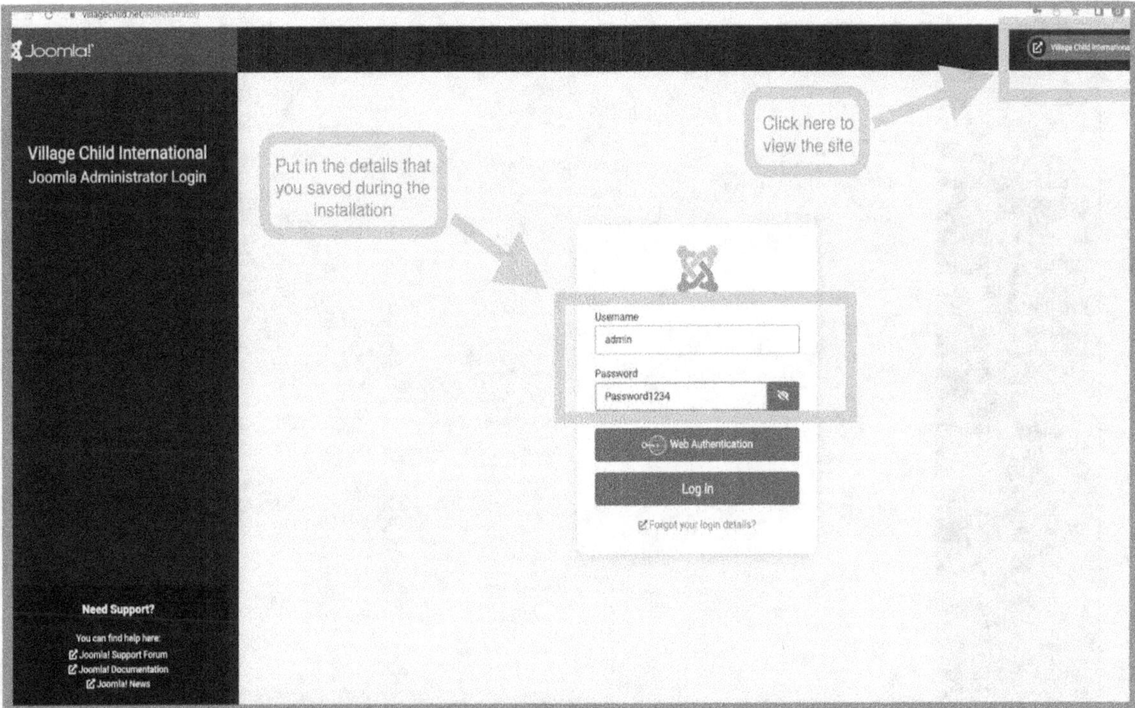

This is Joomla Admin account, for making changes to the site.

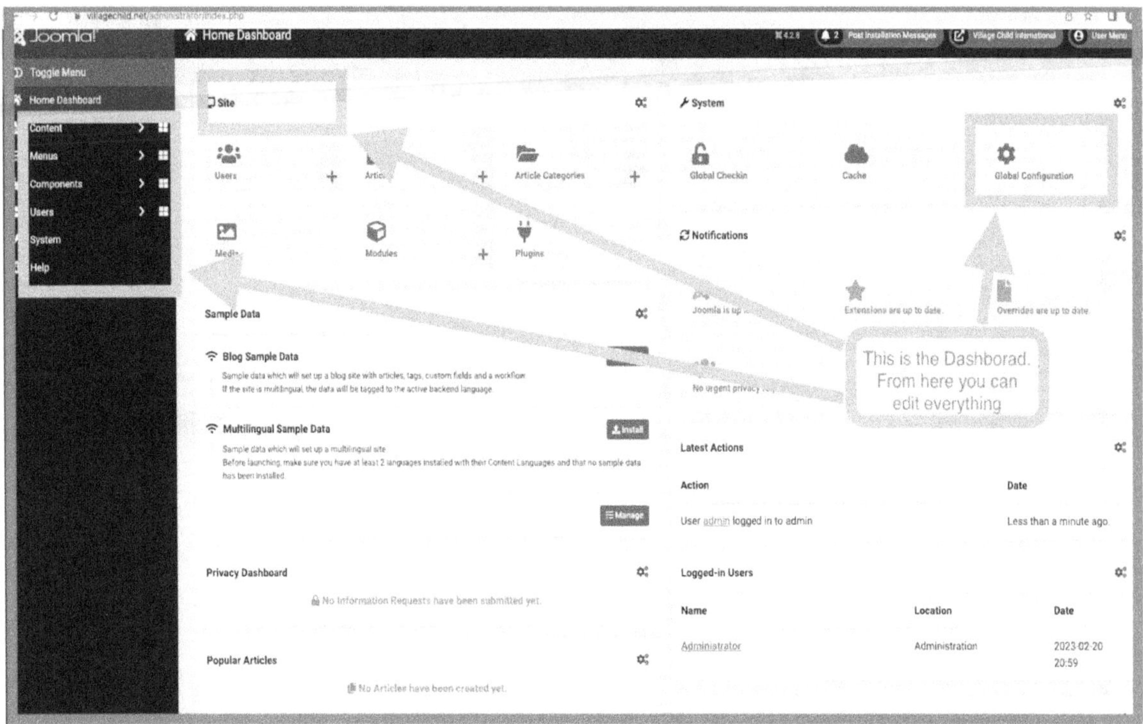

I can change upload new templates or find on one on Joomla to replace the default template.

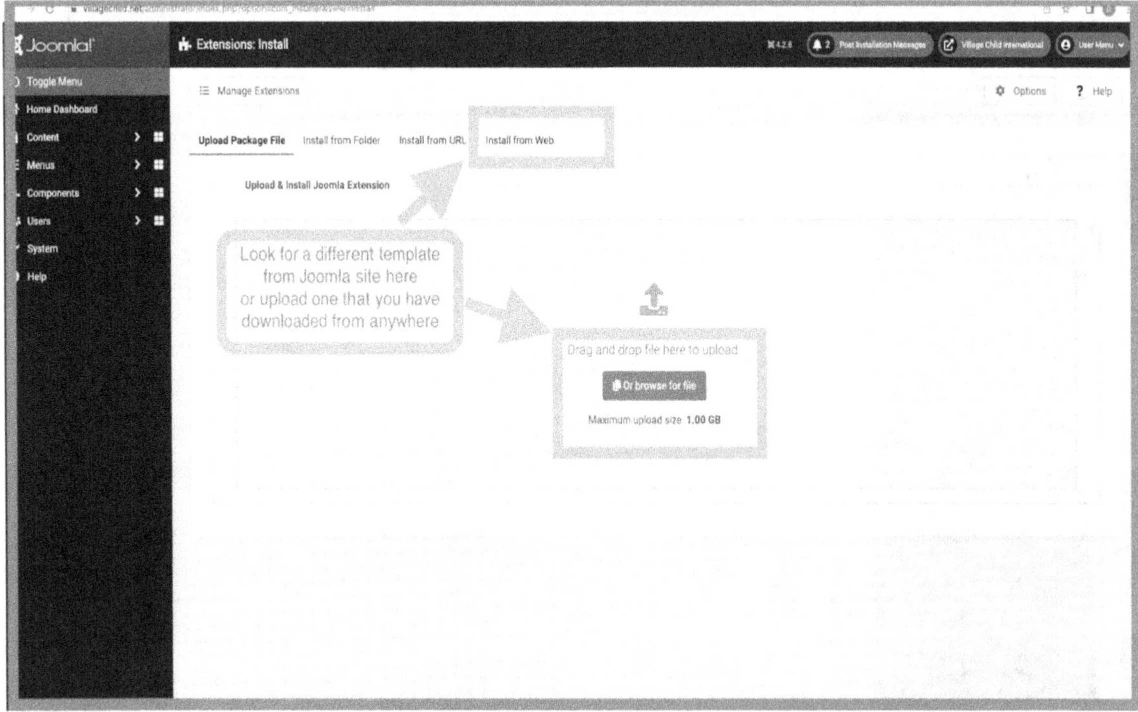

Then go to 'System', to make the templates' switch.

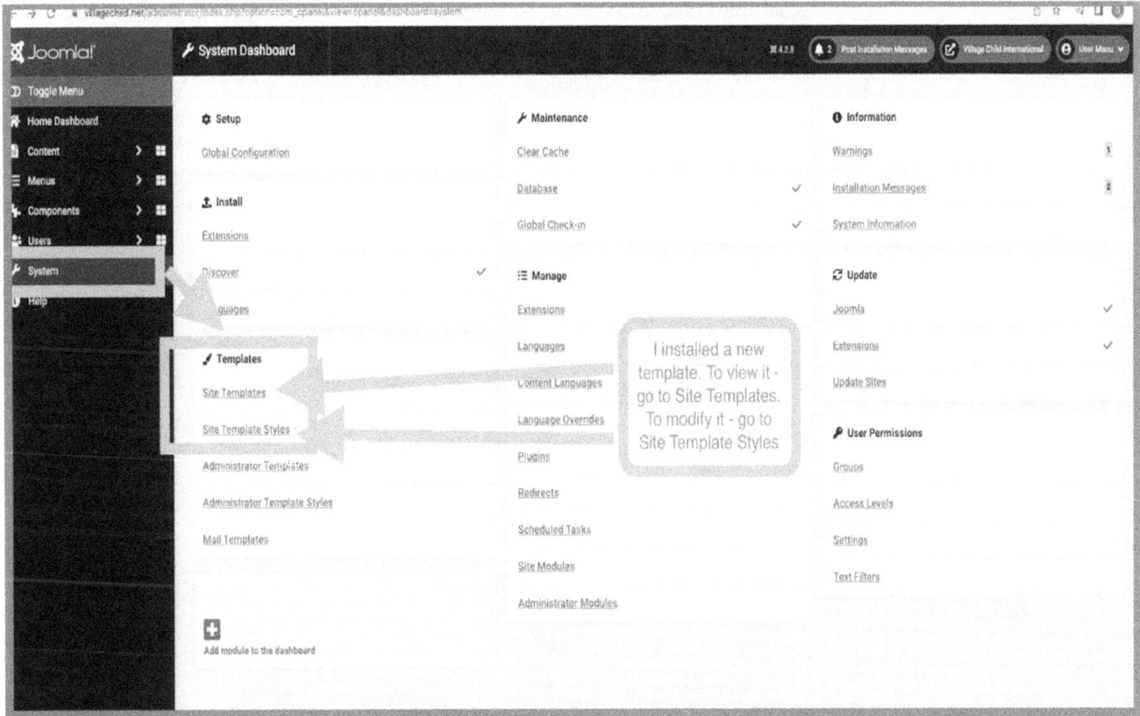

The new Template is called - Lightning. I need to set it to become the default template.

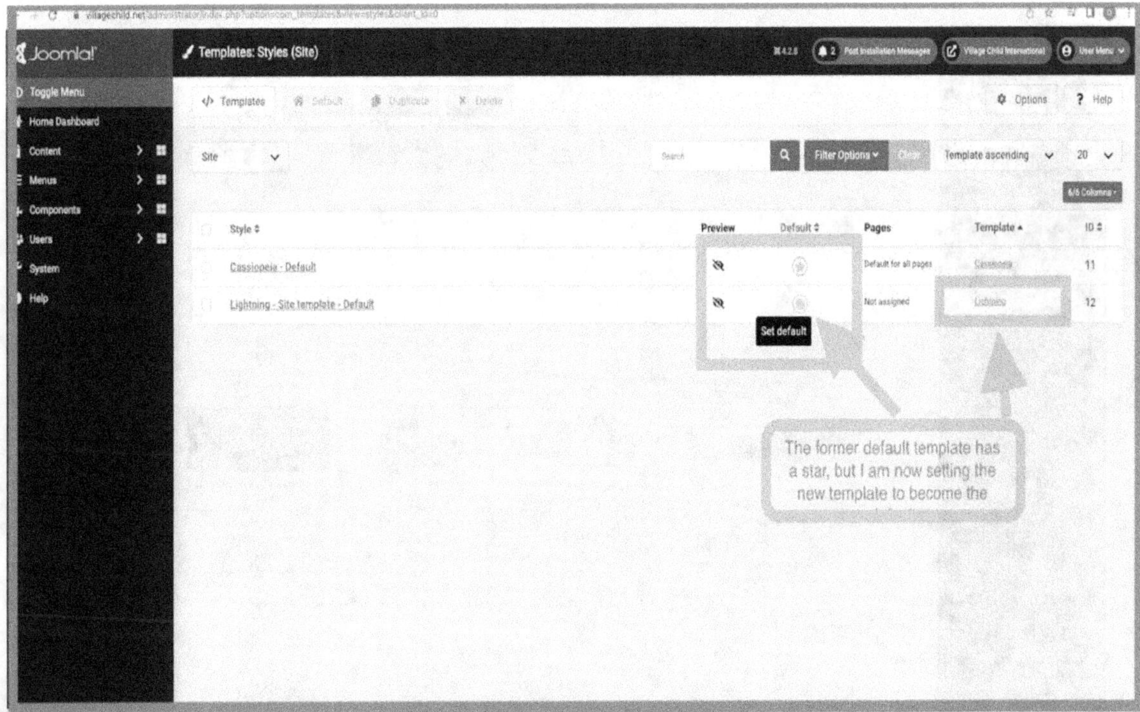

Click on Lighning to customise it to my liking, including changing the logo, colours, etc

Click on Extension, look through to see plugins I may need. I like this free Image Slider

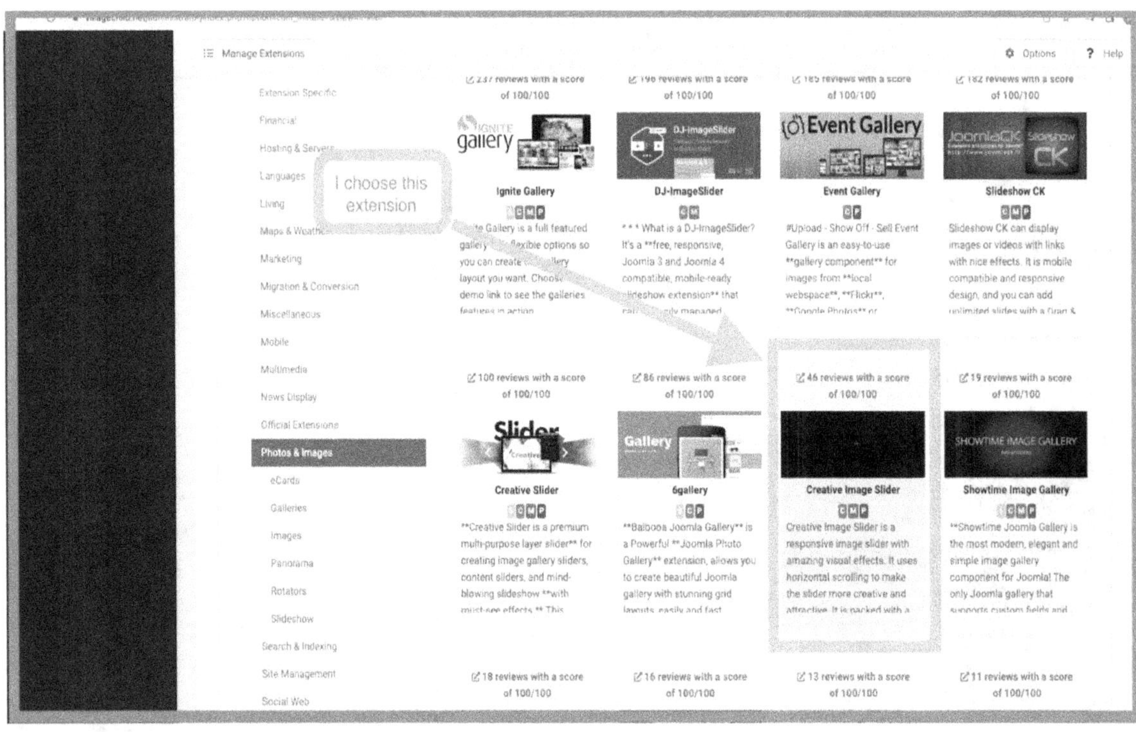

Once installed, I will now set up a Menu item for it, so it can show on the front-end.

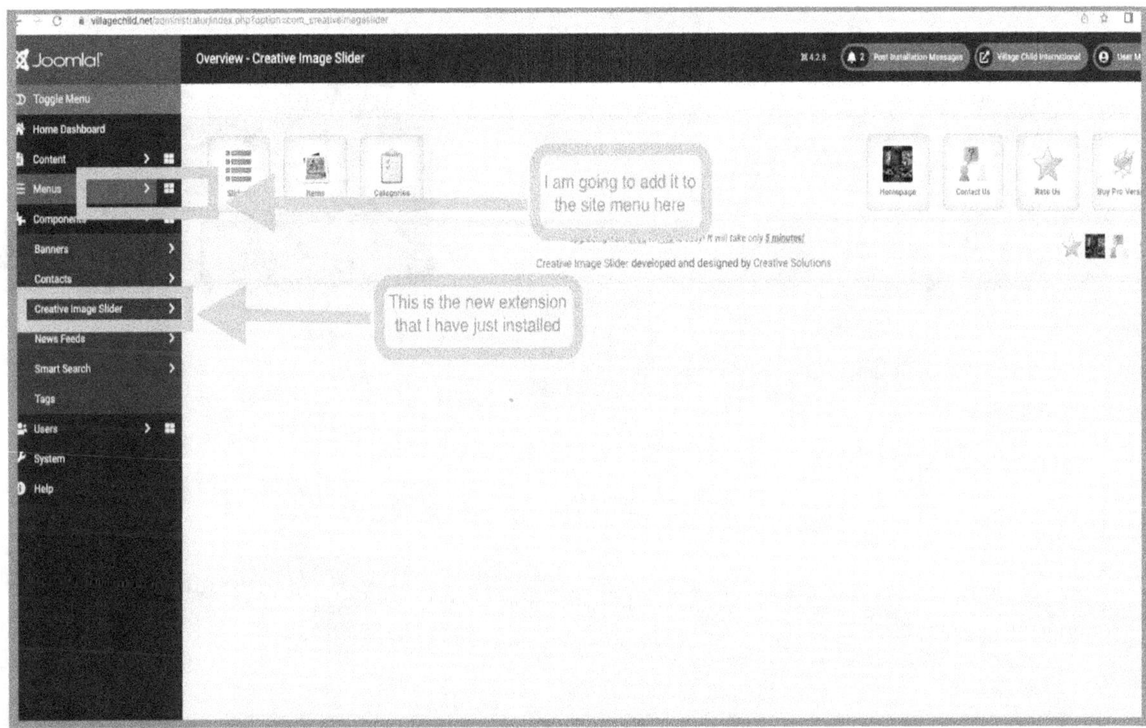

These are the current 4 modules on the front-end (site). Each, on a block position.

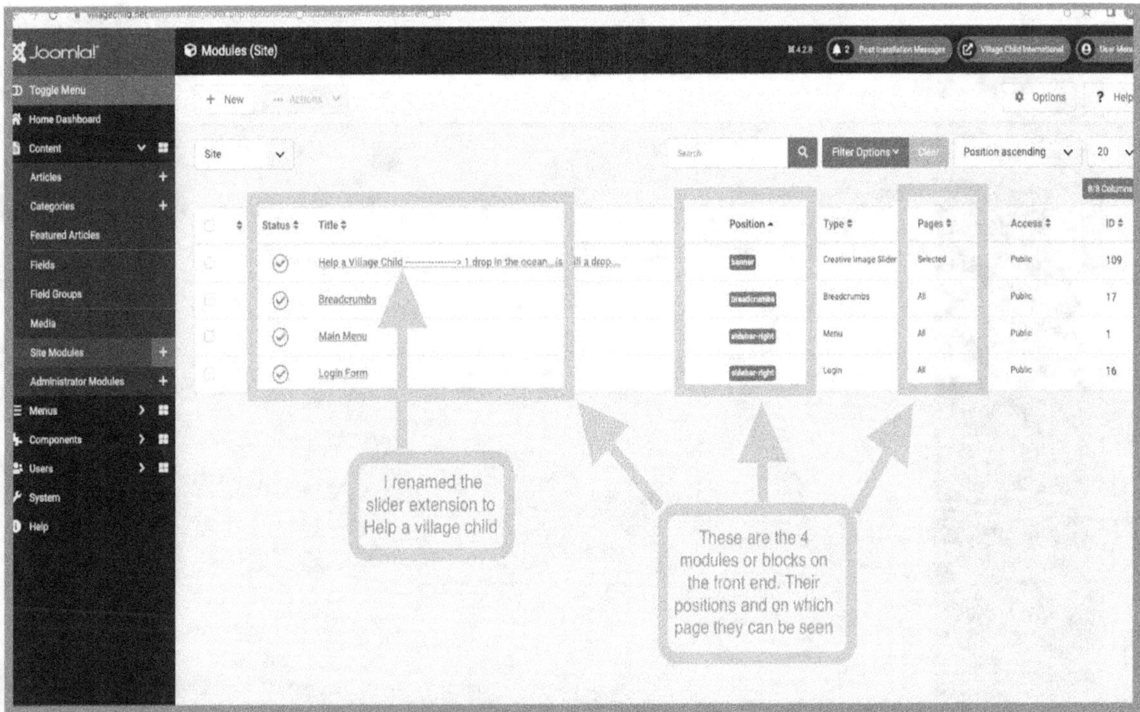

The 4 blocks that are set by the 4 modules above.

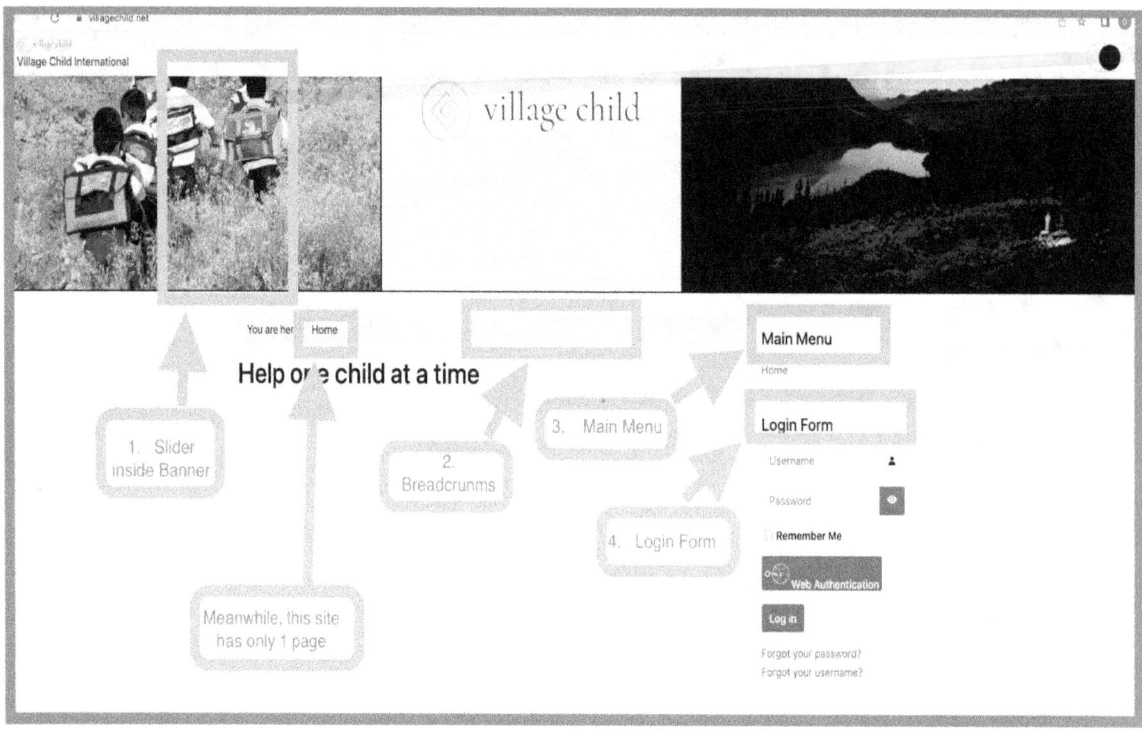

Back to the Admin Panel: here are the modules that we can add to the site (front end).

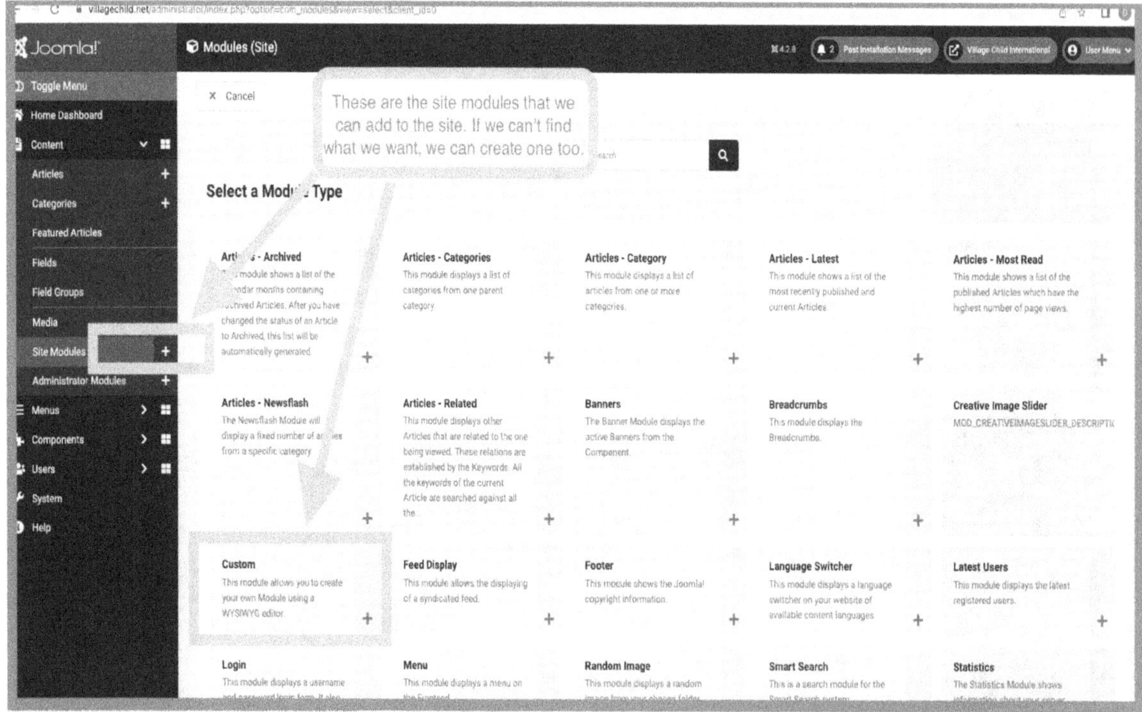

Currently, our site has only one page, that is the Home Page.

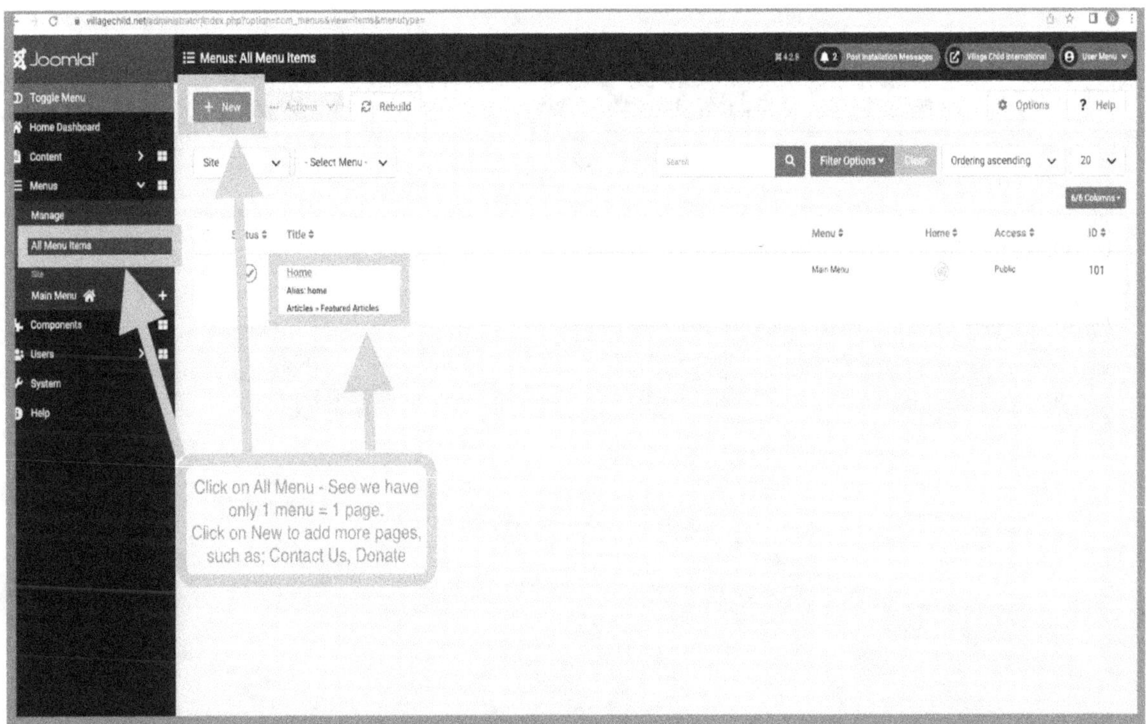

To create more pages, go to Content -> Articles -> New -> Single Article. Then type a name.

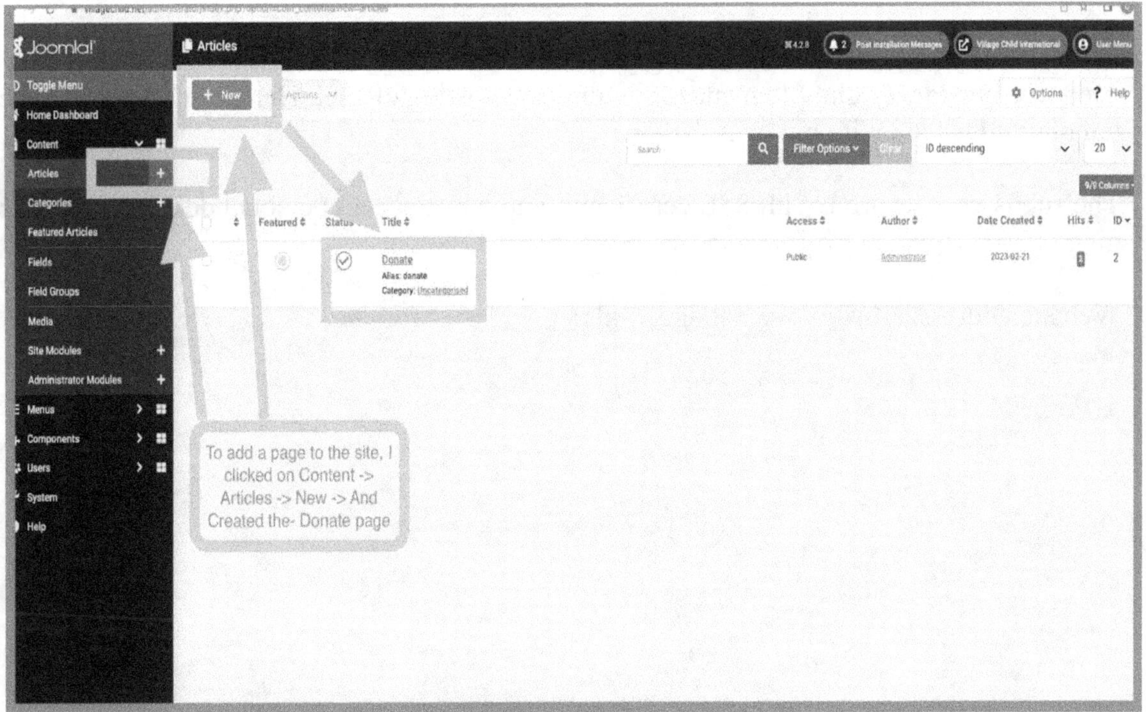

Assign the new article a menu item: Menu -> New Item-> Single Article. Then select the article from Content earlier.

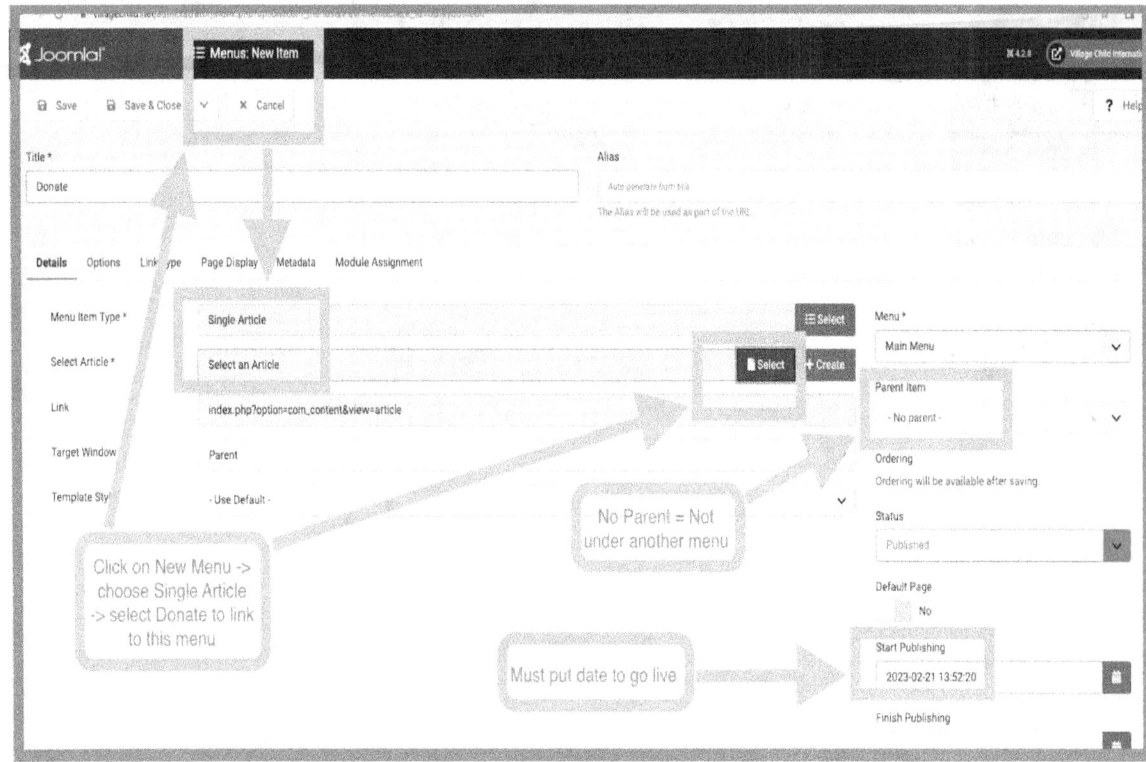

If there is anything that we are finding difficult to edit through Joomla Admin Panel, then we need to come to web site file manager on the web hosting cPanel. Here, I am replacing the template's Favicon with my own.

The site is very secured, with SSL certificates and it can accept personal details of users logging in.

Website address: https://www.villagechild.net

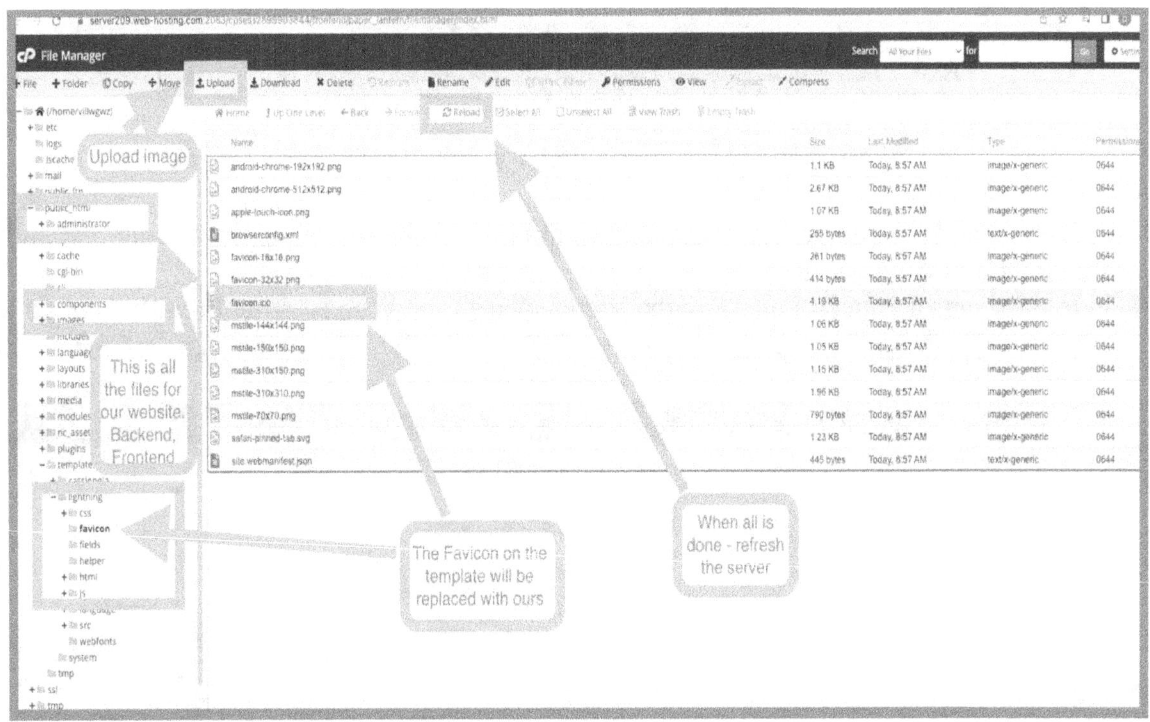

Here is the web site, showing the three pages: Home, Contact Us, Donate.

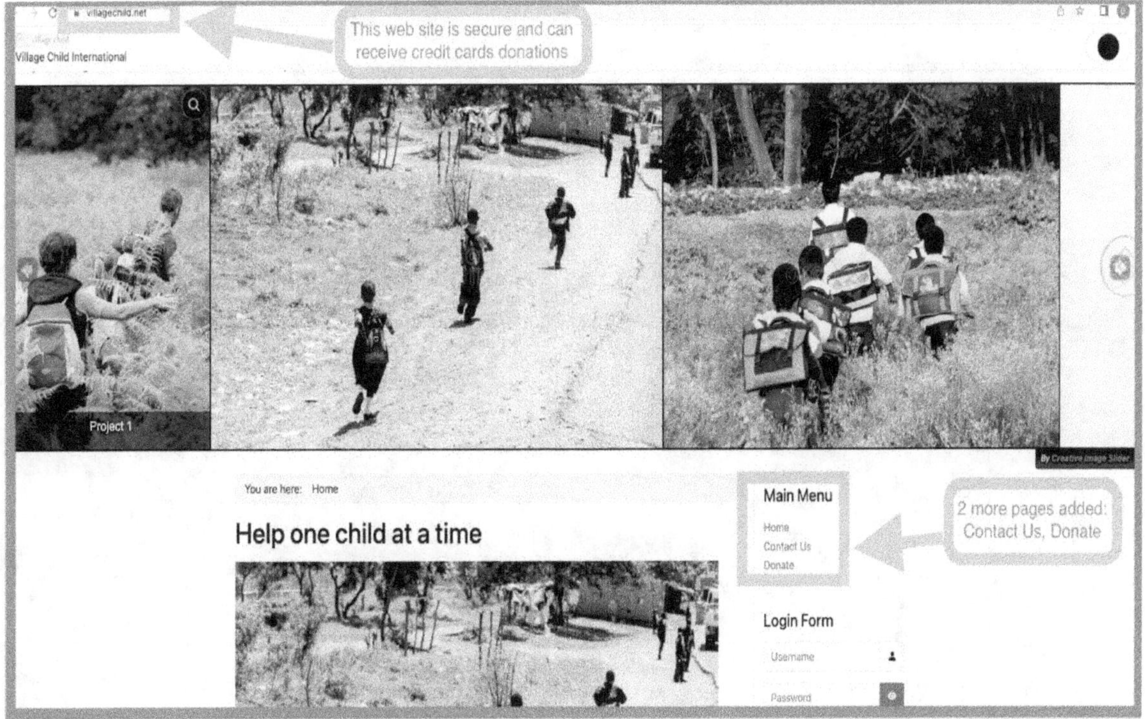

You should now call yourself, a 'Joomla Web Site Developer'. Start applying for similar jobs and freelance work.

Magento Ecommerce Site with PayPal Payment

Magento Ecommerce Site with PayPal Payment

Magento is an E-commerce software, that is, already has built in shopping basket/cart and an interface for payment gateway.

Go to the Control Panel (cPanel) on the Web server of the Web Hosting Provider and go to Softaculous Installer. Look for Magento and install it on the subdomain - gift.villagechild.net.

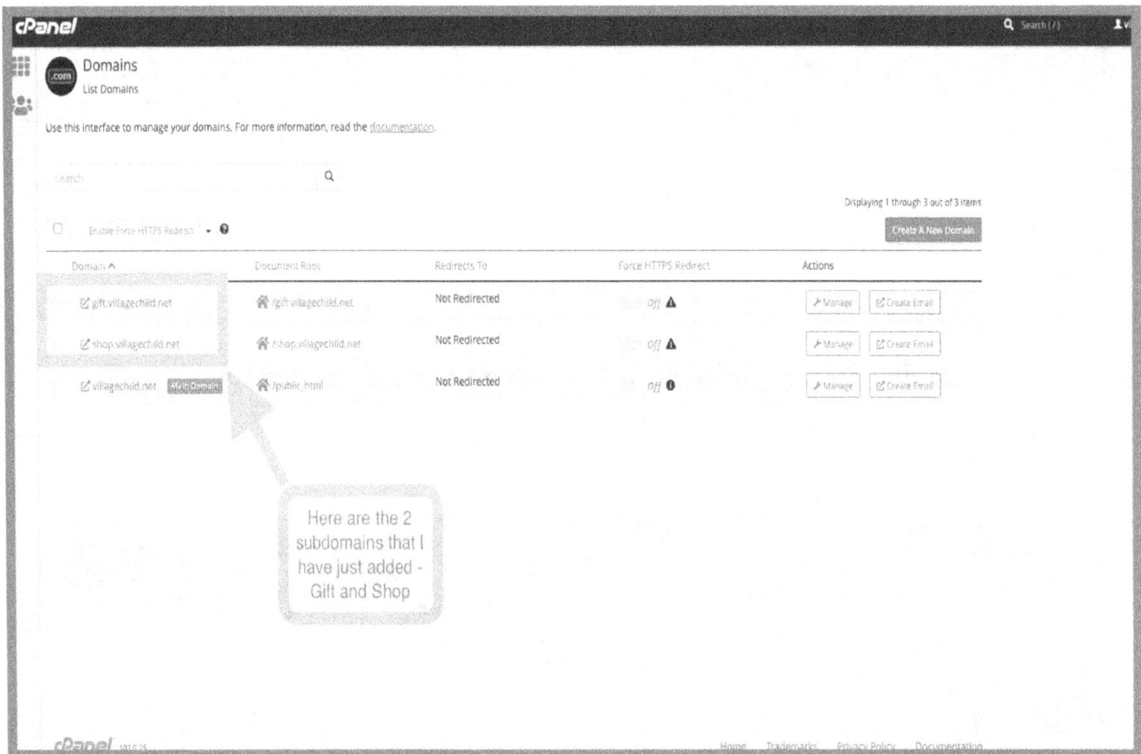

Fill in the details and install Magento

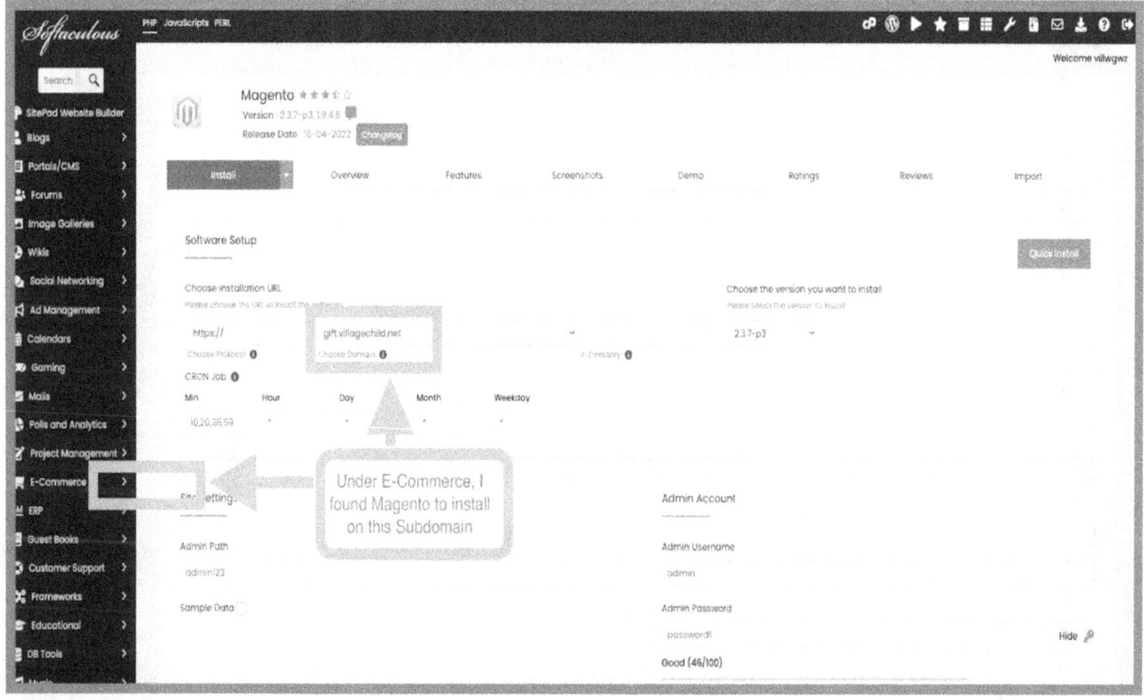

To set up a payment gateway, go to - Stores -> Configuration -> Sales -> Payment Methods.

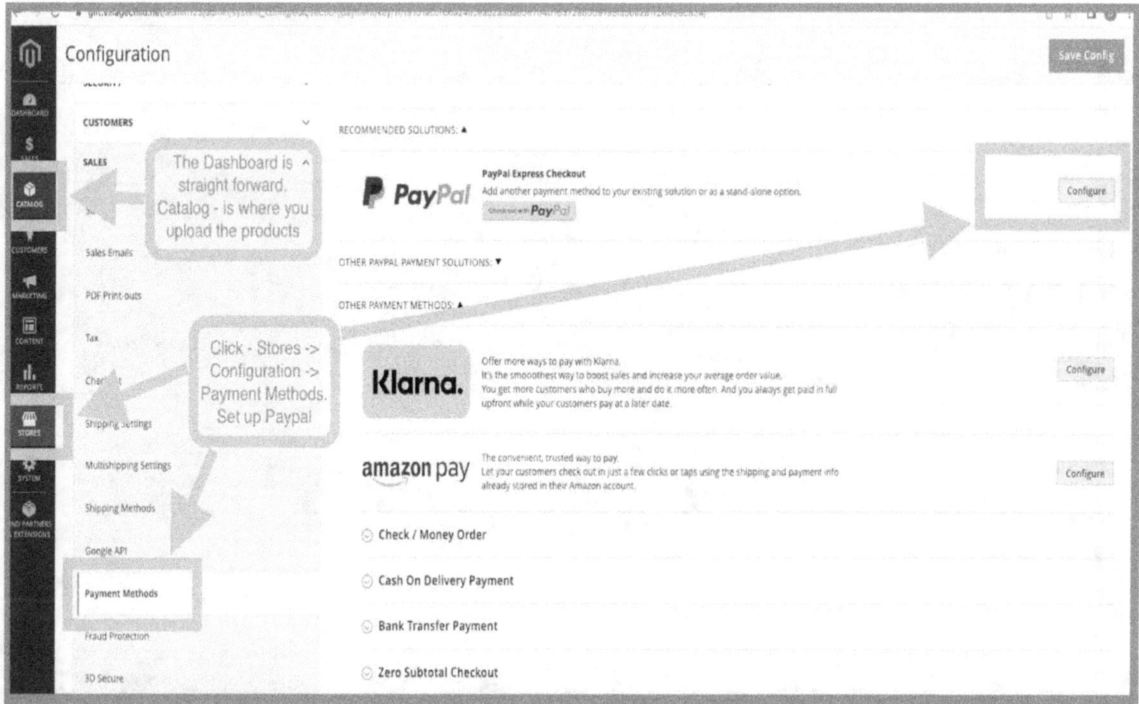

Click on Configure PayPal: Fill in your PayPal account detail or leave blank if you don't have

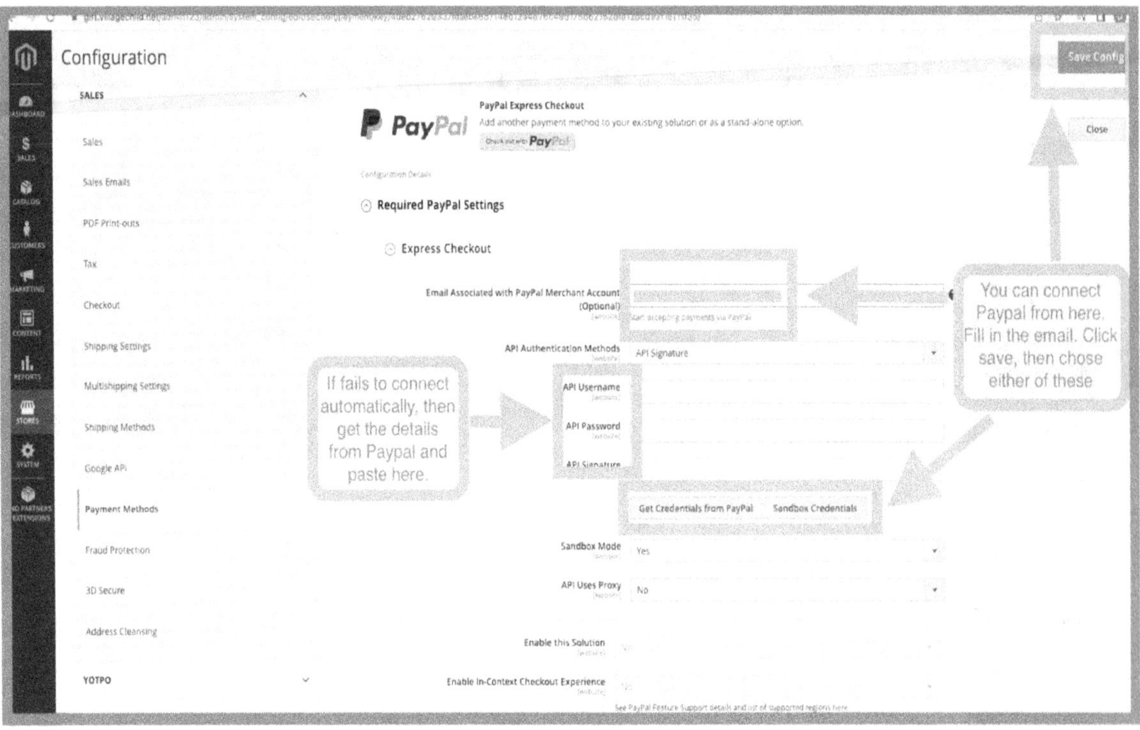

It will take you to PayPal to continue

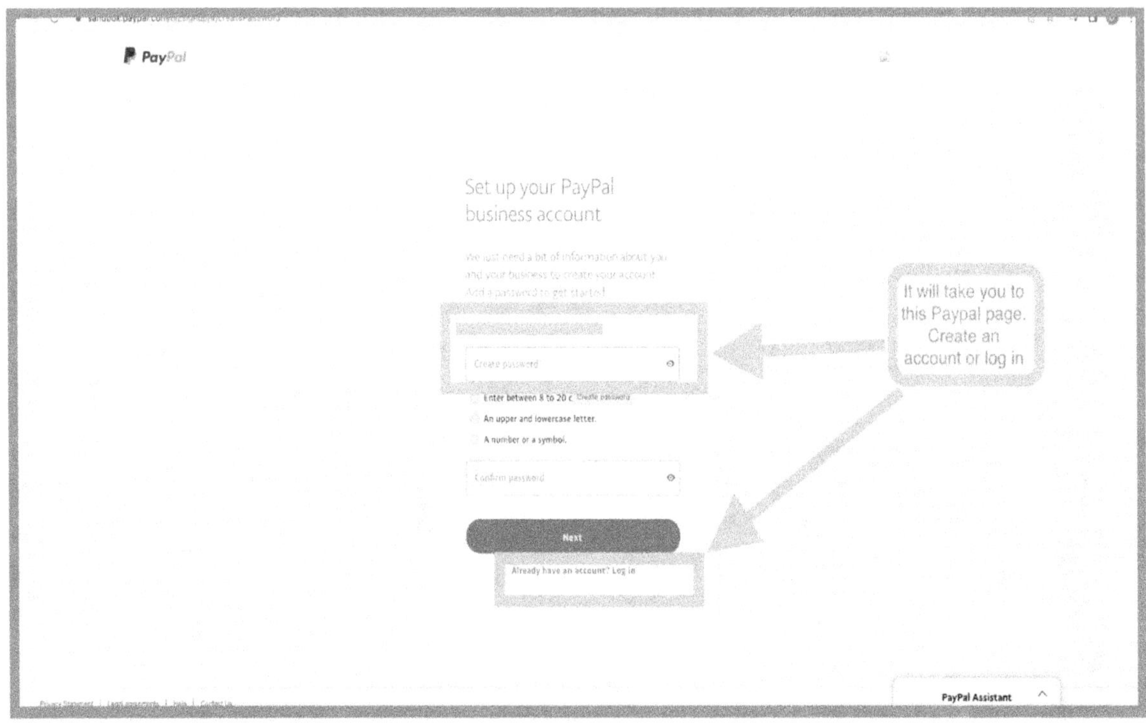

Once you have signed in into PayPal and complete on that site, it should connect Magento

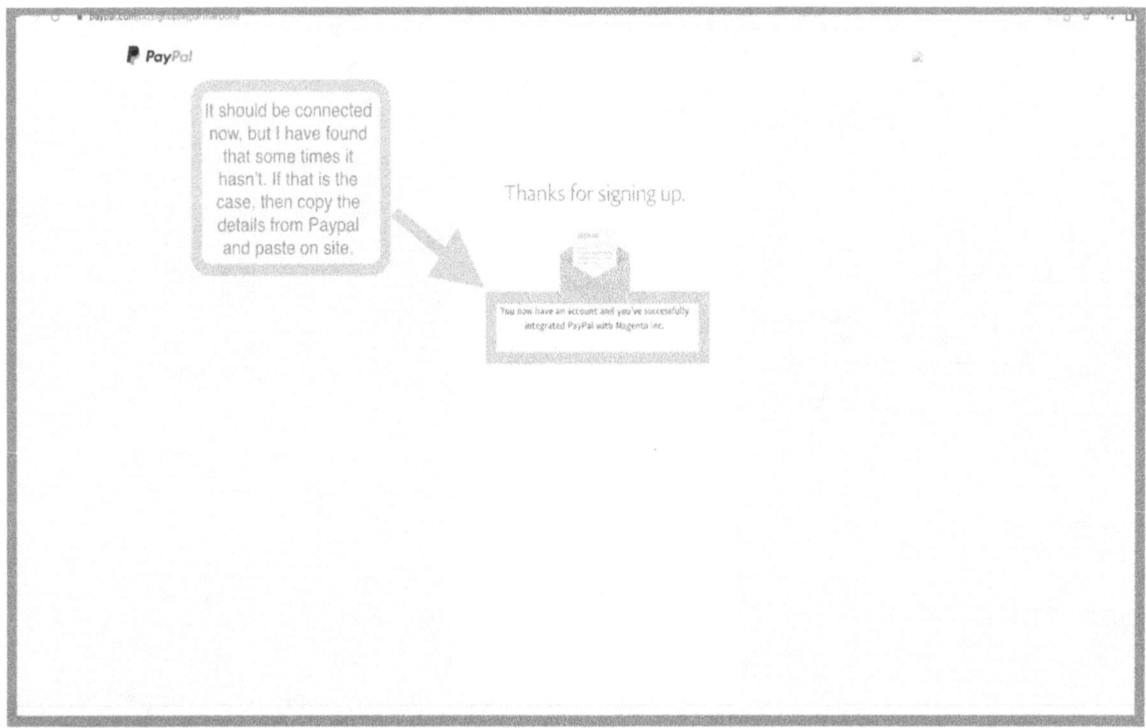

If the PayPal setup failed y going doing it through Magento, then head to PayPal and do it manually.

Let us now head to PayPal and open an account with them, or log into our account, if already have a Merchant (Business) account with them.

https://www.paypal.com/uk/business

Log in and go to the Dashboard

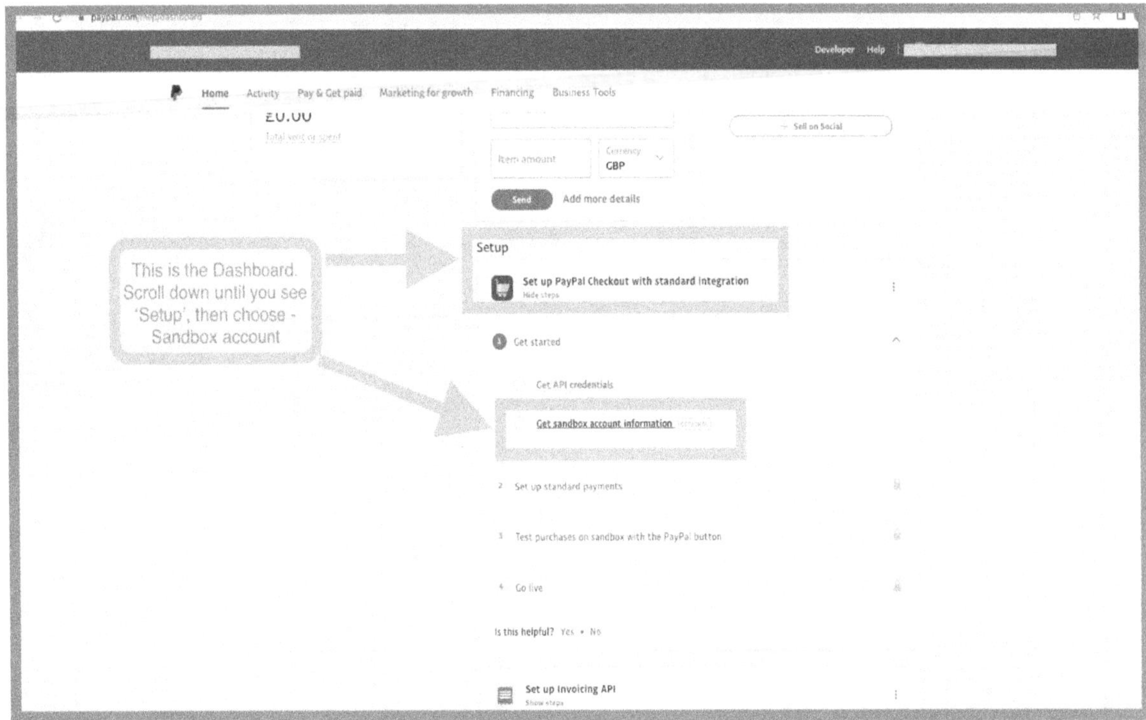

Choose Sandbox account to get the test API credentials.

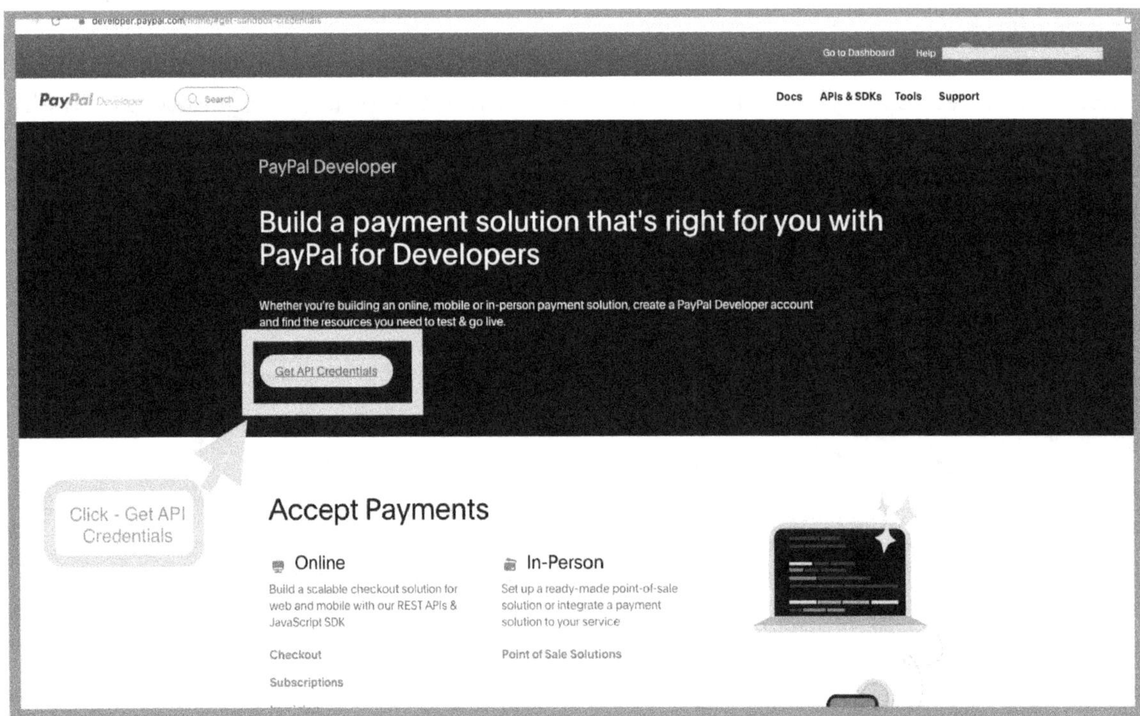

Click on Testing Tools to view or create the test accounts

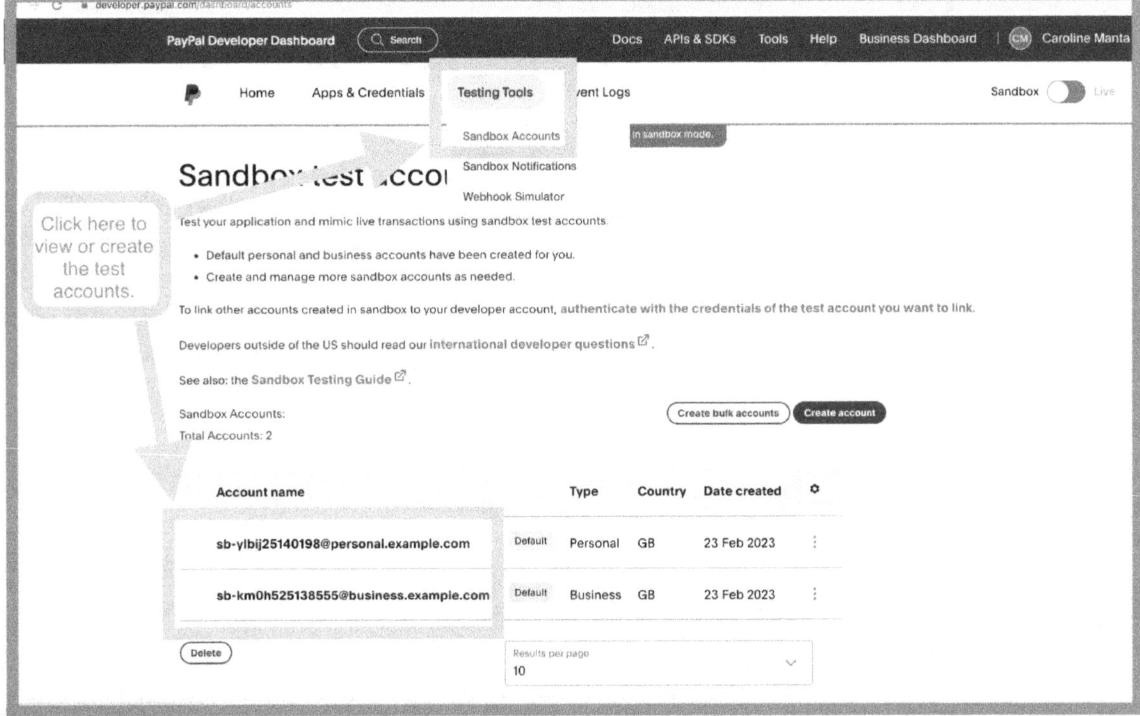

Click on Apps and Credentials, then scroll down to 'Rest API Apps'

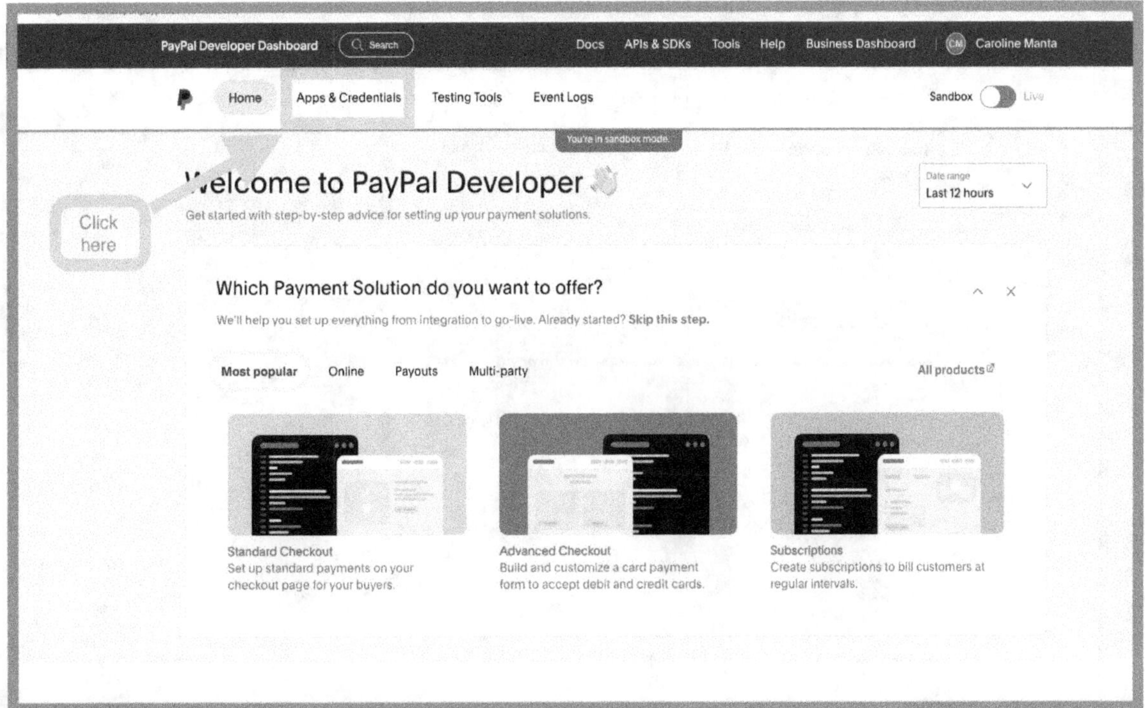

Click on Default Application

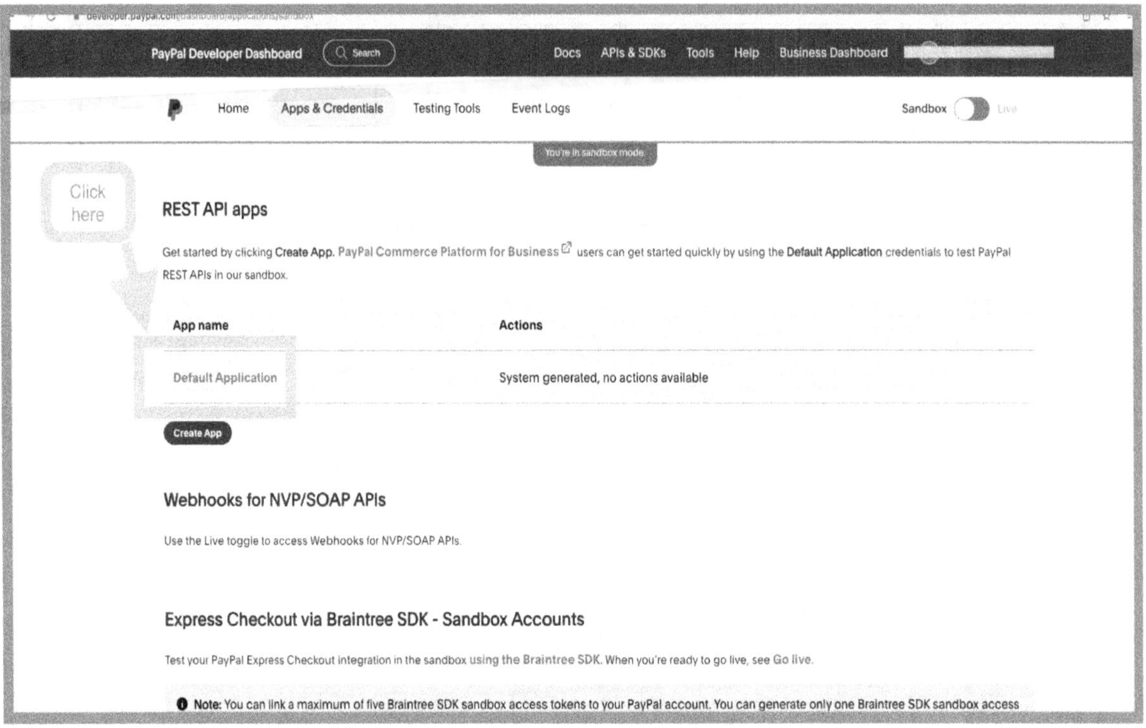

Copy the API keys and paste them into Magento configuration file above

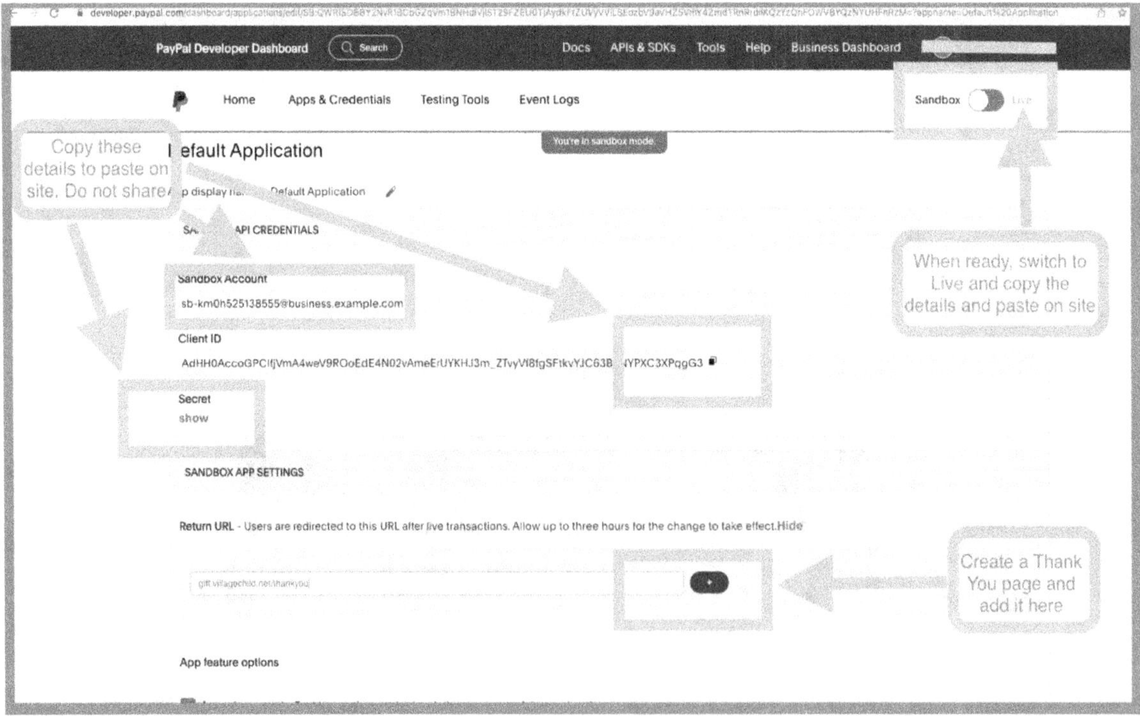

The Return URL should be a page with something like 'Thank you, blah, blah,....'
So, the URL will be = gift.villagechild.net/thankyou

Here is the web site, showing some pages: Home (renamed to 'LUMA'), Contact Us, Subscribe, etc. The site is very secured, with SSL certificates and it can accept personal details of users logging in and credit cards information.

https://gift.villagechild.net
Here is how the front-end (site) looks like.

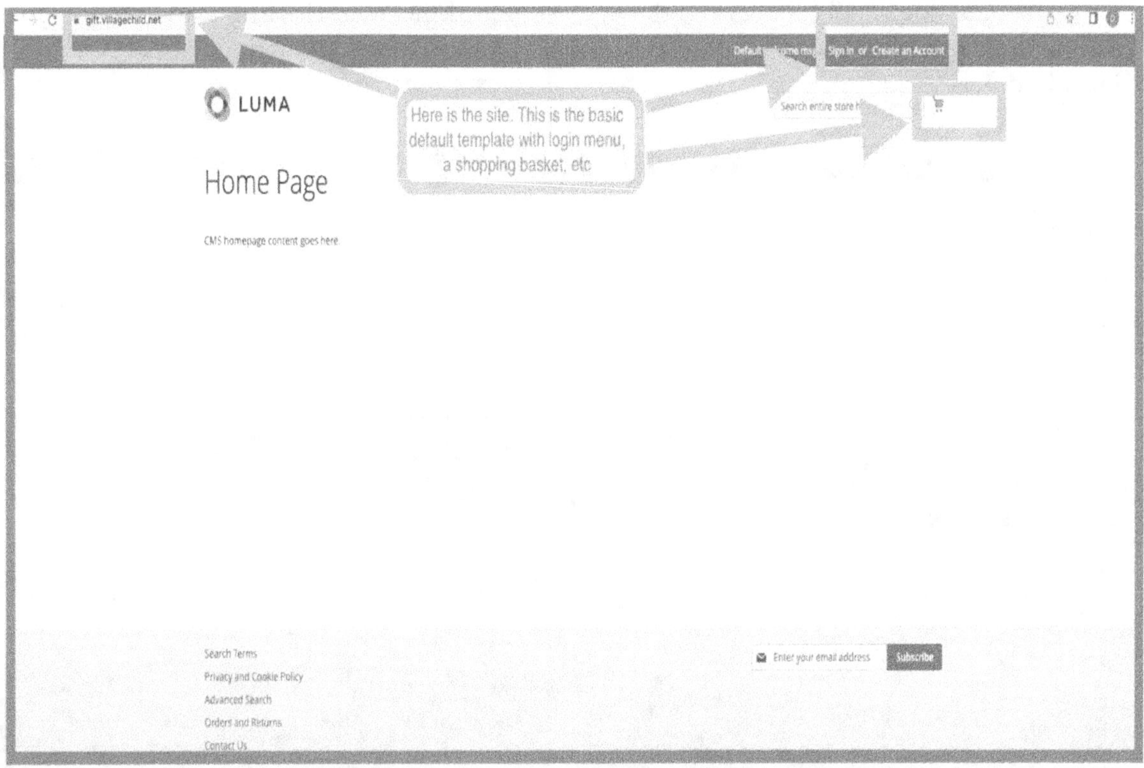

You should now call yourself, a 'Magento Web Site Developer'. Update your profile and CV and start applying for jobs similar to it and also advertise for freelance work.

PrestaShop Ecommerce Site with Stripe Payment

PrestaShop Ecommerce Site with Stripe Payment

PrestaShop Web Site

We are going to use PrestaShop on one of our subdomains:
https://shop.villagechild.net.

Go to the Control Panel (cPanel) on the Web server of the Web Hosting Provider and go to
Softaculous Installer. Look for PrestaShop and install it on the subdomain - shop.vil-
lagechild.net.

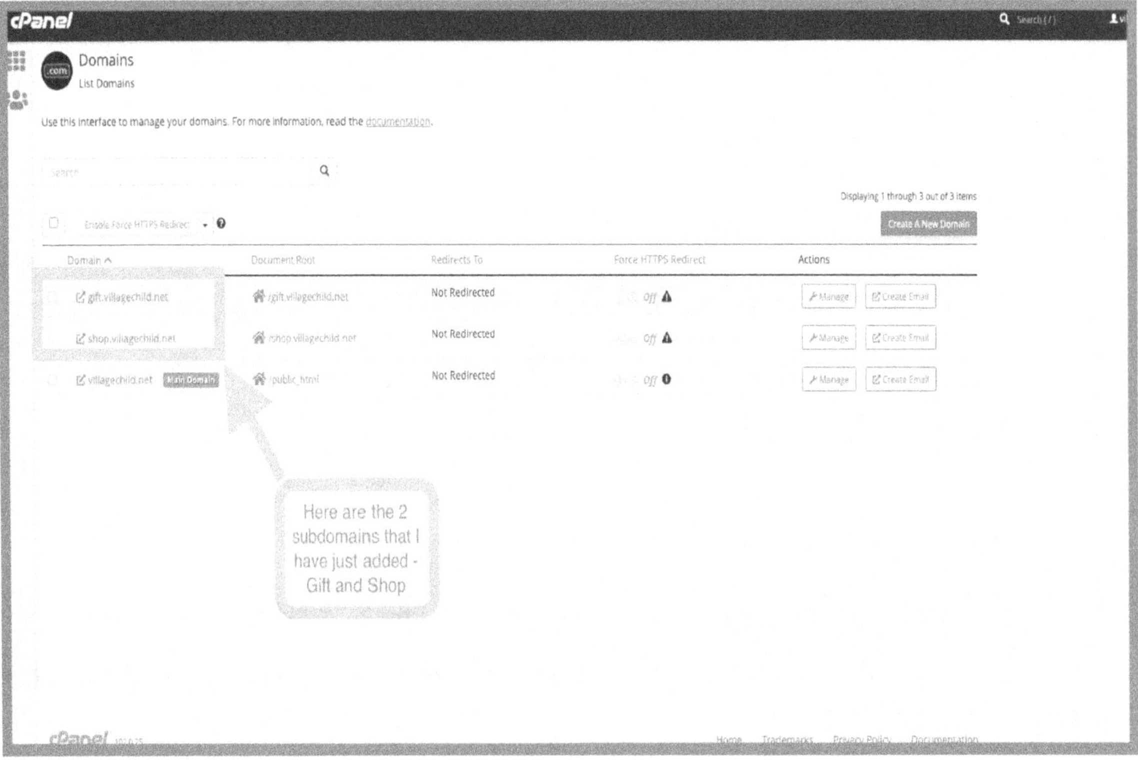

Here is the PrestaShop Admin Panel:
https://shop.villagechild.net/admin123

Log into the PrestaShop Admin Control Panel

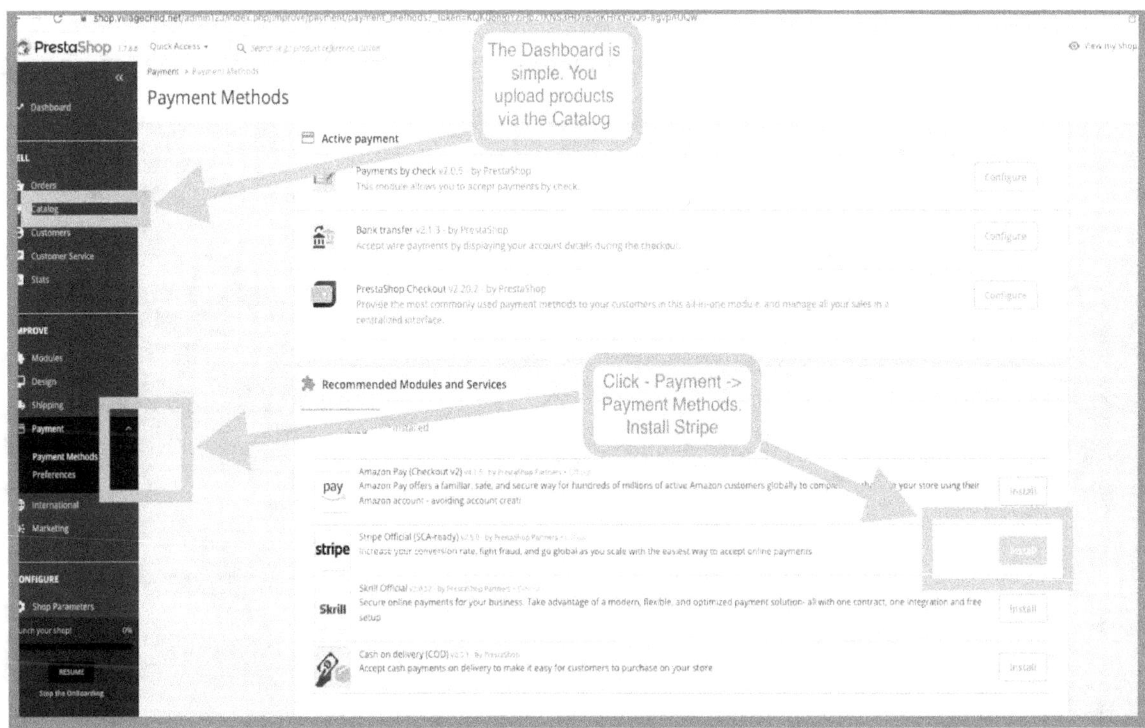

We need to get the API details from Stripe. Go to - https://stripe.com
Sign in into your Stripe account and go to - Developers

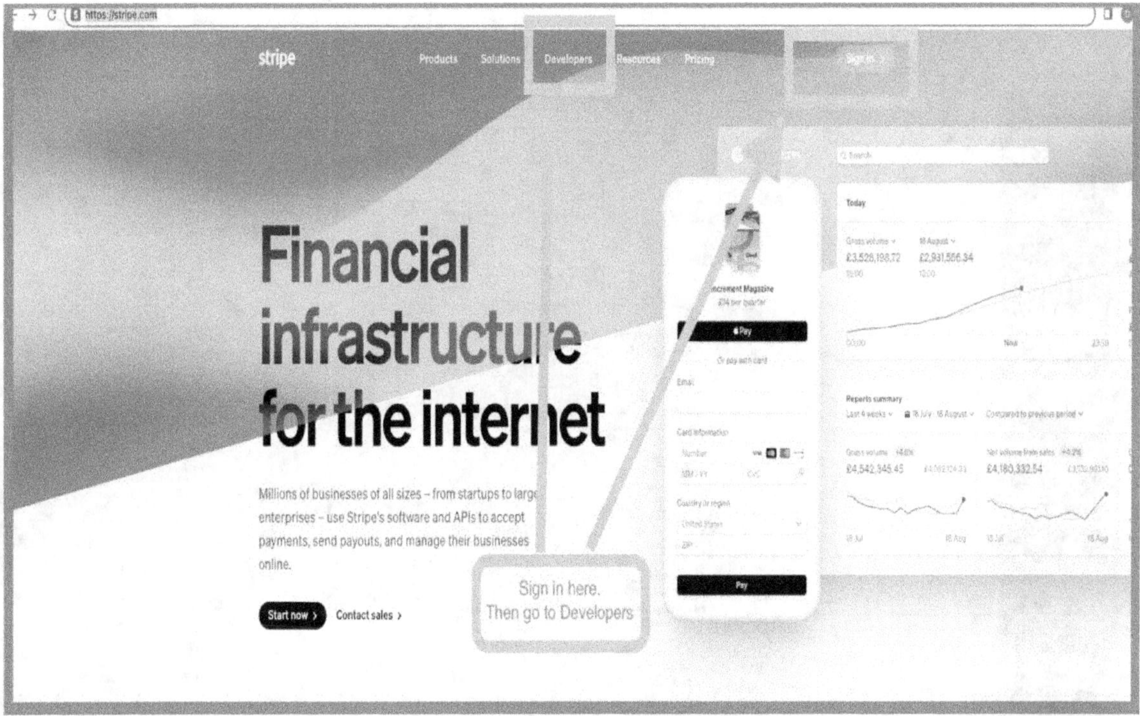

Click on API Keys and copy them. Remember to work in Test Mode first, then later change it.

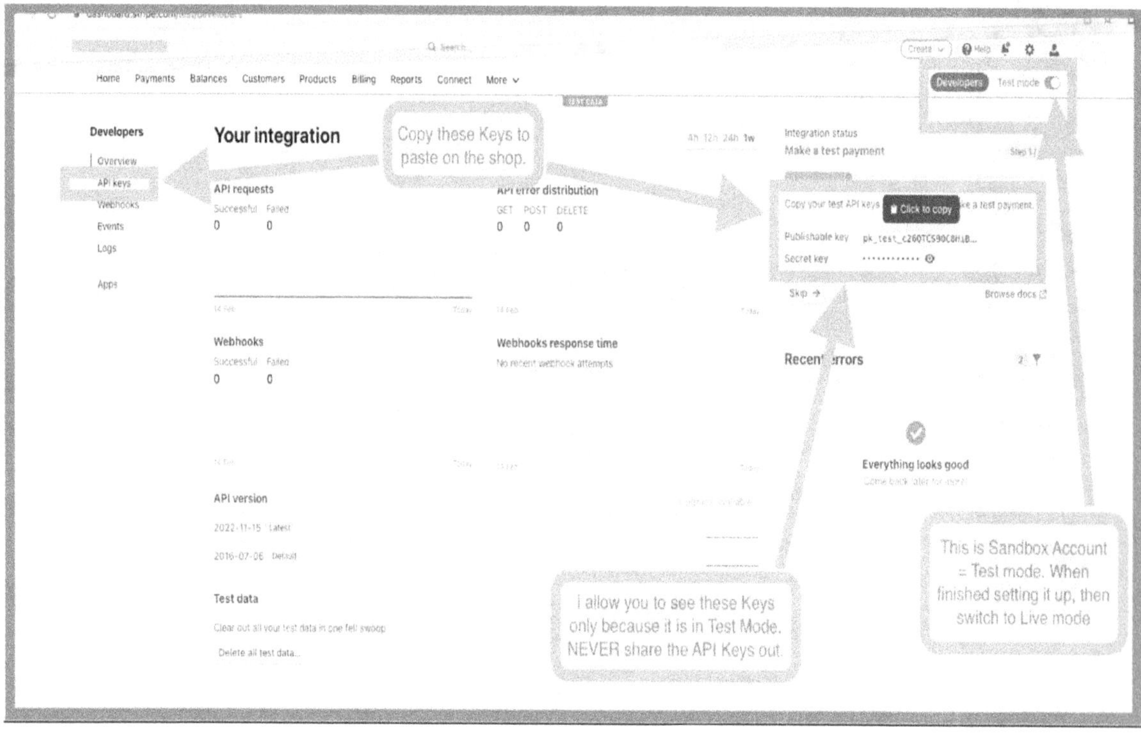

Paste the API keys into PrestaShop and click Connect. Green light - means connected.

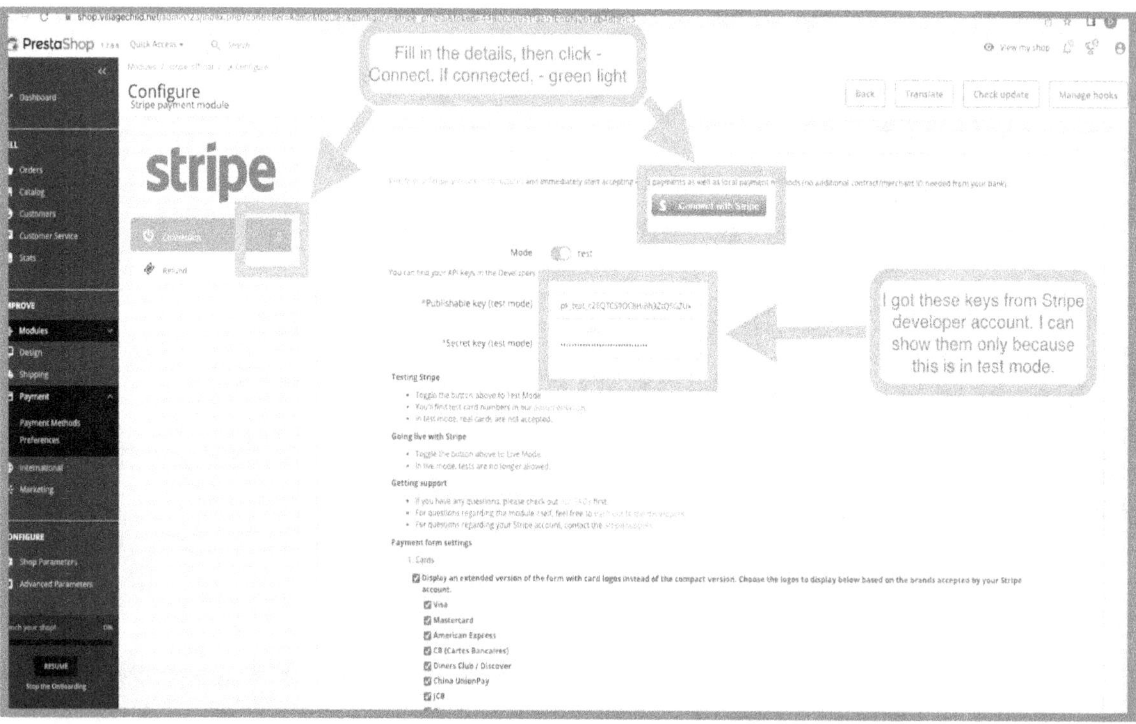

https://shop.villagechild.net

Here is the web site, showing some pages: Home (renamed to 'my store'), contact us, Clothes, Accessories, Art. The site is very secured, with SSL certificates and it can accept personal details of users logging in and credit cards information.

You should now call yourself, a 'PrestaShop Web Site Developer'. Update your profile and start applying for jobs in similar field, and also can advertise for freelance work.

Database, MySQL and PhpMyAdmin

Database, MySQL and PhpMyAdmin

Database is data in rows and rows, in tables that seats on a database server. The common database for our level, is the relational databases. A relational database (RDB) is a type of database that have tables of data that are related with each in one way or another. For instance, Table1 contains customers' names and dresses, and Table2 may contains products and prices. If customer1 buys product1, then the system relates cutomer1 from Table to product1 from Table2.

MySQL

The good thing about using a share-hosting plan, is that the database server has already been configured and set up for us, ready to just put our stuff on. The database server may be using a Microsoft server operating system or a Linux operating system (usually cheaper than Microsoft), or it may be a cloud server of some sort. The Microsoft servers would have SQL as their relational database management system (RDBMS), while the Linux server would use some open-source relational database management systems, which are MySQL, PostgreSQL, MariaDB, MongoDB. For our tutorial, we are using MySQL.

Connecting a Database

Another good thing is that we are using a CMS. Most CMS are structured in a way, that everything will streamline and fit into place - a bit like flat-pack furniture. The engineering of the CMS is such that provision for a database has already been incorporated. The best thing again about it, is that there is usually a script included that automatically set up tables and columns and rows according to the items being inputted. With the CMS, the front-end matter is securely integrated with the back end; that is the server, etc.

From the Web Hosting Control Panel, click on - Databases to view the database sets.

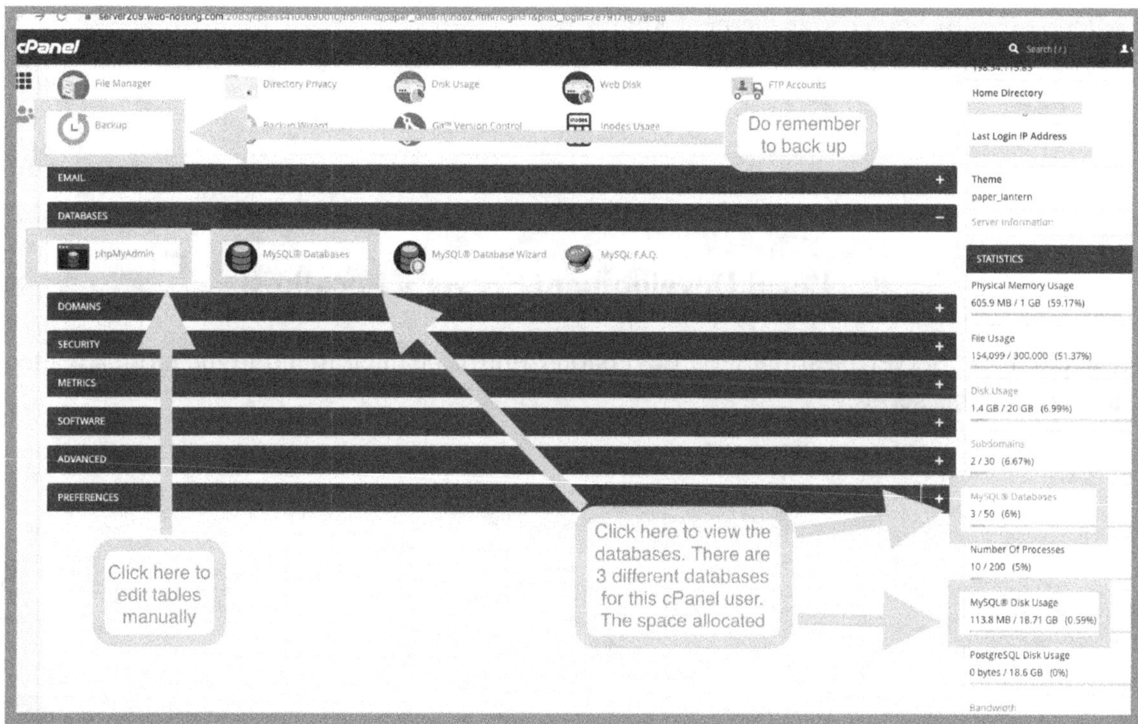

PhpMyAdmin: You can edit the tables and data manually using phpMyAdmin

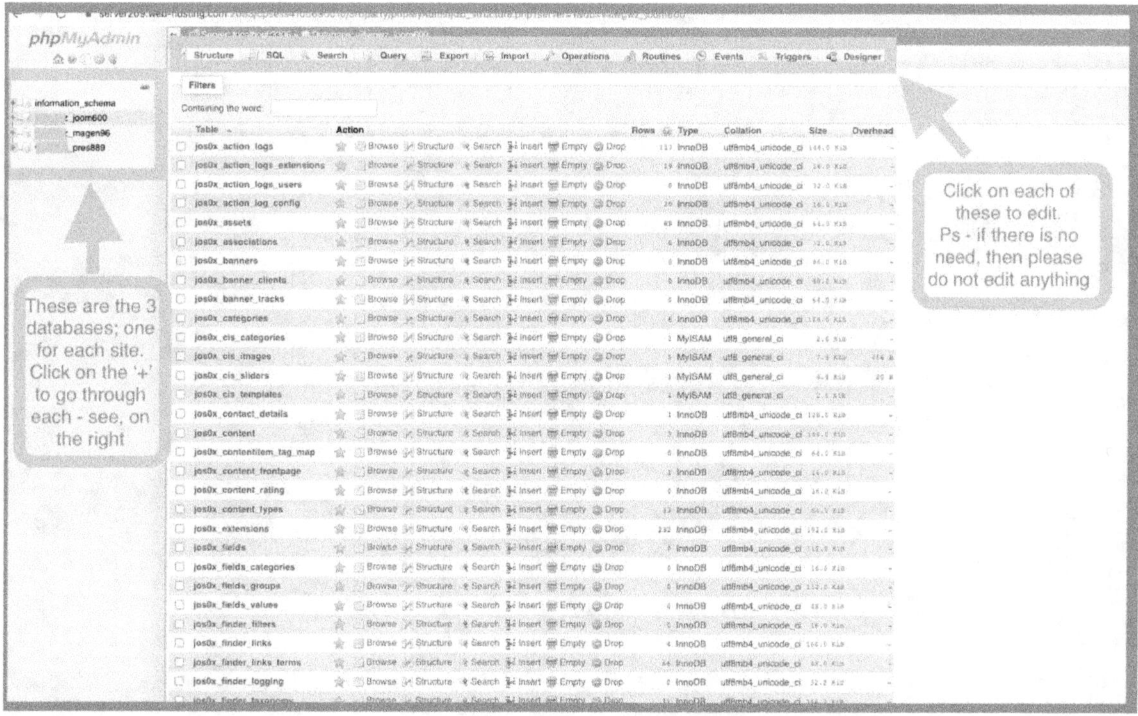

PhpMyAdmin provides a graphical user interface (GUI) to interact with the MySQL database without writing SQL commands. Other SQL GUIs:
Microsoft SQL Server Management Studio
MySQL Workbench.
dbForge
dBeaver
HeidiSQL
DronaHQ

Local Development Server - Localhost

Development Server, Testing Server, Version Control - can be found in the more advance topics book of this series.

Updating Our Skills Profile

Update Portfolio and CV

Update our Portfolio, GitHub, LinkedIn, and CV with the job skills of Web Developer. Do this with every project that you successfully complete. You may leave out client private information and just give a skeletal outline on your portfolio and profile.

Apply for Work

Since, you have successfully completed this project, it shows that you can do similar work and that serves as your work experience to include on you CV. You should start applying for Web design type jobs now.

Freelance Work

While we are looking a job as a Web Site Designer, we can in the meantime, start advertising our skills to accept freelance contracts.

Managing Stress

Working IT can be stressful. Some jobs are more stressful than others, so you need to think ahead of ways that you would deal with stress and manage yourself. Like taking frequent breaks when sitting long hours on the computer to stretch, looking away from the screen every 20mins, going for regular eye test, etc. Why not start a hobby? Remember, all codes and no play, makes Jack a total nerd – so dull.

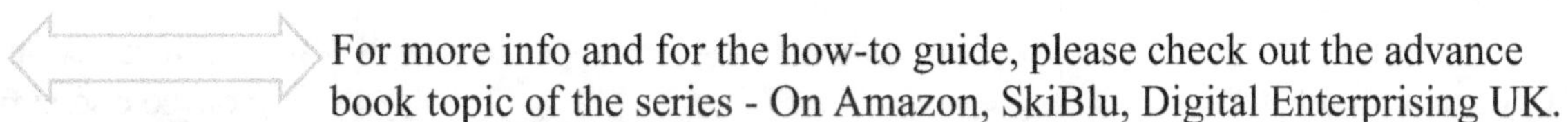 For more info and for the how-to guide, please check out the advance book topic of the series - On Amazon, SkiBlu, Digital Enterprising UK.

The video course material can be found on SkiBlu, Digital Enterprising UK,

http://www.digitalenterprising.co.uk/tutorials
http://www.skiblu.com/tutorials
https://sites.google.com/view/caroline-mant/tutorials
https://sites.google.com/view/digital-enterprise
https://sites.google.com/view/skiblu
https://digitalenterprise4.wordpress.com
https://skiblu5.wordpress.com

Glossary

Glossary, IT terminologies and Acronyms

args (arguments) - When you start answering back to a computer – it calls it argument.

Auto-complete – Completes a typing spelling.

Auto-suggest – Suggests as you type out

Auth = Authentication -Login with Username and password

2-Way Authentication. You put in your password, then you get sent a code to your phone or email to verify.

OAuth2 – Open Authorization. E.g., Google by itself can get your logging details from Facebook. You just clicking on Facebook to continue to your Google account.

Build - Put together the pieces of the

Deploy – Publish it live.

Developers Environment – Where the software is being build.

Test Environment – testing the software.
Production or Live environment – Where the software is open for use to the users.

dll – Dynamic Linked Library. Some applications tend to share libraries with each other.

Db – database

Default – The basic option that holds the place if no option is made.

Drag and drop – copy from one window into another, by clicking and dragging.

Docs – Documents or Documentations

Export – Send out work from an application

Import – To bring into the workbook in an application

Index page – The first page of a website – more like the doorway of the web site.

IntelliSense – The program can sense what lines of codes you are writing and suggests Functions and Methods.

i- installs or to install

lib – library

ls – System library

Legacy – Old

Obsolete – No longer used.

Deprecated – Chopped off

init – Initialise

QWERTY - Refers to a full standard keyboard or keypad
Responsive – The screen adjusts itself to fit everything on its screen, be it a large screen or small screen

RSS feed- A way to get updated content from a website in real-time

schema – blueprint of the network infrastructure or application architecture.

src – Source codes (or source codes files in a folder directory

txt - Plain English text.

Versioning – Trying to see a solution in the bigger picture.

White Label – Software that is generic.
Branding – A generic software given a logo and company's name.

software into one application. **cd** – Change directory **CMS** – Content Management System. A software used to organise blocks of programs	**Dynamic** – Keeps changing **Static** – Does not keep changing. **Hard-coded** – That's it -set in stone.	**lib** – library **Opening Tags and Closings** – To quote what the computer said in its language, you must put it between the open and closing tags.	

www.ingramcontent.com/pod-product-compliance
Lightning Source LLC
Chambersburg PA
CBHW081610250726
48657CB00009B/2529